DARING
to WRITE

DARING *to* WRITE

CONTEMPORARY NARRATIVES BY DOMINICAN WOMEN

EDITED BY

ERIKA M. MARTÍNEZ

THE UNIVERSITY OF
GEORGIA PRESS
ATHENS

© 2016 by the University of Georgia Press
Athens, Georgia 30602
www.ugapress.org
"Greñas" © 2015 by Kersy Corporan
All rights reserved
Designed by Kaelin Chappell Broaddus
Set in 10/12.5 Century Old Style by Kaelin Chappell Broaddus
Printed and bound by Sheridan Books, Inc.
The paper in this book meets the guidelines for permanence
and durability of the Committee on Production Guidelines for
Book Longevity of the Council on Library Resources.

Most University of Georgia Press titles are
available from popular e-book vendors.

Printed in the United States of America
20 19 18 17 16 P 5 4 3 2 1

Library of Congress Cataloging-in-Publication Data

Names: Martínez, Erika M., editor.
Title: Daring to write : contemporary narratives by Dominican women /
    edited by Erika M. Martínez.
Description: Athens : The University of Georgia Press, 2016. | Includes
    bibliographical references.
Identifiers: LCCN 2015036980 | ISBN 9780820349251 (hardcover : alk. paper)
    | ISBN 9780820349268 (pbk. : alk. paper) | ISBN 9780820349275 (ebook)
Subjects: LCSH: Dominican literature–Women authors–History and criticism.
    | Dominican literature–History and criticism.
Classification: LCC PQ7400.5.D37 2016 | DDC 860.9/9287097293–dc23

    LC record available at http://lccn.loc.gov/2015036980

FOR MY DAUGHTER, **ALMA**,
AND MY MOTHER, **MERCEDES**

CONTENTS

2. I'M NOT FROM HERE AND I'M NOT FROM THERE

3. THAT'S NOT ME ANYMORE

one I remember most: A husband and wife, both writers, were at a party chatting with their friends. They were asked how they managed to write, since they both held full-time jobs and had children. The husband went on to describe how he dedicated every Sunday to his writing while his wife looked after the children and other domestic responsibilities. She was only able to write when her family was in bed; her husband didn't have to sacrifice sleep.

In the Dominican Republic the disproportion between the number of books written by men and by women was compounded by the nature of self-publishing on the island, where, for the most part, writers must finance their own publication. Since men have higher incomes than women, they are better positioned to establish their writing careers. The inequality in earnings combined with the inequality of spare time makes it more challenging for women to write, publish, and distribute their books. And, unfortunately, government and educational institutions do not seem to be making noticeable efforts to correct the inequity—the international and regional book fairs I attended on the island showcased many more male authors than female authors, and the classes I audited covered literature mainly written by men.

Despite the obstacles, Dominican women have been involved in the creative process. From early Spanish colonial records, we learn that Leonor de Ovando, a Dominican nun at the Convent of Regina Angelorum of Santo Domingo, wrote poetry in the early 1600s—a fact that remains little known. In light of this history, it was important for the present anthology to include narratives by writers who had not yet published as well as ones who had. This anthology was not intended to be an exhaustive one. Some of the writers are well known, but some are new to international publication. No matter, they are writers, first and foremost, because they write. They dare to face the blank page and fill it with their words. When the world silences them, they turn to their craft to make sense of their reality.

These narratives written by women in the Dominican Republic or women of Dominican descent in the United States were selected because they shine a light on the female experience. In either case, they ground readers in place and time, portraying the rich diversity in contemporary Dominican life. Narratives written in the Dominican Republic are interspersed throughout the anthology with those written in the United States so readers can travel back and forth, as many of its authors do. This arrangement also allows the texts to enter into dialogue with one another.

I have grouped the narratives so that readers can approach them through four different lenses—love, identity, gender, and migration. Despite this compartmentalization, the narratives are complex, broaching many themes at the same time: from mother-daughter and father-daughter relationships to adoption; from identity to discrimination based on color; from migration to religion; from friendship to marriage and infidelity.

The first part, "The People Who Love Me," gathers more than traditional love stories portraying courtship and marriage. These stories demonstrate how much our families and culture influence our relationships. While a few of the stories explore dating, many more delve into marital failure. Some of the women in these stories have chosen a partner on the basis of attraction and love, yet at the same time the narratives explore how class, age, and notions of beauty impact relationships. It is also interesting to note the different perspectives that the writers take: Daughters reflect on their parents' marriages; wives lament choices they've made; and young women realize how much they are willing and unwilling to compromise in their search for love. We see that what ties us to another human being is often beyond what comes from the heart.

Part 2, "I'm Not from Here and I'm Not from There," depicts the struggle with identity. The narrators in this section are asking, Who am I? By immersing ourselves in the location of these narratives, whether it is in the Dominican countryside, Santo Domingo's Chinatown, or New York City, we see how identity is rooted in a sense of place. When a character migrates, she will carry within her the essence of Dominican life, yet the new environment will redefine her. Even when characters remain in one location, their sense of belonging wavers as a new population moves in. We also see how education and social mobility shape a character's sense of self. As we witness these narrators' stories, we experience their transformation. No matter the forces involved, the tension between the self and family, community and ancestral legacy is an undercurrent running through this section.

"That's Not Me Anymore," the third cluster, introduces conflict against the backdrop of gender and sexuality, including sexual orientation. Half of these narratives also probe the impact of infidelity on the family. At the same time, the intersection of gender and beauty is highlighted. Several characters in these stories make difficult choices to satisfy their basic needs, sometimes sacrificing their self-respect, their morality. But we also encounter protagonists who rebel against the confining expectations and restrictions of their families and communities; whether it is in childhood or adulthood, some ultimately do find empowerment.

In the last section, "The Countries Beyond," we are introduced to women who dream of a life abroad or who have already migrated. Most often, they are searching for economic opportunity, not only for themselves but also for their families. Whether they have moved to another island in the Caribbean, the United States, or Spain, they are grappling with changes in their lives. But it is not only their lives that change; the family and community they left behind react to the new character emerging in the foreign land. Some have the opportunity to travel back to the island, while others can only visit through their imagination.

She went on to explain that my father had very important work to do in his life. But, like every man, he had to make a choice to be great or to destroy himself.

—Does your father do addiction?

—Yes, drinking killed him. He was diabetic.

—Do not worry for him. He's very present now in your life. He wants your forgiveness. When you were born, he gave you all his responsibility. He was too cowardly to be a great man. You have been angry at him. Does what I say sound familiar?

I don't remember a time I wasn't angry with my father.

—When you were six, something important happened in your life?

When I was six, my mother left him because he hit her. As soon as she had gotten her papers straight, she applied for visas to bring my grandmother and her brothers to the United States so they could also work and make dollars. When they arrived and moved into the apartment next door, my mother gave my father an ultimatum: If you hit me again, I'll leave you.

He hit my mother and almost hospitalized her. She waited a few days for the bruises to heal. She waited until he was good and drunk and his body was too heavy to get out of bed. The day she left, he called her name over and over. My brother and I, wearing our pajamas, hid inside the closet in our bedroom; the hems of our coats brushed against our foreheads. My mother pulled us out by our wrists and asked us to hush. Our bags were packed and waiting for us in the other apartment where my grandmother and uncles stood guard. For a very long while, my father banged on the door of our new home begging my mother to return to him. Each time, she called the police. She did this until he stopped banging on the door.

The psychic continued to talk about my father. I tried to change the subject by asking about my mother, who was alive and well and who I projected was a more important figure in my future. She answered me:

—You look toward your mother for answers, but your father is your guide. When you were about fifteen, something important happened in your life, no?

Although my mother left my father when I was six, my father never gave up on my mother. In fact, when he was in New York, when he was not working, he stood in front of our apartment building waiting to make sure my mother arrived home alone. He tried to charm my brother and me to let him inside, and at times he succeeded. My father then waited inside my mother's bedroom wearing only his boxers.

My mother had to call her brothers to help her get him out. That was after she prepared him dinner, and he drank half a bottle of rum.

—Why did you feel the need to feed him when he was making your life impossible? I asked her on many occasions.

—Because he's your father. And I want you to love him, despite everything.

Every day, my father waited for my brother and me to arrive from school. He waited for my mother to arrive from work. He stood in front of our building as if holding up the walls. One day, when I was fifteen, I walked toward him. My friend David walked in the same direction. When I saw my father, I moved away from David, slowing down so he walked ahead of me. He, like everyone else on my block, knew about my father, the man with a restless fist who heated up quickly. Like me, they feared him. But it was too late. When my father got close enough to me, he grabbed me by my ponytail and flung me toward the building. My face smacked against the wall.

—You whore! he yelled out in front of the crowd that quickly formed around us. You're a whore, just like your mother!

My aunt swept me into her arms and took me to safety, into our apartment where she could treat the place where the skin had scraped off from my face.

The next day, he left carnations in front of our apartment door. He telephoned every few hours asking to speak to me. My aunt and my mother took turns picking up the phone and told him to call later, another day.

—I'm never speaking to him again, I told my mother.

For once she didn't insist. He had gone too far.

For years I kept the videotapes I made of my father in a drawer. When I decided to transfer the footage to DVDs, I watched them for the first time. I noticed how with each visit, each interview, there was physically less and less of him. In the end, my father could no longer walk on his own, he had lost four toes, he was completely blind in one eye and legally blind in the other. With each transcription, I was less certain how I felt about him. I also no longer wanted to be angry with him.

When I was a teenager, my mother's insistence that my brother and I spend time with my father despite his violent behavior was infuriating. My mother continued to assist and care for my father up until the day he died. She did this even after they were divorced, living in separate apartments. She defended herself by saying:

—He's a sick old man. When you're well and have your wits about you, people will always come by to look for you. But when you're like your father, who's falling apart, no one visits with him now. It's the least we can do.

Having my mother as a role model—a woman who can find compassion for someone like my father by putting his actions in context and also by creating boundaries with him (not letting him inside our house) while still being open to the possibilities of change in their relationship—has made me realize that she was right when she said:

—He's your father, and you'll regret not knowing him.

Even though I can't remember a time when I was close to my father, he said that when I was two years old, I would sit on his fat belly and never ever want to leave his side. He bragged about the trip we took together when I was six months old. He flew with me to the Dominican Republic all by himself.

—By yourself, really?

Now that I have a child and understand what it takes to travel with a baby on my lap, I can't imagine my father carrying me, changing my diapers, feeding me when I was hungry, soothing me when I cried. When I asked my mother if he did all those things, she said:

—He wasn't all bad.

My father has been the elephant in the living room of my work. The more I tried to push him out of my life, the more present he became in my imagination and fiction. For four years I've been working on my third novel, *In Search of Caridad*. The first few drafts of the book characterized my mother as a saint and condemned my father. With each revision, the process of turning my father into a full-fledged character with his own struggles and ambitions has allowed me to sympathize with him, as a writer and, ultimately, as his daughter.

MARIBEL AND EL VIEJO

FICTION BY JINA ORTIZ

Saturdays are baseball days for El Viejo. He sits in front of the flat screen, legs wide open, extended on the lazy chair, unbuttoning his Hawaiian shirt and unbuckling his pants. I'm left to wash the dishes, away from the screams of the crowds around the diamond. Cooped up inside this small kitchen, I've served him for the last twenty-five years, cooking meals, wiping countertops, and scrubbing aluminum pots.

I peek into the living room. Viejo rocks in his chair, forgetting that the footrest gets stuck because the iron rods are stiff. His legs lift into the air and press against his chest.

"Necesito ayuda, Mari. Come on, Vieja, help me! This thing don't work no more. My favorite chair, qué jodienda . . ."

Even though I'm fifteen years Viejo's junior, he calls me his Vieja. The name has stuck like any other title: wife, mother, sister, or daughter. As usual, I have to unsnap him out of the lazy chair. He attempts to roll out of the fetus-leg-up position. All this time, it is his arthritis that makes it hard for him to move, not the fact that the chair is as old as our eldest child and that the springs pop out from the sides.

"Did you think the Red Sox were gonna win after Pedro left? You know it's not the same without having three Dominicanos on the team. Qué carajo were they thinking?" Viejo lifts his right leg over one of the chair's arms and, sliding off of it, drops to the floor.

I shake my head and ignore his clumsiness. "Viejo, remember you have to take esas patillas para la presión!"

He was diagnosed with high blood pressure and cholesterol five years ago, and, not adhering to his diet, he's been sick ever since. All the while, I've been his walking alarm clock, ticking whenever he needs to pop a pill in his mouth.

He picks himself up and nudges his large butt into the same spot on the chair. Luckily, his can of Presidente is still standing inside the custom-made beer holder designed for his chair. I'm not going to be his cup holder, too.

"¿Tú m'está escuchando, Vieja? Did you hear me? My team is losing." Viejo presses the buttons on the remote control, flicking it straight at the screen. These days he only has energy to watch baseball. Before he got sick, he used to take me out dancing, and now we barely touch each other, only on game nights, and his team has to win. "Bueno, I don't need to be taking them pills at three in the afternoon. El doctor me dijo, well, he told me after dinner."

I'm worried about him. His doctor's visits have been more frequent, and he's been too sneaky lately. Last time I caught him smuggling Ding Dongs into his lunch pack for work, I told him he was en route to getting diabetes. He doesn't listen to me. He no longer calls me on his lunch breaks or when he is on his way to see the compadres for a game of dominoes.

"I'm cooking pig's feet con moro."

Viejo gets up, pauses the game, and reaches behind me in the kitchen as I set the table.

"Remember that Eusebio y Chepe are coming over for dinner. They gonna be watching the second game from Santo Domingo on NDTV. It's a good thing I didn't get the cheap TV service," Viejo says.

"I know."

But he knows that even with the cheap services he could have gotten the D.R. programs. He just wants to watch the nudie channels. He thinks I don't see what he does when I fall asleep from my long days working at the factory. ¡Ese Viejo, con esa bolsa larga! Es verdad that I married a dirty old man. I should have listened to my mother, who always said, "Maribel, look, that Alfredo Alcantara is a good man." She insisted I marry someone my own age, like that nice guy Alfredo. Maribel Alcantara. Too late for that.

He starts reaching for my butt; even with my bata on, he still wants it.

"I smell like oregano, Viejo!"

He looks over my shoulder and stares at my breasts. After three kids, I wonder what view he is getting. They haven't been perky in over twenty years. "Well, you always been mi Vieja," he croons, squeezing me, trying to pull me closer. Then he presses his hand against the stove.

"¡Ay, mi madre! ¡E' verdad, Maribel, tú sí eres mala!" Viejo screeches, kissing his hand and running to the faucet. The electric stovetop is still hot, even though I turned it off to cool. The cold water runs, spraying over the kitchen counter. My red and green bell peppers ready to be chopped for the seasoning fall to the floor, one by one, rolling like dominoes on a fold-out table.

I laugh.

"Ay, Vieja, I love you so much, and this is how you treat me." Viejo wipes his hands with one of my decorative towels, the one with large polyester bows on each end. He smells my hair and unpins it, unraveling the curls that then drape onto my shoulder. Walking back to the TV, he says, "You know, I was going to tell you a surprise, but I'm going to keep it a secret tonight."

"Okay, if you say so. The last time you were able to keep a secret we were still living in the campo." Placing la paila de moro on top of the stove, I know exactly what the secret is. I know he is getting us plane tickets to go back to the island for Christmas. And for this he'll deserve all the kisses he wants, which aren't many these days. We have not gone to the D.R. since my cousin Raquel's wedding in Salcedo; it's been three years. Valgame, she has a toddler now.

"Nope. I know what you thinking. It's not plane tickets to Santo Domingo for Christmas," yells Viejo while snacking on his conconetes and gulping his beer. "¡Mira, los Yankees, lo malvao Yankees!"

The phone rings.

"Alo, ¿quién es? Who's this?"

"¡Soy yo, Mercedes! You don't have to answer in English for me." Mercedes was born here in the States, yet it's like she was born in Santo Domingo. She always speaks in her Dominican-cibaeña accent, adding a strong and long "i" sound to almost every word that doesn't even have an "i" in it to begin with. El Viejo does the same thing, but he *is* from El Cibao.

"Maribel, you don't know lo que pasó up in la factoría!" Mercedes chews on some food; I can hear her in the background fussing in her kitchen. She's even used the malvao bathroom while on the phone sometimes. That irritates me. This is how I know for sure she was not born in Santo Domingo; her American ways confuse me, like when she told me she pops her underpants in the laundry basket after she's used them. Unheard of! If our husbands found out that we threw our underpants in the laundry, none of us would be married. Every woman on both sides of the island washes her underpants by hand the minute she takes them things off. Pero, Mercedes is crazy like that, and she keeps on talking and chewing her food.

"Did you listen to a word I was saying, girl? Elena got caught sleeping with one of the managers. The head of the department in the factory found out, and they fired her and the Puerto Rican guy," she says, then declares her ay-dios-míos and qué-vaina-más-dura before finishing her last lunch bites. She talks as loud as car speakers; her next-door neighbor can probably hear what she is telling me, like the time her sister's husband told her he had fathered a daughter by another woman back on the island. This child was supposedly conceived before Mercedes's sister married the guy; he's a big pendejo.

Mercedes is always the one to call if anyone wants to know any news about our jobs, layoffs, or any scandals at the factory. Since she knows English and got a degree from some fancy college, she is the manager of the manufacturing small goods department at the Webber Price and Company factory; they are the folks whose jingle is "Good Stuff, at a Good Price, is the Right Choice. Save with Webber Price Accessories and Apparel Products."

"You know I am still here! Are you listening?" she says.

"Yes, I am. Between you and El Viejo's TV blaring the baseball games, I'm about to go deaf."

"That may not be a bad idea, when I tell you what's next. Get this," she says, switching to her New York attitude, which hasn't changed even after being in Massachusetts for years. "Did Viejo tell you his surprise? I know ever-y-thang!"

"M'ija, just tell me what it is! Viejo is in the other room, belching and pigging out on the conconetes. He's not gonna hear you. Trust me." Even though the base of the phone hangs against the wall jack, the cord extends all across the kitchen. I walk toward the door into the living room and peek in to make sure El Viejo doesn't listen in from the cordless in the bedroom. Nope, he's glued to his lazy chair and, from the looks of it, about to snore his way through the fifth inning.

"¡Dime ahora!"

"Chepe told me that you guys are moving to Florida because the doctor told Viejo that he got some kind of gastritis and pancreatic cancer. He didn't want you to worry and lose you to a younger man."

"A younger man? Mercedes, ¿pero está loco El Viejo? Tengo que colgar; I have to go. I have to wake him up before he misses his entire game. We'll talk later." My pink apron with the strawberries stitched on each pocket still has pig grease stains on it from the last meal I cooked, but that doesn't keep me from using it as a handkerchief to hold my tears back. The pot is bubbling vapors from the rice and pigeon peas. I'm so distressed that I forget to wear my potholder mitten to pull out the casserole dish from the oven and come close to burning my hand.

Dinner is almost ready, so I fix the plastics on the sofas, putting the cushions back in their place. Soon Viejo will toss them aside to make room for all his snacks and Red Sox paraphernalia. He wakes up to his own snort. As the baseball game announcers report that David "El Papi" Ortiz has just injured his shoulder, he dribbles beer on his hairy chest, now exposed after taking off his cheap cotton Hawaiian shirt.

"Ay, Vieja, is there a clean shirt? Mira, El Papi. Ya se jodió la vaina. We gonna lose for sure."

His case of Presidentes is about finished, so he looks for more. His hands wave down at the carpet where all the empty beer cans lie, his face full of disappointment. The announcers keep talking about El Papi's injury and reminding the Red Sox fans about the losing streak, but all I can think about is Viejo and his health.

"Viejo, tenemos que hablar," I say even though Eusebio and Chepe, Viejo's two drunkards for friends, may walk in any minute.

Viejo already knows. He walks around with his potbelly, rubs the sides of his love handles as if he's slapping Bengay on them. I follow him to our bedroom. He avoids eye contact with me as he handpicks a clean top from his accordion-style closet. A newer version of his favorite Red Sox T-shirt. The last one never survived the baseball party Eusebio had at his apartment last month—El Viejo splashed the entire bowl of punch on his clumsy self and spilled the jug of piña colada that Candidad, Eusebio's poor wife, made for them. He puts on his sad little shirt, focusing on the buttons. This is how I know he is afraid to face me.

"Mercedes told you. I wanted it to be a surprise," he says matter-of-factlike, as if the days of picking low mangos were here again.

"Viejo, a surprise heart attack?" My arms rise toward the ceiling, angry and scared all at the same time.

"I know, Maribel. I shoudda told you. Perdoname."

"¿Cómo es que tú piensa? How come you couldn't tell me, but you tell your buddies?"

"Déjame explicarte. The doctors—"

"Doctors, there's more than one?! Carajo, Viejo. Tú sí me tienes de pendeja," I swear at him.

"I was gonna tell you tonight, after Chepe and Eusebio watched the next game with me." He returns to his lazy chair. He can't even face me without looking inside his beer can, his gaze on the alcoholic drips left unsipped on the can lid, slurping his way out of the conversation. I'm not convinced that he's even telling me the entire truth. His eyes tick back and forth like the pendulum of a grandfather clock as I pace in front of him.

Again, his slurps irritate me. "Is there more, Viejo? Before the kids and I have to ship you to the island in a casket?"

His head is down. I can tell he's starting to feel like dung.

The air is dense in the living room. Luckily for El Viejo, the timer rings, reminding me to take the pork out of the oven. I want to jump out of my bata and tell him how dumb he was for keeping his illness a secret for who knows how long. But I don't; I feel sorry for him. Ese pedazo de platáno is mine, old and big now, but he is all I have. To think someone else might pick up after him in a hospice makes me even angrier. "So, what do you want? Florida. A nice retirement home?"

"Vieja, I'm not dead yet. And you know we have our ranchito en Santo Domingo. There is no way I am retiring in this country. All people do here is work, no hay vida. And you know it's true." He gets up from his chair to kiss my cheek, but I pull back and walk toward the kitchen.

"It's not the point. What do you want me to do? Gracias a Dios, the kids are in college and are paying their own bills, and the eldest is married. They have their lives and families now. ¿Pero y yo? You're the only family I have here." I look straight at him, and he slouches back to his seat. This time he plops his beer can inside the cup holder embedded in his lazy chair. Like a second instinct, he gets up and follows me into the kitchen.

"No ponga esa cara así. Let's go to Santo Domingo!" He squeezes me tightly.

"I thought we weren't going for Christmas, remember?"

He always changes the topic when he gets too sensitive about something. When he knows it's getting bad for him, he scratches his head, rubs his right hand across his face, and says coño, like the time he told me he lost all his vacation savings at a cockfight. Back then, we were still living in New York, and I told him to stop betting the household money. He always said we should have moved to Lawrence, there's more Dominicanos up there. But we're here, in Worcester, so he has to deal without having someone come over our house on Saturdays to collect for the Sunday numbers game. He pretends he doesn't gamble anymore, but I heard there's a man from the D.R. that takes numbers behind the Sazón Especial Restaurant on Copper Street. Sneaky Viejo, gambling seems to still be too easy for him. And here he is again trying to pull another fast one on me.

Viejo hugs me even tighter, pressing on my greasy strawberry pockets. I push him away.

"We can retire out there." He tastes the pork, rice, and pigeon peas, and the pastelitos lined on the counter.

"You can retire, Viejo, not me. But you're only fifty-nine years old. You're too young. We make too much money. And what am I going to do with all my spare time?"

He sticks out his bemba to press his puckered lips against mine. I'm not in the mood.

"What you always been doing, Vieja, lavando, planchando, and, essentially, taking care of me," he says with a smirk on his face.

"Like I said, Viejo, what am I going to do while you vegetate and let the rest of your pancreas become shredded broccoli?" I want to tell him I'm afraid he won't be able to eat whatever he wants like a healthy person or go out to a restaurant that serves spicy foods. I can see this cancer taking him over like a bear that grabs a person from the back, scratches and claws him to death. He starts to cough more often now and goes to the bathroom with frequency. No more pasteles or pork dishes, no more rice and beans. He'll eat more green and orange vegetables like the doctor ordered. How did I not notice, with all the belching he does?

Viejo continues to talk, raising his voice, "I'll live longer there in my country rather than here. And if I'm gonna die, you know where I bought my plot in the cemetery in Santiago on the way to Guayabal. You know my family is from there."

"I know, Viejo, I know. That's where we met. I was nineteen years old, and you were thirty-four. I lost my inheritance because of you."

"Am I worth every parcel of land? Every cow you could have sold to the American or European businessmen?" He inches closer toward the stove to get more pork, dangles a piece to my face. Smiling, he looks desperate for attention, or just hungry.

"It's taking you too long to answer my question, Vieja."

I doze off, if not for a second, maybe a lifetime. And then I say: "I'm still thinking about you, Vi-e-jo! How you kept this cancer info from me."

I laugh at the pork stains all over his shirt; I married a big old kid who wears his baseball T-shirts to bed.

That Saturday, Viejo went back to just watching baseball on TV, lying in his lazy chair with no beer stains on his shirt. I heard only a wordless snort. After his friends went home, he caught one last game. That time the White Sox won, and Viejo, I know, felt satisfied because the Yankees weren't even in the match. He died several days later, lying there on that lazy chair. His cancer had spread very quickly to his vital organs. Viejo's body gave up the way the Yankees caught the last baseball pitch of the season that year. Nothing seems the same without the noise of his belching or the high volume of the sports channels on a Saturday afternoon.

Maybe this is all I'll remember from my Viejo, the Saturdays, when the biggest event in our house was those baseball games, watching him evolve into a big bowl of rice, beans, and pork. We never made it to Santo Domingo, where we were going to retire and spend our later years with our families.

In his casket, he wears his Red Sox hat and his nicest and only suit, which he wore to birthday parties or for others' funerals. In my memories, our conversations always end this way:

"¿Y qué quieres, Viejo?"

And he replies, "I want the Red Sox to win another game and get smart and put another Dominicano back in there."

THE BIG NEWS

FICTION BY DELTA EUSEBIO

Translated by Achy Obejas

"I've got big news for you! The girl who lives around the corner in the pink house, Papo's daughter, she got pregnant! Guess whose it is," Amancia says as she comes to greet me. Her voice is so loud everyone in the colmado can hear her.

When she sees me it's always the same, she talks about everybody's business. Her high-pitched voice and the clacking of dominoes confirm that it's break time. I come up the main street. I approach the two doors on the east side—they're open, as if to welcome everyone who comes in. I sit and ask Rafelito for a small, really cold one. "Bésame, bésame mucho, as if this was our last night . . ." I love that bolero by Lucho Gatica. My nephew says the only people who come to this colmado are P.M., post meridiem, that we're all over the hill, both because of our age and our taste in music. He's right, because the customers are all friends of Amancia, and we've all gotten old together, although young people are coming by again these days, especially on Fridays.

"Juana, I don't know why you always have to say 'really cold,' with that sarcastic edge in your voice. They're always really cold here, whether there's electricity or not, that's why we have a fifty-kilo generator. You know who made that belly on Laurita, Papo's daughter?" Amancia says as she sits by my side.

"No, I don't."

"Hold on to your seat. It's Dr. Pimentel's. That blonde woman who thinks the whole world is her oyster? Her husband. She's gonna have to climb down from her pedestal now. Imagine, Laurita's a minor."

Amancia keeps on talking. Her voice reaches me like a murmur. I don't pay much attention to her. At sixty, the gossipography of the neighborhood no longer interests me, but I do like coming to the colmado, it's like hanging out with family. The music's good, none of that reggaeton, and it's not so loud as to hurt my ears. Ever since my kids went to live in New York, I close up my sewing machine after turning in my jobs, take a bath, and walk over here to my second home. I sit and look at the bottles, all neatly aligned in rows on the shelves—beer, rum, whiskey, juices, there's everything here. The blue Formica countertop is always clean and shiny, and the whole place smells of tobacco and pine essence. Amancia's lucky because Rafelito is a good worker. The colmados today are so different from back in the days of my youth. Then, their main function was to sell groceries, but now they sell liquor, though I think that, more than liquor, what really attracts people is the company. People to talk to and share with without having to spend a lot of money, because these aren't times for spending a lot of money.

"Juana, you have to go to the doctor. You're worse every day. It's almost as if you aren't here. You're either in love—and I doubt that—or there's something wrong with your brain. If you want, I can talk to Doctor Mateo so he'll see you. You should take advantage of the fact he always comes by, and he's so nice. He probably won't charge you."

"I wish I could fall in love, but that's impossible in this day and age. Men my age are looking for younger women. I'll let you know if I decide to go."

Amancia is always tearing down or building up. She uses the same passion to destroy the reputations of her friends and neighbors as she does to help when any of them is sick or in trouble. It's been thirty-six years since she opened the colmado, and she's worked mostly by herself. Her husband, Joaquin, is good at taking orders, and she's good at giving them. I remember she moved here a year after I got my house. Who could have imagined that the houses President Balaguer built for teachers would someday become residences for the rich? Back then, I was a teacher; later, I was forced to retire because of my heart condition, and I had to dedicate myself to sewing. Amancia bought her house from a teacher, Benigna Castillo, who sold it to go to New York and struggle.

"I have a second piece of news for you. Guess who was here last night?"

She answers herself before I get a chance to speak.

"Hold on to your seat, cuz the surprise is gonna knock you over. Rosa. The saintly one, the dark-skinned girl who spends all her time in church," she says gaily as she takes a sip of beer, holding it up as if she were toasting a prize she'd earned.

"Rosa! You must be mistaken. I don't believe it."

"No, my dear, I'm not mistaken. She was wearing a very tight, short red dress. She sat on the bench under the awning, asked for a small one and drank it, savoring each and every sip. I never took my eyes off her. Every once in a while, she'd comb the colmado, as if she were looking for someone, and it seems that someone was also looking for her. Want to guess?"

"Cough it up, Amancia. Rosa is a serious churchgoing girl. This surprises me. She's not the kind of girl to hang out at a colmado."

"I suppose you can imagine, with that body of hers, my customers were drooling, looking her up and down, but she just looked back as if nothing was going on, as if she was an innocent. Rafa, the deputy, Colonel Guzmán, Juan Pablo, the eye doctor—they all approached her like a flock of flies homing in on dead meat. They chatted her up and ended the evening by teaching her how to play dominoes. She conducted herself very well. She was neither unsociable nor overly friendly, and after about two hours she left with the excuse that she had to take care of her mother."

Amancia keeps talking, describing looks and gestures, interpreting bits of conversations. The truth is I can't believe it. The voices, the sounds of the bottles, the laughter, the movement of the chairs—it all seems vulgar and distant. This makes me restless. I know Rosa doesn't belong in this place—she's neither easy nor crazy.

In the last few years, I've always said nothing makes me lose sleep, but last night I slept badly. I can't get Rosa out of my head. She's a different kind of girl, with a good job. She's a teacher at a school for rich kids and a private tutor. She reads a lot, and you can talk with her about anything. If she hasn't married yet, it's because she hasn't wanted to. She was in a two-year courtship with Nelson, Ángela's son—it's true he's a very serious and hardworking young man, but he's also duller than an oyster—and she's had a bunch of admirers. She dedicates her free time to reading and working with the kids from the Café neighborhood. I'm very close to her because, with the scraps left over from my sewing jobs, we make quilts and sheets for the old folks' home.

Like every afternoon, I go to the colmado, and unfortunately confirm Amancia's news. There's Rosa, in a tight dress, laughing heartily, being provocative. A stranger. I'm embarrassed, for her and for me. It's a strange feeling, as if something inside me were telling me that I, too, could have done what she's doing. Amancia signals for me to come over. I avoid her and push my chair behind the counter so Rosa can't see me. I don't want to embarrass her.

"You can't stick your hand in the fire for just anybody. I always tell you, and you never learn. You still believe in innocents, that's why so many customers take advantage of you. Open your eyes, Juana, and don't be such an old fool," Amancia says as she takes a seat by my side.

"You're right," I answer, though I could have just as easily said "uh huh" or "yes."

She doesn't hear a thing. She's like one of those voice-overs that narrate soap operas.

The laughter and noise of the clientele is hurting my ears. The sound of the bottles snapping open. Everything is amplified. I'm overwhelmed by sadness. I feel heat and an ache in my throat. Miguel–so many years married to Miguel, so many lost years without either security or love. He gave me nothing, although perhaps I shouldn't be so unfair–he did leave me a slew of bad memories. I think if I were young again, I'd laugh like Rosa, and I'd come to the colmado to have fun with the deputy and the colonel, who'd humiliate and hurt me, but who'd at least provide financial security.

The days go by, and Rosa's laugh becomes increasingly strident, the dresses get tighter, and the comings and goings with the deputy more frequent. She sees me and greets me quite naturally, as if nothing is going on. And maybe nothing is going on. The truth is that times have changed, and I'm an old-fashioned woman, "left behind," as they say these days.

I'm coming up to the colmado. Amancia runs toward me, gesturing with her arms as if she were drowning. I start to say something, but she beats me to it.

"The devil has gotten into Rosa's body. Guess what happened yesterday after you left?" she asks, taking me by the arm and leading me to the stool farthest away from everyone.

"Just tell me; you're killing my heart."

"Rosa came back from her usual stroll with the deputy around ten o'clock, and in about a half hour a car came and honked its horn. She ran to it and got in. I couldn't see who was driving, and I ordered Rafelito to follow them. I'm still crossing myself. The devil's on the loose."

"Tell me who the hell picked her up."

"You're not going to believe it. Father Moisés, the same priest we confess to and who gives us communion."

"You're lying. I don't believe you. I'm sure Rafelito made a mistake."

We decide to organize a surveillance network. I stay until eleven p.m. several days in a row with the excuse of wanting to learn to play dominoes. Amancia sets out a table in a spot where we can keep an eye on all the entry and exit points. On the fifth day, I confirm what I didn't want to accept–Father Moisés is the one who picks up Rosa. There's no doubt in my mind whatsoever. I know him well, and I recognize his car.

I get home and go straight to my altar. Facing an image of Almighty God, I pray for them and for me. I pray about disillusionment and for all the young people who are lost, for the priest's great sin (because he is supposed to be God's representative on earth), and for Amancia to hold her tongue and not talk about what we saw.

It's been days since I've been to the colmado. My head hurts. Perhaps it's from being inside. I want to cry. I don't even have the energy to bathe. I'm going to go out for a little while to see if I can get rid of this heavy weight in my stomach. It's like a fear that got stuck.

"Juana, open up, quick—the devil is in us," Amancia screams as she pounds on my door.

"Jesus Christ, Amancia, what's going on? What are you doing here at this hour? Come in already."

"Oh, Juana, we have to go to confession. We are sinners," she says, coming inside with such haste that she has to hold on to a chair for balance. "Doesn't your conscience bother you?"

"What are you talking about? I don't understand. Why should my conscience bother me?"

Amancia pounces. "Don't you know about Rosa and the father? Haven't you heard the news?"

"No. What news? I don't know anything," I answer, while I feel my stomach clench as if in a vise.

"Damn, Rosa and Father Moisés turned in a child prostitution ring that the deputy was running."

"What?"

I lose my balance. Amancia takes my arm and helps me sit.

"It's just like I'm telling you. I got tired of calling her house and being told she's out of town. The colonel told me the police are protecting her. Father Moisés was the one who gave details to the media."

I get dressed, and we head for the colmado. I drink more beer than I'm used to. I toast Rosa, my heroine.

A lot of time goes by, and I don't hear anything about Rosa. Father Moisés was sent to Rome. I hear that they both left out of fear of what could happen to them—it seems there are people involved in this thing who are way more important than the deputy.

I approach the colmado slowly. It's a special day. I'm turning sixty-two. I'm glad to be alive, but I feel a little empty because I've spent all this time on earth without doing anything of importance.

"The devil's on the loose, Juana, I have big news for you," Amancia says as she catches up to me and brings me back to reality.

"He's always loose as far as you're concerned. C'mon, tell me. Who's the gossip about?"

"Rosa."

"What? You heard from her? Is she all right? Tell me slowly. Wait until I get comfortable."

"C'mon, it's not like she's your daughter. Change that foolish, old-woman tone, cuz she's doing a lot better than you and me. Rafelito, bring us a couple of frosty ones," Amancia yells.

"For the love of God, tell me. You're killing my heart."

"Pilar called this afternoon. She just got back from New York and says she ran into Rosa there, with her husband and son at the McDonald's on Grand Concourse and 182nd. Rosa and her magnificent husband, the former Father Moisés. I'm telling you, the ones who seem the most innocent end up being bigger sluts than Herminia."

"Rosa and Father Moisés! It's like something out of a soap opera!"

Amancia tells everyone who comes in the colmado. "Big news!" she says, as always. The big news is a good birthday gift. I can imagine a thousand ways that romance could have grown between Rosa and Father Moisés. It's my personal soap opera, and I enjoy it, I go over it as I sew, seam by seam, as I'm cooking, bathing, as Amancia's talking away. I enjoy love stories.

THE DAY
I LOST MELISSA

NONFICTION BY ERIKA M. MARTÍNEZ

Rosie combed my hair before going to bed as she told me a story about a girl in high school who fell in love with a boy on the last day of school and had to wait the entire summer to see him again. I looked forward to the day I'd be older, like my cousin Rosie, so that I could get my hair relaxed the way she did. Then I'd be beautiful, and one day a boy would fall in love with me and want to get married. My tíos and tías would admire me instead of Melissa.

Mami was never as gentle. She'd fought with my curls ever since I was a baby and reminded me of it by taking out pictures of me at two or three years old wearing a bandana over my head with pink sponge rolos underneath. It was embarrassing to think about myself walking the streets of Brooklyn when my head looked twice its normal size.

Rosie's grandmother, Adín, had been watching my sister, Melissa, and me since Mami had gone to Santo Domingo nine days earlier for Abuelo's funeral. Francisco, my four-year-old brother, was at Minerva's in Hoboken; we'd left him there for the weekend so that he could play with our cousins, Rob and Raymond. It was Sunday, January 3, 1982. When Mami returned to Union City in the evening, neither Melissa nor I wanted to walk the sixteen blocks back to our place.

In the kitchen, as Adín cooked, the adults tried to dissuade us from leaving. Mami could not afford to miss work the next day, and she did not want Melissa or me to be absent from school on the first day after winter recess. But Adín knew our refrigerator was empty, that when we woke up in the morning there would be nothing for us to eat. She wanted us to stay until Mami had had the chance to pick up her food stamps and go grocery shopping.

I wanted to stay at Adín's to enjoy the pasteles she had made for us. I loved being in a home where the fridge was full. When I served myself a glass of water, my eyes feasted on the fresh parsley, red tomatoes, and plátanos. To me, the sight of colorful food on every shelf was beautiful. Adín knew we didn't always eat well, so she often gave us a Tupperware filled with beans to take home as a complement to the white rice I'd made every day after school since Papi left us. I also wanted to stay because I wanted to sleep in the warmth. Unlike our rent, Adín's included heat—she didn't monitor a thermostat the way Mami did to keep our bill low.

One by one, they resolved the complications. I would get to school in the morning taking the number 19 or the number 22; Adín would put Melissa on either of these buses at noon, telling the driver to drop her off on 39th Street; when Melissa got off the bus, I would be there waiting during my lunchtime recess to walk her to the kindergarten trailer. Melissa had never walked to school alone or taken the bus by herself, because when Mami was not around I brought her wherever she needed to go. The next day, as soon as she descended from the bus, I would make certain she got to class and did not miss her half-day of school.

We were staying.

Nearly thirty years later, I reach out to Adín about this very evening, the day before I lost Melissa. Her voice on the long-distance call sounds like it did in 1982—high in pitch, sweet. I imagine that the pauses in between sentences help her travel back to the past. She tells me about how difficult that period was for Mami because Papi had left right after Thanksgiving, and Abuelo died in December. From her tone, I sense her remembering Mami's sorrow.

But on that night we weren't thinking about Mami's sadness. The adults were smiling, not because we were sleeping over; they were smiling at Melissa. Along with the rest of the family, I stared at Melissa's green eyes, at her pale skin, at the way her straight hair fell limp on her shoulders. Mami noticed everyone's delight and took a sip of her beer. She beamed the way she did when she looked at pretty pictures of herself. If Mami had created such beauty, then she was beautiful herself.

In the winter of 1972 I was in my mother's womb. Although Mami and Papi did not want to start a family until they had moved back to Santo Domingo, I was a planned pregnancy. She was happy that she had not experienced morning sickness. Papi protected her and me at the same time. So that we were both nourished well, he tried to coax her to eat fruits and vegetables, even though she hated them. As Mami walked around her kitchen in New Jersey, she held on to her belly so that I would not bang against the edges of the countertop.

I was wanted and loved before I was born, before she saw what I looked like, before my mind formed memories.

On Wednesday, August 15, 1973, my mother spent the night in Room 23 at Christ Hospital in Jersey City recovering from a breech birth as President Nixon gave his second Watergate speech. America was wrapped in scandal the way I was swaddled in my blanket. With the help of Dr. Coronado at 9:55 that morning I arrived in the world feet first. This was the first of many things Mami held against me. She was in labor for over twenty-four hours. I weighed five pounds, fourteen ounces.

Eight months earlier, the U.S. Supreme Court had ruled on *Roe v. Wade*. This was the year that women started thinking out loud about abortion. I had thought about it every time Mami reminded me about my difficult birth, when she told me what a challenge I'd been since the beginning, as she repeated all the sacrifices she'd made for me. In 1981, 1984, 1987, 1988, when Mami said she wished she'd never had me, I wondered why I had not been aborted.

On January 4, 1982, I arrived home from school alone on one of the coldest Monday afternoons of my childhood. As I walked through the glass vestibule door of the two-flat apartment building, I heard our phone ringing on the second floor. I raced up the rickety stairs covered in green shag carpet, unlocked our door, leaving the key in the deadbolt lock, and took the call. In Spanish, Adín asked if my sister was with me as I panted.

"No. Melissa never arrived," I told her. I had gone to the bus stop, as planned, but she was not there. When the bus doors closed, all I'd seen was the reflection of my brown winter coat in the glass doors, the one Papi had bought for me when we'd moved from Santo Domingo in December 1979. He had brought two of the same coats to the airport, the bigger one for me, the little one for Melissa. When we'd slipped inside them on that snowy day, Papi had tied the leather belts for us at the waist. He'd dressed Francisco in a plaid coat. "I thought she stayed with you."

"I put her on the bus at noon. Go back to school and get her," she said. "Go."

I dropped the phone, took off as if I'd heard a gunshot at a starting line, a firing that sent a rush of heat through the currents of blood in my body.

My feet skipped steps, two and three at a time, thumping. I raced down the cement stairs and across the street to the tall red-brick buildings—their playgrounds were empty. I stopped, caught my breath, searched for schoolmates returning down the hill, but they were already inside, watching afternoon cartoons, doing homework, or eating a snack.

Just minutes ago, I'd been happy to walk home alone at three o'clock—without Melissa, that is. When the bell rang, I'd raced out the door with my friends Mirelys and Ivette. I hadn't had to pass by the kindergarten trailer, since I thought Melissa had stayed at Adín's. I hadn't had to listen to messages from her teacher and deliver them to Mami. I'd been free to spend time with my friends and had the liberty of walking as fast as my legs could go without having to wait for my little sister. Mirelys had shown Ivette and me how to skip like Dorothy in *The Wizard of Oz*. We'd pranced down the yellow brick road toward home until we crossed Kennedy Boulevard. There it had become too hard, because the momentum pulled us downhill faster than we could coordinate our feet.

The thought of now running up the hill overwhelmed me, but the fear of what Mami would do to me if I didn't find Melissa forced me to run. My breath was visible with each exhale. At the top of the hill, the crossing guard was gone. What would Mami do to me if I didn't bring Melissa home? Melissa—Mami's favorite.

It was 1984 when I shoved Melissa to the bottom of our neighbor's three-foot pool in Long Island. She was afraid to go underwater, so I forced her to try it. Then a rage from deep within me wanted her to never resurface. My hands kept her head down longer than she could hold her breath, as her friend Bernadette and her brother Bryan watched. They called their mother, who ordered me to stop.

"Get out," Mrs. Peterson said. "All of you."

We climbed out and lined up in front of her, dripping. Her eyes squinted, not from the summer sun but from disbelief.

"You two are never allowed in the pool together again," she said with a finger pointing at Melissa and me. "Everything has a consequence, Erika."

I left. Melissa stayed with Bernadette and Bryan.

On that Monday in January at the corner of Kennedy Boulevard and 39th, the light turned green. When all the cars stopped, I ran across the street. I rested at the gas station, caught my breath again, but I started coughing. I coughed so much my throat hurt. I couldn't stop. I had to go. I had to get to Melissa.

I got to Bergenline Avenue, and the crossing guard wasn't there either. The light was red. I squeezed my eyes shut trying to will it to turn green. But I could not make it change, the way I could not make my skin lighter or my hair straight, the way I could not make anyone love me.

Mami was going to kill me if I didn't find Melissa. I raced to the kindergarten trailer, and she was not outside waiting for me. I pulled the door to her classroom, and it was locked. I pulled and pulled and pulled until I couldn't keep myself from crying. It's all my fault, I told myself. Melissa, where are you? I lost Melissa; I lost my little sister. She was so beautiful, and now she's gone because of me. "Somebody let me in," I screamed. But nobody could hear me. There was no one there. I was all alone.

I roamed the streets. I repeated Melissa's name in between sobs. There was no use in trudging around the baseball diamond once more or under the basketball hoops. When I went around to 40th Street again, the shopkeeper of a rug store saw me walking alone and crying. "What's wrong?" he asked.

"I lost my sister."

He warmed his hands in his breath, then rubbed them together. He took my hand. We walked around the school and stopped at every door. He tried to pull each one open. Even the main entrances on New York Avenue at the top of the long stairs were closed, locked. The lights were out behind every window. He pounded on the doors with his fists, but no one answered. He even put his ears on the door to see if he could hear anyone inside.

On 39th Street, he found an unlocked door. When he opened it, my breath stopped. He waved me inside. We heard the sounds of children playing, sounds coming from the basement. We walked downstairs and entered an after-school day care center.

The shopkeeper spoke to the director, a woman I'd later know as Connie. She led us to a kitchen, where Melissa sat waiting with her head down on a round table, forehead nestled in the nook of her crossed arms.

She lifted her head, and I saw dried-up tears on her chapped cheeks. She was still wearing her brown coat with the belt tied around her waist, like me.

January 16, 1990, was a Tuesday. I came home from my closing shift at McDonald's after midnight, and instead of going to my bedroom, I stayed in the kitchen with the lights off so as not to wake up my family. I needed to talk to my friend Howie. We'd made it a ritual to exchange notes folded into little triangles every time we worked together and to call each other when we returned from the restaurant, but Mami had recently forbidden me to use the phone.

Because Howie didn't work that night, I didn't get a response to the last note I'd given him—my eight-page suicide letter. I stood over the sink with the phone in my left hand and the cup of Tide laundry detergent I would drink in my right. Starving myself to death was no longer a viable option; at sixteen, I needed to end my pain.

I cried as I told him my reasons for wanting to die. He didn't know that I was poisoning myself as we spoke. I didn't tell him about the thick cold liquid, how it stung in my throat and made me gag. Mami entered the kitchen and turned on the light.

"I'll call you back," I said and hung up the phone.

My back and shoulders tensed up because I thought she'd come forward to hit me for being up so late, for talking on the phone, but she got closer to take away the laundry detergent. As she screwed the top back on, she asked if she should bring me to the hospital. I shook my head no. She turned off the lights and went back to bed.

I called Howie again, trying to control the volume of my sobs. "She doesn't even care," I said into the handset.

Howie realized that he had to read me what he'd written, that the message couldn't wait until we saw each other again. "Remember in your last note you said if you only had one good thing to balance out the bad? Well, you do. Me. I'm always going to be there for you, Erika. . . . Your problems aren't a burden to me. I'll read one hundred of your eight-page notes and let you cry on my shoulders seven days a week . . . our friendship means the world to me. You mean the world to me. I love you. . . ."

I gasped, then wept even more as he continued to read, because without knowing it this was what I needed—to hear those words, to believe them, to feel someone love me. His promise to be there for me felt as real as the telephone cord spiraled around my index finger. The phlegm in my throat made me cough; then I began to throw up the detergent into the cold stainless steel sink.

When he was convinced that I wanted to live, we hung up. I spent the dawn in my room, vomiting into a garbage can next to the bed, following Howie's instructions. Like he told me to, I imagined a place with no mothers, no school, no work, just fun.

In 2002 Melissa called to see if I'd felt relief from my depression. The entire family, then scattered over five states, had been in communication about my condition. Melissa filled me in on several phone conversations. Papi had called Mami and asked her to be nice to me because it was evident I'd suffered a trauma. Mami had then called Melissa to say that Papi caused the trauma when he left in 1981. Francisco had called Melissa and asked her to have compassion for me because Mami had always treated her like the favorite. Melissa had denied it. She didn't remember the past.

Francisco had reminded her of a day in 1984. "The two of you were fighting over a blanket for hours. Erika was lying on the couch, and you were on the floor by her feet tugging at the blanket. She kicked you. Your lip started bleeding, and you ran to Mami, crying," Francisco had told Melissa. "Mami then rushed in from the kitchen, pulled Erika by the hair, and started slamming her head on the dresser. Mami almost killed her that night."

As I heard Melissa repeat what Francisco said, I was taken aback. I had a witness.

"Mami did almost kill me that night," I said to Melissa. "But she didn't slam my head on the dresser. I remember she pulled me to my bedroom, threw me to the ground, straddled me, grabbed my neck, and started choking me. Doña Julia and Aidita ran in and had to pull her off me. They saved my life."

At around five p.m. on that Monday, Melissa and I walked home. I held her hand the entire way. I wiped my sticky face at the stoplight and remembered how I took off after Adín's phone call.

"I don't have keys," I said. "I left them in the door lock when I ran out. I left the phone off the hook, too." I started to cry again.

"Mrs. Mary will let us in," Melissa said.

If Mrs. Mary wasn't there, we couldn't get through the vestibule door. We'd have to wait outside for Mami, who wouldn't be home for another three hours. If we had to wait for Mami, she'd know everything. I wouldn't be able to hide all the things I'd done wrong.

Almost three decades later I talk to Mami on the phone about this day. We disagree about many details of the plan to get Melissa to school, but she tells me she remembers what happened because this was why she had to go on welfare. The school administration gave her a letter to take to Social Services so that she would qualify for public assistance and stay at home. They didn't feel that Mami should leave us at home alone, especially Francisco, who was only four years old and spent the entire day with no one around to watch him. I ask Mami if she stopped working, even though I know the answer. "Not really," she says. "No. I worked under the table."

That Monday afternoon when Melissa and I returned to our building, Mrs. Mary wasn't there, so we sat on the cold cement stoop. We huddled together in the corner to try to stay warm, but we couldn't hide from the wind blowing through the holes in the porch walls. We took our hands from our pockets to warm them with our exhalations the way the shopkeeper did. Our breath shimmered in front of our mouths. Melissa heard my stomach growl.

I prayed for Mrs. Mary to get home first.

We spent a few hours in the dark before Mami came home with Francisco. She walked up the stairs, pausing at each step. "¿Qué hacen aquí?" she asked. Her voice was hoarse, tired from talking over the sewing machines.

Unable to hide what had happened, I told her why we were outside. "Mami, I'm sorry. I left the phone off the hook and the door unlocked upstairs with the key in it." Tears fell down my face. "I couldn't make dinner. I'm sorry."

Mami fixed her eyes on me. In those long seconds, I waited for a scream or for her hands to come at me. Instead, she pulled out the keys from her purse, unlocked the vestibule door, and held it open for the three of us to go inside.

In February 2002 I was living in Chicago. I sat in the dining room of our new condo, constructed according to our specifications: walls painted mint green, hardwood floors, and stainless steel appliances. Everything was as I wanted, yet I was in one of the deepest despairs I'd experienced in my twenty-eight years of life. I was on the phone with Mami, who could not understand how I could be depressed, because I had everything—a college education, a good job sitting at a desk all day adding numbers, a wonderful blond husband who she was waiting for me to procreate with, hoping our children would be born with his blue eyes and blond hair (my entire family was hopeful), and we owned our home.

Her response to my sobs was the same: stop listening to classical music, because it darkens anyone's mood; stop crying, because I'd lose my husband (she thought everyone was afraid of tears); and pray—God could save me. When I hashed over the past, she insisted I was wrong. I wanted to understand how a parent could favor one child over the other.

"But she's your hermanita," she said. "You love her. You've looked after her since you were three."

The earliest times I remembered watching over her were between 1977 and 1979. We'd lived in Santo Domingo then, and I'd made sure she didn't swallow the coins she found or pick up cigarette butts and bring them to her lips. I clutched the handset. No wonder I could not keep myself from telling Melissa which foods were best for her. Mami told me this made me good.

"Your sister needed to be watched over extra carefully. Even now she needs more support than others," she said.

But I was the one on the phone asking for help, and it was as if Mami couldn't hear me through the music playing. She was not listening as she recalled the memories. I did not yell at her for leaving me in my current darkness. In that moment, she approved of me, and that pulled me up for a breath. Her last words to me that night were to pray. That was the best she could do.

THE IMMACULATE FINGER

FICTION BY FARAH HALLAL

Translated by Achy Obejas

When I saw my neighbor sitting in the park, her eyes fixed on Christopher Columbus's back, we hadn't planned to meet. It happened by chance—in this case, a very thin and weak chance, almost nonexistent, with a smooth, reddish copper finish from being turned over so many times over the years. For all the gossips who hang out on the streets of Vietnam, I'm going to be perfectly clear: my presence in that ring, where the sane and insane fight for a crown of ignorance, happened without any planning on either of our parts. It was as much a coincidence as the threat of rain that had forced me, moments before, to dismiss my first-level English students that Saturday afternoon.

Well, the truth is I gave my students the pleasure of being let go before six not because the sky threatened to rage outside, but because it was also threatening to rain inside the classroom due to a problem with the drainpipes on the fifth floor that affected the fourth and would end up drenching all the rooms, as often happened with the midday rain. In any event, I wouldn't be able to justify staying to practice the verb "to be" to the mothers, who are cultured people but become much less so when their offspring are threatened with pneumonia because water drops are hitting their backs with the sharp insistence of a voodoo priest jabbing his needle into a rag doll's body.

That was the only reason I had to get out of the institute. Even though I always go home after I finish my classes on Saturday afternoons, this time I had no desire to buck the crowds in the streets. That's why, when I descended the last step which spit me out onto El Conde Street, I decided not to go to

Independencia Park, from which carritos depart for anywhere in the world. Truth be told, I couldn't be turned on by a city whose funereal aspect foretold the continuation of a soulless rain.

At that hour, when passengers were fleeing the Colonial Zone with the desperation of slaves fleeing their yokes, I preferred to flee the dreadful lines of people dying to find a way to get to Los Mina. Anybody would agree that Saturday afternoon is no time to get into a shoving match with whoever wants to steal my turn to climb into a carrito battered on all sides, with no glass in the windows, and a driver who forces you to press up against other passengers, encouraging you with the famous phrase "Squeeze tight like you did last night!" That's on top of the fact that because it's me, they always end up charging me two or three fares for one ride, and no other passenger wants to be next to me.

Walking struck me as a better idea, especially because walking in the drizzle and over puddles of unpredictable dimensions always awakens my memory to faded images of my brother, Camilo, who died from meningitis at Robert Reid Cabral when they still called that hospital "El Angelita." It was unclear just how bad the storm was going to be, but the forecast changed for me when I saw my antisocial neighbor, Inmaculada, just as I was walking by Columbus Park. Without a doubt, that day held a secret I never would have believed if anyone had told me, even if they'd been from back in the neighborhood.

In the neighborhood where I live, Vietnam, any homeboy would kill to come to El Conde Street to learn English. And not just because there are various institutes to choose from. People know that because there are tourists around, they can practice. But if kids from neighborhoods like Vietnam had the money to pay for the course, they wouldn't have money for commuting or to buy themselves a two-for-one deal during recess. If they had any luck at all, they'd just come and go, dying of hunger, just as they were born. Given that scenario, Inmaculada wouldn't be the right age or have the money to be here in El Conde taking classes either. The "what she was doing here" or "since when" was impossible to know from seeing her. She wasn't carrying a bag or notebooks to hint that she might be studying around there. I often tell my students (those who have someone to cover their expenses but no desire to learn), "Go down to Columbus Park," better known as Pigeon Park. That's how they practice their English—they talk to tourists, helping them take photos of themselves when they're alone or giving them directions when they look like they're lost.

It strikes me as almost amusing that the day I saw Inmaculada, I was the one who was lost. I walked as if I had a purpose without actually having one. I was merely trying to get out of my own head, taking my hands out for a stroll, pulling them out of the pockets of my plaid pants where I'd been hiding them. I'd been struggling for some time to find my odd and ample size in clothing.

I wasn't apt to have very many options, and I'd been reduced to these plaid trousers now so faded that their exact colors were hard to remember. These were supplemented by a pair of prewashed jeans and some black pants my mother called the lint magnet. When it comes to clothes, my mother knows what she's talking about, because she was once a washerwoman, a real one, back in the day when women who were any kind of poor didn't have Japanese washing machines, and her being forced to rub the dirt out of all those strangers' clothes with a measure of her own resentment supported my desire to get ahead. That desire was rare in the neighborhood I lived in before I got to Vietnam. Back there, winning at dominoes and knowing how to dance salsa really well were much more valuable than an eighth-grade diploma.

Well, it turns out that Inmaculada, who is actually, cruelly, known as Culá, was sitting in the park quite comfortably as if nothing was going on when the sky opened up. She didn't have an umbrella or an open newspaper, as the man who'd been sitting next to her a few minutes before did. She seemed not to notice that terrible sensation of having wet feet inside one's shoes. Didn't she realize all the sky's anguish was coming down? No, Culá did not betray any signs of flight, unlike the others, who were clearing out of the park like pieces off a chessboard after the players have tired of the game, or when it's more than evident who's been defeated.

First, I noticed her gaze, which was practically a straight line to the statue of Christopher Columbus. She looked at it in the cordial way you look at someone you're sure you know but can't place. The next thing I noticed was that she lingered for a long time on the admiral's raised finger. I'm not going to deny that when Culá moved her hand and pointed to Columbus's index finger, I was frightened. What the hell was going on with the statue? Was she going crazy? Couldn't she tell that somebody had noticed her behavior, someone who knew her from the neighborhood and was well aware that what he was seeing was none of his business and that he was getting wet just to play along with her? Actually, no, I wasn't getting wet just to play along with her. I did it because if something had happened to her I didn't want it on my conscience.

While Culá delineated in the air the quickest route to the nearest loony bin, I stopped to take in the vanity of America's first cathedral, which by virtue of being the first is not necessarily the best. Its wet walls stood with the same assurance as always, as if no one ever noticed that in every hole left by a missing brick, in every point-blank shot it ever took, there was a common pigeon taking a shit. Surely it had begun by appropriating a hole in the wall to make a nest, but in time any pigeon (no matter how dumb it might be) would have figured out you can't just lay an egg in any basket. With its ill-calculated dimensions, the cathedral holds—aside from all the live bodies that come to pray on Sundays—a good number of dead in its discreet marble crypts, dead who evidently deserved much more compassion than all the natives who were exterminated.

Wiping away the drops that could have fallen in my eyes, I turned back to Culá. If she'd been aware of her surroundings, she might have noticed the smell of wet earth (and wet shit) that was overwhelming the park. And she would also have noticed the silence quickly descending now that the kids were leaving, not just because the rain had functioned like a scarecrow for the cathedral, but also because the cloudy skies were swathing the park like a child who'd been sent to bed early.

My neighbor's obvious derangement made me step back a bit so I could call Doña Fredes. I needed to let her know what was going on. Culá had lived with Fredes for many years (everybody knows that suffering and compassion go well together). This woman, who'd become her mother from one day to the next, would come get her as soon as she realized that Culá was sitting like a lunatic on the edge of the most atrocious rainstorm this side of the world, making delirious gestures with her finger. I couldn't see much difference between this and a total breakdown.

I used the last few minutes on my cell to call the very Catholic Fredes, who made all of us in Vietnam get baptized—me twice because she didn't believe I'd been baptized before I came to the capital. Unfortunately, I couldn't find her back in the neighborhood and neither could my mother. "Doña Fredes meets every Saturday with the other church elders, and no one ever sees hide nor hair of her then," she said. I didn't want to leave a message with my mother because she has the power to hurl a rumor into the world with the force of vomit. If I told my mother—forgive me, mother—Culá would be the target of far more ridicule than she'd been in her whole life.

In adolescence, Culá had twisted teeth and a prematurely worried expression. Since she was pretty much a stick (in both her figure and disposition), the homeboys would whistle at her in a flirty fashion, and then when she turned to look they'd say the most disgusting things. Before they went away to jail, El Bigote would call her "Big Pussy," and El Guandul would steal her panties off the laundry line and hang them off the railings on houses all over the neighborhood.

Since Culá only has a birthday every February 29—in other words, every four years—old Fredes tried to do whatever she could to throw her a little celebration. One time, she had a party with the absurd notion of marrying her off. She had the bright idea of inviting all the homeboys to see if one of them might get interested in her. Even I got an invitation, not on a proper postcard, but screamed at me through the tiny space between my living room window and my neighbor's. "Don't even think about missing it, Don Vicente!"

It didn't occur to Doña Fredes that, with my gray age, my bachelorhood, and my interests—as dusty as antique books—I would not enjoy a party organized by two or three matchmakers. Only they ended up attending the party. No one else was interested in Culá and her sexless thirty-seven years, with her bony and unwanted body. There was cake for days; they sent me some three times that same week.

"It's just that there are so many power outages, Doña Vicenta," Fredes told my mother, practically apologizing for coming by the house with yet another piece of cake, now almost gone bad.

Even though I realize that a lot of the rudeness Culá experienced was rooted in ignorance, when I saw her out of her mind sitting on that park bench, I asked myself if she was going to end up as the local crazy, as part of the panorama that you get used to in the Colonial Zone. Since I haven't gotten married either, and I'm close to fifty, I know all too well that being alone is like getting hit with a ball right in the chest. It's like having a weight inside, something heavy that you can't get off no matter what. But it's been a while since I stopped caring when people pointed me out as an oddball because I'm also lucky in that, as a professor, as someone who got ahead, I get respect, even if I still live with my mother in an iffy neighborhood.

It's well known that there are no secrets in Vietnam, and if there were, it would be a minefield. There, every infidelity—no matter how delicately handled—ends up exploding like a headline that doesn't need to be printed on the front page of a newspaper to reach everyone. Because of this neighborhood's talent for gossiping, it was well known that Culá was looking for love. And if she wasn't looking of her own volition, it would have been because she was pushed to do so by the neighborhood women, who were determined that she not end up as alone as she had been when she was born, orphaned by her mother at birth, pulled out alive by such luck the doctors might have thought she had something big in her future. When she was three her father died, and from ages three to fourteen all her aunts clamored to have her as their ward so she could clean up after their miserable selves. And, well, at fourteen, when one of those aunts discovered her husband about to rape Culá, she beat Culá and threw her out of the house, dumping her at Caribe Tours. Doña Fredes was coming from La Vega and found a penniless Inmaculada at the bus station, crying and with nowhere to go. I know this story—which I heard so many times in my kitchen—better than the protagonists themselves. And so there, in the park where nobody cares who sits and who gets up, I made a space for myself by her side, knowing that she might not notice anything. I didn't even greet her. Because Inmaculada never spoke to the neighbors again after that party and hardly ever let herself be seen (me neither, to be frank), I remembered her mostly as a figure concocted by the neighborhood boys. I was astonished to find she had almond-shaped eyes that were an almost clear brown. I bet that if I could have seen them closer, with lashes and expression, they would have revealed everything she carried inside. You could say I had magnifying lenses for eyes, allowing me to see up close her arms, as long as the misery that she carried through this life. Her arms had whip marks, probably from when she didn't finish washing the dishes on time or chose to watch a soap opera on TV while the aunt on shift was out of the house.

After a while, I forced myself to look at what she was staring at. My teacher's curiosity led me to also point at the raised index finger of Christopher Columbus, a much more bronzed admiral than he imagined himself in life, when he encountered new ideas in his search for a better-drawn world and found only simple souls in little clothing. There he is, still, after five hundred years, pointing north without the slightest regard for poor Queen Anacaona, who's also there, but who hardly anyone notices in passing. No one sees her bronzed pain, dragging herself like a lizard toward "the king" of the Spanish seas. The pitiful demise of the indigenous people has always been clear, so I never thought it necessary to have that sculpture as a reminder, like a stake in the heart.

Anyway, I don't think Inmaculada and I were having the same artistic appreciation. It didn't take long for me to figure out that she expected something extraordinary to happen, but nothing did, except that she said hello. I think she said hello because I almost pushed her off the bench. I thought it was kind of silly that I was asking myself if she'd recognize me, if she'd mind my seventies salsa singer mustache or my fiftyish belly. Inmaculada knew my name and my profession. She even knew the nickname my mother used whenever she sat me down to read or to listen to the classical music station or to prepare for my classes. The windows in my room look out at the windows in her room, though it never seems as if anyone's there. I had begun to doubt that this woman could even properly articulate, but my doubts dissolved in the puddle beneath our feet.

"I raised my finger like this one day, and a ray of light bounced off the bronze finger. It looked like the light came from my finger. It felt beautiful, as if it were magic." Her voice seemed angelic, maybe because she used it so rarely. Her words made me realize she could tell I'd thought she was a little off and that her gestures in the air with her finger deserved a good explanation. Embarrassed, I lowered my eyes to find my copy of Maupassant's short stories lost in the loud design of her skirt. It was my favorite edition, a 1965 hardcover, orange with gold letters.

"Your mother lends me books now and again. I'm sorry we didn't ask your permission," she added, and her cheeks reddened with shame.

"Surely it'll be sunny next Saturday," I said, to keep the conversation going because it interested me. What else could I say? I found myself lifting my finger in the air like a crazy person. I'd just turned into a big-bellied fool in front of this woman who didn't seem any crazier than me. Why had I thought I was better than her? For example, at my age, why was I still single? Why do I run away from women, incapable of flirting with any of them? Anybody could have read these questions in my gaze. They flew past my eyes like a banner trailing a plane where it was plain and easy to read: I'm a confirmed fool. As I sat there, imagining the color of the letters that would spell out my most obvious folly, that of trying to make someone else seem crazy even though I clearly fit the bill way more, Inmaculada stood up and murmured that it was about to rain or something like that. She extended the book to me, which I refused to take as I noticed how her slight weight and heavy skirt made her seem like a woman from the century before last. It seemed her skirt had fabric enough to make a curtain that would enclose the whole park, and I laughed when the idea came to me. Either she didn't like my laugh, or her virtue opposed any continued conversation with me, because I saw that she hurried her departure. Thinking that perhaps some other Saturday we could sit and talk about bronze fingers or, better yet, stolen books, I asked her if someday we could sit together again, with a bit more sun, and see if I could figure out the thing with the light and the finger.

"Maybe," she said, and that "maybe" brought a slight glow to my eyes, the kind you get when a small wish has been granted.

"And when would that be?" I asked, not sure where to look when I faced her.

"When Columbus lowers his finger," she said, and she laughed like a typical girl, the kind who knows she doesn't need a miniskirt or red fingernail polish to turn the world on its head.

HALFIE

FICTION BY ANA-MAURINE LARA

I peel my thigh from the plastic covering his mother's couch. I let my hair cover my face as I sneak a sideways glance in his direction. Angel's talking about something, but I mostly focus on his face, the way the golden brown skin has turned a sallow beige. He holds his hands open, like big nets swatting at the air as he speaks. Trying to catch something. Something. The spring light coming in from the window plays on my curls. I shake my head back and forth to study the reds and blonds peeking out through the brown and black threads of hair.

"You know what I mean?"

He's asking me a question. I shift again. My bra feels hot and uncomfortable under my sweater. I can feel his eyes scanning my calves—my mom's thick calves—as he waits for me to answer. I cross my legs and look up. A slow nausea creeps its way up from my stomach into my throat. I gulp so as not to choke on it. I think to myself, "Why am I here?" but I say something else out loud.

"Yeah, yeah—that's crazy."

"What? It's not crazy. I think I'll make it big one day. My homedog Nest has got mad connections."

Oh. He's talking about his music again. Just like the last time we talked on the phone. Right before I decided to come here to hang out with him. Even though I knew that, really, we don't have much in common. Except that our dads are from the same place—but I live with mine. He hasn't told me about his. I feel my chest getting heavy with boredom. The nausea sinks back to its little cave in my belly. I look at his little afro and dark brown eyes. Don't get me wrong, I mean, he's so cute. Especially those thick, pink lips of his. But . . . well, I can talk about music, I listen to the radio. And my girls and I even freestyle from time to time, but it seems like he can only talk about himself.

I pull my gaze away from him and look out the window to my right. I can see the buildings across the way. The dirty red brick and steel gray doors, the graffiti tags and R.I.P.s. There's a big one with a Boricua flag in the shape of Puerto Rico. It reads, "Chino a.k.a. Danny Velez, 1975–1990." Shit. He was my age when they popped him. They just shot him, too. An R.I.P. already. I feel my eyes swelling in their sockets and an unfamiliar sadness rising in my throat.

"You okay?"

I feel his hands, Angel's hands, his thick fingers on my chin, urging me to look in his direction. Okay, I think, here it comes.

"Yeah, I'm okay."

"You get enough to eat?"

Eat? Oh yeah, that's right. I can sense the Wendy's fries and salad thick in my stomach. I try not to feel embarrassed as my stomach growls.

Almost right after I got here, he had taken me for a walk around his 'hood, as he called it. We strolled across the field littered with chicken bones and trash. My shoes got sucked down into the spring thaw mud camouflaged by patches of neglected grass. Even though now I'm gonna have to throw my ruined shoes out, I didn't say anything. I didn't want him to think I'm some uppity girl from the suburbs. It's bad enough he thinks I'm from upstate, even though upstate is much further away from here than he knows. I'm trying not to think about my shoes. About how ugly they were to start with and how much uglier they look now covered with mud. About how my mom's gonna kill me for ruining them.

It was bad enough trying to get here. My mom had a fit when she saw me walking into the kitchen with a miniskirt on. Apoplexy, as she calls it. I don't care, though. She doesn't really get it. It's clear she doesn't. Even though right now I wish I had on a pair of cute sweats instead of this ridiculous mini. Earlier this afternoon, before she had agreed to drive me here, we even fought about it.

"Where do you think you're going in that piece of cloth?"

"I'm going to Angel's. You can take me, right?"

"Angel's?"

"You know—Angel—the boy I met at the mall last week. He lives in the South Bronx."

"You're not going to the South Bronx wearing that."

"Why?"

"Two words—your father."

She had turned away from me as if the conversation was over. I knew she wasn't going to say anything else unless I provoked her. She'd just have one more thing to hold over my head—for when the time came to fight with my father.

"Mom, Dad knows that I'm fifteen and old enough to wear this. I mean, back on the island, girls my age are getting married. All I'm doing is wearing a skirt and hanging out."

She shot me the look of death that only she can do. It's this eagle-eyed look that cuts through my bullshit and makes it stink.

"Back on the island, girls who are getting married at fifteen aren't generally going to college, either."

"Well—you don't understand. I mean, how could you? You've never been a black girl in this country. We have to dress like this to even get any attention."

That shut her up. The race card. It worked every time. I knew it hurt her feelings, so I walked up to her, speaking softly.

"Mom, I'm sorry. It doesn't mean anything. Other girls my age wear miniskirts, too."

She waved her hand in my direction, indicating "conversation over" and walked into the living room for her purse.

"Let's go."

Our nosy neighbor, Mrs. Emilio, looked out her window as we got into the car. One more file for her case against my bohemian family and how we were corrupting the neighborhood—my mom, the race-traitor Mrs. Mendez, taking her slut daughter out of the house in a miniskirt. As we sat in the car together, I tried not to think about how cold I felt.

I had let my thoughts wander as we rode along the boulevard, the wide streets and tree-lined sidewalks dotted with houses giving way to narrower tree-lined streets crowded with buildings until we got to the part of the Bronx where there were building-lined streets spotted with gray remnants of trees covered with plastic bags for leaves. The South Bronx. Even spring seemed to forget about the projects. I looked over at my mom, who stuck out more and more as there were fewer and fewer trees.

I covered my eyes against the dust and trash flying toward us from the ground. I stared straight ahead, ignoring the looks into our car as we pulled up to Angel's building. These boys on the corner smiled to each other as my mom stopped the car and looked down into her lap to check the address.

"Well, here we are."

I glanced out the window and saw Angel walking down the stairs, all cool and stuff, running his hands down his smooth cheeks. His afro was slicked back, like he had straightened his hair. I stifled a laugh at the thought of Angel trying to act like a white boy. Before I had a chance to say anything, he was standing by the car door, looking in. He knocked on the roof of the car.

"Hey, Maria."

"Hi, Angel. Mom, this is Angel. Angel, this is my mom—Clarissa Mendez."

I watched his face as he looked from my face to my mom's and back to mine again. A knot formed in my stomach as I waited for his reaction, for the words to slip from his mouth and hurt me. But he was cool. He stuck his hand in through the window.

"Nice to meet you, Mrs. Mendez."

"Yes, well, it's good to meet you, Angel."

There was a long pause until I realized I was supposed to be getting out of the car. Angel stepped back as I opened the door and got out. Two of the boys on the corner whistled, and Angel's eyebrows went up in less than a second. I slammed the car door shut and, readjusting my clothes, stood there feeling stupid. Like there were a thousand eyes and hands on my ass.

"Maria, I'll be back at five-thirty to pick you up."

"'Kay, Mom."

"Angel, can you tell me the easiest way out of here?"

I watched the curve of his neck as he leaned into the car to give my mom directions. He was like a mallard duck, sleek and shiny. My mom was really just checking him out. She grew up a couple miles north of here. But he didn't know that.

He stepped back from the car. I ignored my mom as she waved and pressed the automatic window button, the passenger window squeaking as it shut. Angel turned to face me, a big cute smile plastered on his face. The minute annoyance I had felt about our prior conversation gave way to little palpitations in my chest. Damn, he was fine. We started walking.

"It's nice to see you, Maria."

"Yeah, you too. Sorry I'm a little late. You know how it is."

He licked his lips and smiled.

Sitting in front of me, he smells like mint bubble gum and detergent. Tide and Bounce. Even now as we sit on the couch, post-Wendy's, I can smell the mint on his breath tickling my nose. Earlier today, he had taken my hand in his and led me away from the pack of boys on the corner. I felt my shoulders relax as we walked. Just me and him.

"You hungry?"

We had already crossed the field by the time he asked, and I saw that we were walking toward a restaurant with a dark white and blue sign. "El Cibao" was painted on it in large, hand-stenciled letters. My mouth watered at the thought of rice and beans and platano. My dad's food. Oh yeah.

"Definitely."

"Cool, there's a Wendy's close by. It'll be a nice walk."

Wendy's? I tried not to let the disappointment show on my face. Maybe, I thought to myself, El Cibao is too expensive. Maybe the food's not good. Maybe he's sick of eating Dominican food ... but it hadn't helped. I smiled faintly at him, feigning excitement.

"That's cool."

He smiled again and pulled me closer. I felt the heat from his hands warming me up as he started talking, and disappointment gave way to a feeling of victory. Here I was, with a boy who maybe could be my boyfriend. As we walked, he started telling me stories.

"Thanks for coming down here, baby."

"It's no big deal."

He looked at me sideways. I saw his eyes shooting glances from the corners, while his face looked straight ahead.

"I bet you didn't know that this place has got some crazy stories."

"I bet you don't know I have a crazy story."

There. I had put it out there. I thought maybe now he would ask me something.

"Yeah, man. One time this crazy old man. He was crazy, fought in Nam and stuff. Well, he stored up all these cans of tear gas, and then one day BOOM! it all went up in smoke. It was crazy. The whole neighborhood was crying."

As he talked, I thought about my dad's stories. How when he was in school back on the island, the U.S. invaded. During that time, the air was nothing but tear gas and bullets. That's what my dad had told me. I almost said something, but for some reason I got the feeling that Angel wouldn't get it. He seemed like he'd never gone back home to the island. Or maybe he had, but when he was little. It sure didn't show now. He was definitely a Bronx boy.

"Here we are."

We walked into the Wendy's with the wallpaper falling off the walls, the bulletproof glass with bullet holes, and the packs of children hanging out with their moms.

"Go ahead and take a seat, Maria. What you want?"

I had sat on the cool plastic chair, warming my hands with my thighs as I waited. I pushed my hair out of my face, tried not to think about my Dominican cousins as I watched the glazed, bitter glares in my direction, asking, "What is *she* doing here? Rich bitch from the suburbs. Twirling her good hair like it's something." The girls' glares that echoed my cousins' envy. As I sat there, I remembered the time my cousins cut my hair till I was bald, and then how they shrank away from me when they got in trouble. Inevitably, they got in trouble. For cutting my hair, for wearing my clothes, for messing up my books. It wasn't that they tried to get in trouble, they just hated me. And they hated me because my aunt was always telling them that someone with my good hair and white mother didn't belong in the same category as they did.

That my cousins should always try to be like me. But they didn't know how she laughed at me, too, telling me I deserved to look ugly so I could see what it feels like to be like everybody else. As we got older, my cousins' envy only worsened whenever I showed up to visit. Just like the daggers that threatened to jump over the seat and stab me as I sat waiting for Angel. I smiled. The daggers turned away from me.

"Who you smilin' at?"

"Just at that girl over there with her kids."

"Oh, her." He leaned over the food to whisper to me. "She's crazy. We call her Lupi, short for crazy."

I started to laugh, but he put a finger to my lip and winked. I nodded, even though I didn't quite get why he wanted me to be quiet. I looked into his eyes. He swallowed and raised his eyebrows.

"What?"

"Nothing."

He gnawed off half his burger, and in between bites I could see bits of lettuce sticking out between his teeth.

"Your mom seems nice."

Shit like that always makes me suspicious. Just like back on the island, when people'd ask if my mom was Cibaeña, knowing full well she's a gringa.

"Yeah. What seems nice about her?"

"Aw, nothin'. I just didn't think white moms let their daughters hang out in the 'hood."

"Are you for real?"

"Hey, I ain't insultin' her or nothin'. So she's white. And? So's every other Dominican."

"Well, I'm not. White, I mean."

I looked at him dumbfounded, my mouth falling open as he looked over his shoulder. Lupi was pretending not to listen, but I could see her suckin' her teeth and laughing. Angel took a huge bite out of the burger and chewed slowly before answering.

"Yeah, okay. So what? Me either. Big deal. Where I'm from everybody's mixed with something."

"You mean where we're from."

"Yeah, well—I'm from there, definitely. Both of my parents are from there. You, you're only half from there."

I bit my lip and looked down at my fries. Somewhere deep inside I felt a light fading, the glow that I had seen around Angel's head diminished. I cut my eyes at my fries.

"So wait, even though I was born on the island, just like you, I'm only half from there? So even though you left when you were, like, two years old, and I left there when I was nine, you're more from there than me? I don't get that."

He shook his head at me. "It's not that serious."

"Well, to me it is. I'm tired of people saying shit like that."

"Okay, okay—I take it back! Come on, Maria. Relax, baby. It's cool."

He had said that then, and he's saying those same words now. I'm trying to keep from throwing up, and I haven't even noticed he's eased up to me, his hot breath moistening my neck as his fingers move from my chin down to my shoulder. His hand searches the space between my thighs. I turn just enough so that our mouths catch, latch onto each other, and I feel his tongue pulling mine, swallowing my lips and teeth. That hand on my thigh holds on tighter, and even though I didn't know this could happen, the heat in my panties is burning.

And as he presses me back against his mom's crinkly, plastic-covered couch, I look at the porcelain figurines decorating the shelves and coffee table. My mom hates those kinds of tchotchkes. At the thought of my mom, the burning turns to pain, and I push him back.

"What's wrong?"

"Nothing, Angel, it's just too fast for me."

"Too fast? We're just kissing."

"Can I use your bathroom?"

He falls back to his corner, his mouth a big red pout lined with pink, his breath hard. He turns away from me and puts both his feet down on the ground, pulling his pants out away from his thighs and legs. Finally, he clears his throat and decides to say something.

"Yeah. It's over there, down the hall on the left."

I stand up and pull my skirt as I walk down the hall. The bathroom is small, smaller than my closet at home, and I twirl in one spot as I look at myself in the mirror. I look at my behind and feel myself turning red. My panties are showing. Angel was probably watching me with my panties showing. Shit. And my miniskirt and sweater are all wrinkled, too. I run my hands over my clothes to try and straighten them out.

"Stupid. What you making out with this boy for, anyway?"

I look at my face. The face an echo of my mom's features, only my brown eyes and light-brown skin make me a negative of her image. I pull back my curly hair and inspect my neck for hickies, smack my lips, bat my eyes, and smile. My lip gloss is gone, and I can tell I look as annoyed as I feel.

"Now what, Maria?"

The pain between my legs has turned into a strange, almost pleasant throb. I shake myself and open the door. Walking into the living room, I see Angel leaning out the window yelling something at somebody. I only catch the end of it.

". . . be right down."

"Angel?"

He turns around and looks straight through me. He walks past me into the hallway.

"Your moms is here. She's downstairs waiting."

"Five-thirty already?"

I feel so relieved. This date or whatever you wanna call it was getting to be a mess. Angel's standing by the front door, holding it open as he stares at the wall in front of him. Jerk. I walk up to him and look at his face.

"Thanks, Angel."

He lowers his gaze to look at me, but only for a second. I can find nothing else to say to him. He half bows and makes a sweeping gesture out the door. "You know how to get out."

"Yeah, I do."

I walk outside to the car where my mom is sitting with the engine running. The dark blue evening sky has just started to peek over the tops of the buildings, and I stare out across the field and the glimmery project sunset. I take one last look up to the window of Angel's apartment, but he's not standing there. Just as well. I get in the car, looking away from my mom so she won't see the sadness hit. I stare at the boys still standing on the corner. They're snickering now, hiding their mouths as they laugh in my direction and slap each other's hands. I roll my eyes and instantly feel better. I can't believe I ever thought Angel was cute.

"Thanks for picking me up, Mom."

"Oh well, you're welcome. Did you have a nice time?"

"It was all right."

I turn the radio on, find the salsa station. We start driving north on the boulevard, back up to where the trees are.

THE GAME
OF EXHAUSTION

FICTION BY SHEILLY NÚÑEZ

Translated by Achy Obejas

"I'm furious, dammit!" I muttered. Indeed, I whispered it, practically swallowing the words, because the only thing I had left was my dignity. Two big tears ran down both cheeks, dissolving what was left of the foundation I'd forgotten to wash off the night before. No mascara, though—I'd learned years before that any woman who falls in love should use only the waterproof kind, because there's nothing more vulgar than waking up with your eyes ringed in black.

"Dammit, I'm so angry it's eating me up inside!" I had breakfasted, lunched, and dined on those rancid words so many times in my life that this poison-turned-tears was consuming me little by little, my tears no longer of pain but of impotence.

I tried, unsuccessfully, to stand up. The sheets, stuck to my body with the alcohol distilled in my own sweat, pulled me back into the same position in which I'd fallen into bed. A hangover promised to nail me with a headache that made me avoid getting up right then, forgetting all about the insomnia I'd been going through the last few months. I managed to drag my right hand along the mattress and felt something. With my blurry vision, I couldn't see the details of the object. I lifted it just enough to see it was the bottle for my sleeping pills—empty. My eyes began to awaken, to adjust to the lighted contours of the furniture in the dark they'd been submerged in since I'd arrived at the Hotel Bellagio. The light coming from behind the half-opened curtains ran through the room, invading my privacy. Its presence overpowered my being, which had been drunk and unconscious in this room for I don't know how long. I adjusted myself on the pillow. Only the space occupied by my body interrupted the flat, still-smooth surface of the bed. I was a person-object, quiet, immobile, waiting for something to cause me to jump up, to reactivate the force of my muscles for a few minutes and make me—in spite of myself—get up and amble like Lazarus, barely aware of being resurrected, deader with each day, more like a specter, less of what I was like in life, until I wasn't anything at all. I can't really say it was a good day to get up.

The sound of the music vibrating a little on the walls made me forget my misfortune, bringing forth the memory of the many times we had come here together and gazed upon the impressive spectacle of waterfalls and lights from the balcony of this very room, reserved every year, on the same date, for the two of us.

I felt humiliated—he didn't even do me the favor of being with someone of my level, instead cheating on me with a peasant, a shell of a woman, an illiterate nobody—it's the worst insult of my life. I felt a pressure on my chest that just flattened me, reminding me that, in spite of the dye jobs and exercise, I wasn't so young anymore. I let the spasm pass and started to slowly make my way to the bathroom. Elegance can't be hurried. I entered the Jacuzzi filled with warm suds, still smelling of rose petals.

When I moved, I accidently knocked over an object that unrolled on the floor, like my disappointment which could well have been measured in meters and cut with a pair of scissors. I watched that white thing on the floor for a few moments and had a glorious epiphany. I stretched out my arm and took hold of the roll of toilet paper and finished unrolling it, making big, irregular balls. I patted down my entire body with the paper until I was dry. I cleaned off twenty-five years and tossed the tissue into the toilet like the shit those years had been. Twenty-five years of playing the same game.

I'd bet on "forever" with that man. I had been too young, I barely knew the rules, I had no malice, I was in love, intoxicated with feeling, and, like all beginners, I took advantage of the luck that came my way without realizing it wouldn't last. I lost my freedom in the first round, I threw it to the wind like thousand-dollar bills and saw it float to the sky like a soul looking for eternity, making its way through the air, carrying with it the heavy weight of my body, leaving me with an emptiness in my chest, there, exactly where I'd staked my will, where I still hold my desire to fly.

Then came doubts and misery in the second round. In the bathroom, I shook my first bottle of sleeping pills, betting that in spite of everything I'd finally get some sleep, and I've been doing that for the past ten years. The stupor produced by the drugs prevented my tears, thickened by various anti-wrinkle creams, from drowning the sheets when I extended my arm and felt the empty space by my side, and a quick thought, like a wisp of smoke, escaped while I imagined another bed in which another woman played the same game and, unlike me, found sleep without assistance.

I had abandoned the idea of having children and raised his as if I'd birthed them myself, living as we were then in a sad little apartment like poor people because we were newlyweds and couldn't afford anything else. It seems he forgot how he first arrived in my country with nothing, and even though we treat foreigners like gods, if it hadn't been for my family's political influence—which would always have shielded me from difficulties—not even his light eyes would have saved him from starving to death. Without my involvement with the political party, passing out little bags of food, toys, and all that other stuff that they come up with during electoral campaigns, putting up with all those people desperately climbing all over me, hugging sick and sniffling kids, he would never have gotten government contracts for his miserable little construction company.

He took a chance that I wouldn't notice his infidelity. He bet big time that I wouldn't ever find him out. "He's going to be screwed," I said.

I was constantly attacked by the same thoughts: What had gone wrong? What had I done wrong?

And what if I left him? I asked this not thinking about how my life would be without him, but rather how his life would be without me. Would he be happy without me? Could he be happy without me?

I hadn't wanted to call anyone before I got on the flight to Las Vegas. I didn't want to hear pitying words from my hypocritical relatives, nor did I want to hear advice from girlfriends who'd tell me to leave him while they kept their own faithless men. That's why I came to make my last bet with every intention of losing. I wanted to lose myself, to see if I could win that way, to let luck leave me and see if, that way, I could rescue what I didn't have, to walk out with empty hands from the casino, unafraid because this way nothing could be taken from me. I was going to play like that, to lose. This would be a game with a different deck of cards, not like that time years before when I smiled after I won a hand a couple of nights in a row, while the other woman savored her great victory. When I saw her on the street, I pretended everything was okay in order to keep up appearances. I put up a front with so many people, even those whose comments meant nothing to me. Whenever I found myself wanting to speak freely, I'd bite my lip and swallow my spit. I'd heard all that talk about "happiness." I think I'd even felt it at times—a few times, maybe at the beginning, I couldn't remember anymore. I was tired.

Everything was flashing where I was. The lights helped my memory with quick scenes of all I hated, all those people I hated who'd let me play stupid without saying a word. I calculated and recalculated everything in my mind— the possible solutions I'd already tried that hadn't worked, sleights of hand, lawyers, the shame from which I was fleeing. I didn't know the man I'd loved anymore. I'd believed all his "It won't happen again," "I swear I love you," "I'm sorry," over and over like a roulette wheel announcing the same insipid winner again and again. I told him that I trusted him, that, yes, I believed him, and then I had the phone tapped to be sure—oh, it's illegal? The only thing that's truly illegal is whatever you don't have money in your pocket to buy— and that's how I came to hear that conversation. I'm not a woman who holds grudges, but to hear that my dear sister-in-law was the procuress, the one who was behind his affair with that nobody, that was just too much. That hurt me deeply. I'm forever poisoned. I rubbed her out of my life with cat shit.

I finished getting ready in the bathroom and left the hotel room prepared to bet it all. And I smiled, laughed with a cackle from an old-time movie. I looked at myself reflected in a Technicolor mirror. I wrapped a scarf around my neck, then let it fall down my back as I looked over my shoulder at my designer purse bursting with big bills. My heart stopped when I saw the woman I used to be fade into the shadows forever, that woman who put up with so much all those years without doing a thing. A vaguely erotic scent came through the air. It was me, it was my revenge. I let its urgency envelop me.

"I'm going to the casino," I said, turning back in my own footsteps as if I could unwalk them.

Before I left the room, I grabbed a recently uncorked bottle of champagne. As the elevator went down, I drank the foamy liquid and saw myself reflected in the mirrorlike golden doors. Thousands of dollars worth of creams and makeup had erased all trace of my suffering. Unquestionably, they were worth every penny. I could see a beautiful woman, mature, with a shiny head of blond, wavy hair showing not a trace of gray, and a firm body. No wonder the surgeons who'd worked on me had charged so much. I looked at my eyes, free of any sign of aging, with no dark spots, as it should be. There are eyes that don't say a thing, but mine are the eyes of a powerful woman. No one else—no matter how young—could even touch the soles of my feet. What had happened was absurd. My rejuvenated eyes returned to the shiny metal with a look of disdain for all the images playing in my head.

I walked through the Grand Ballroom full of slot machines, unaware of the time. Sometimes I think it's never nighttime in Las Vegas. The table I was looking for was on the far end, beyond the reception desk. I moved a bit indecently, trying to be provocative, feeling the champagne bubbles go to my head, feeling light, so light that, dizzy and confused, I dropped into one of the elegant lobby chairs. My body swayed from side to side in rhythm with the laughter that had restored a joy now turned into excitement. My head rocked on the armrest while I continued hearing voices inside like a swarm of bees that just kept humming without daring to sting. I kept laughing because the time had come! Because it had gone on too long to be wrong; now it was just a question of waiting. Surely there would be more tears, and I'd be sorry about what happened, and I'd come out of it filled with shame, hiding behind a pair of Dior glasses.

"Beautiful glasses, lovely accessory," I said observing—my head upside down on the chair—the showcase of the shop across from me. This was the perfect mask to wear to the carnival dance of divorce terms.

"Maybe you should forgive him! It's the only way to experience that satisfaction again, something like dying to be born again, an emotional resurrection."

Seeing me twisting in the chair, a bellboy approached wearing his impeccable velvet uniform. He looked like he'd stepped out of an ad. He seemed astonished, as if he wasn't sure how my face and my ass could align like that, or maybe it was just a momentary indiscretion on his part. He helped me up, and I put my arms around him, pretending to need support just so I could touch his chest and strong arms, not out of any sick motive, but to know what it's like to caress a young man.

If I were just a few years younger, I'd have the world by the tail, I thought.

The young man looked at me unsurprised. He could tell I was drunk.

"I want to go to the casino, I came down to bet it all," I whispered, like a secret, staggering but with the calm assurance of someone with nothing to lose.

The young man held me until I could keep my balance standing. He didn't say a word, just smiled as he backed away and gestured with his white gloves at the entire vastness of the casino.

I went on, like a slug oozing a wake of chiffon from the gown I wore, too dressy for the occasion. And there it was, the exclusive blackjack table, right in front of me. There were only two players, a sweaty man and a very old woman, both not quite there, numb from the hum of the shuffling cards. I bought the most expensive chips, put them in a circle, and watched them disappear little by little with satisfaction. The waiters came by to serve me whatever I wanted. After I'd been there a little while, it ceased being much fun. The pain, settled in its favorite spot, there in the center of my chest, was too much. I felt the need to breathe—but real air, not this asphyxiating perfume. I looked all around, but there are no windows in a casino. That's also part of the game—the beautifully decorated walls without openings, and the lies. The dealer kept shuffling. It hurt to lose. What was I going to do? (a ten) end it all? (a five) show my hand? tell him that I knew everything? (a two) a tear escaped my eye.

"I'm in great pain," I said with the voice of someone who's about to lose their life, but the couple at my table barely noticed me, so I pursed my lips and lifted my chin, because I wasn't going to let myself fall. What I said would happen was the only thing that mattered because, in the end, all this was also mine—my money, my husband, my life. I heard myself hiccup, and it was my sign to double down. I was sick of everything, but I wasn't going to just walk away. They were dealing the cards again. No woman likes to be replaced, even less so by trash like that. The last card was turned over to decide the game.

From the other side of the salon, the figure of an older man—a bit overweight, with glossy gray hair that invited touching, dressed in a fine linen jacket, with a cigar in his left hand, the same hand on which a gold ring shone—approached the table with annoying calm. There was a chill in his bearing, maybe from worry or fear, but he maintained a relaxed smile. He went around the table until I lost sight of him. Maybe it was just another illusion of my hysterical state. I decided not to turn and look for him. I was never going to follow a man again, not even with my eyes. Then I felt his lips kissing my cheek, without a trace of the perfume that would usually give away his indiscretions. He whispered that he loved me as he took a seat next to me at the table while the dealer swept away the chips. The losers got up, disappointed. The sweaty man angrily threw down his cards and knocked over his stool. A confident smile returned to my lips upon seeing my husband again, in his eyes the look of someone who's traveled many hours just to be by my side, just to keep up our exclusive annual tradition. I understood that, in the end, at every well-regulated gaming table, it's always the house that wins.

I'M NOT FROM HERE AND I'M NOT FROM THERE

IDENTIDADES/
IDENTITIES

NONFICTION BY RHINA P. ESPAILLAT

One day in May 1939, the steamship *Leif Erikson* docked in New York harbor. The air smelled of sea and gasoline, and the silhouette of the city gleamed on the horizon, huge and alien. Two familiar figures greeted me from the pier, smiling and waving to attract my attention, but also weeping. My parents, whom I had not seen for almost two years, dressed in what seemed to me odd, heavy clothing.

I disembarked with Doña Ligia Cabral, the friend whom my aunt Rhina had entrusted, back on the pier in Santo Domingo, with the care of her little niece—I was seven years old—and I took leave of her and entered the embrace of my parents, who persisted in looking at me and caressing me, obviously moved by the changes they noted in their daughter, her height and weight, the growth in her vocabulary.

They, too, had changed. I found them—how shall I say it?—less cheerful, as if time had robbed them of some of their playful self-confidence, or rather replaced that confidence with a new and somber courage. As the days passed, I learned their new lives—the way my mother did, quickly and without question, what maids and a cook once did for her, and the way my father washed the dishes after dinner and even wore an apron to do so. They had arrived in New York in 1937 as political exiles during the Trujillo dictatorship with nothing more than the scant contents of their valise, planning to send for me after finding work and lodging.

When I saw the apartment in which they lived—a first-floor railroad flat on 49th Street in Manhattan, in the heart of the theater and tourist area of the city—I sensed at once the difference between the life that awaited me and the life I had left behind in La Vega, an intimate city in the green Cibao Valley where I had spent my early childhood in the home of my paternal grandmother, surrounded by a large, loving family. Here, there was no garden where flowers, coconuts, and limoncillos grew; there were no cousins in the house across the street, no aunts and uncles in dozens of the neighboring houses, no ancestors' names on sculpted busts of national heroes in a park surrounding a bandstand. Instead, the faces of strangers passing our windows sometimes turned casually toward us and turned away again without a sign of recognition or interest.

My father took me walking in the neighborhood I would learn to identify as mine, pointing out stores and a church, large buildings he said were filled with apartments like ours, and a strange staircase descending under the sidewalk to a vault-like cavity lined with steel columns. There, to my amazement, trains came and went with people spilling out of them or sweeping past us into them through a dense, complicated arrangement of gates and stiles.

I spent the first difficult days longing for the home I had lost, the old people who spoiled me, the maids who looked after me, the streets I knew like my own face in the mirror. And I understood, without being able to put it into words, the change I had noticed in my parents. They were, in fact, no longer the same people they had been; or, maybe the same but with another layer, a new stratum of the self that had altered it forever. And I understood that I, too, would be subjected to such changes in the future as I learned to navigate the city that was now theirs and master their schedule of unfamiliar duties, which I would soon share.

My father worked at a factory that made mannequins for department stores and studied at night to improve his English and qualify for a job as a bookkeeper. My mother, a skilled dressmaker, worked at home making dresses for English-speaking women, some of them singers, dancers, and actresses in the theaters that abounded in the neighborhood, and others wealthy women who lived in a very different neighborhood on the east side of Central Park. Eventually, after I had learned to travel through the city well enough, I shopped for zippers, threads, and other sewing supplies for my mother, carrying small swatches of fabric in order to match the colors. Later I even helped with the hemming and finishing of garments, which had to be done by hand. Almost every day, as I returned from school, I would find a list of items to buy or chores to do before turning to my homework and then helping to prepare and serve dinner.

Our weekend luxuries sometimes included, after we finished the marketing and housecleaning, a visit to one of the city's big museums, or, as a special treat, a trip to the Roxy Theater or Radio City Music Hall for a movie and a stage show. Most often, we walked in Central Park if the weather permitted and occasionally rented a rowboat on the lake there.

The following years taught me that I had two homes—the one I remembered and the one that surrounded me daily—and two families. There was one that wrote me letters, which I always answered, first in printed capitals and with drawings, and later in cursive, sometimes with poems. And there was the second family, the group of children around me in public school, most of them immigrants or the children of immigrants from every part of the world.

Those Dominicans who would arrive later during the fifties and sixties would find neighborhoods populated by Hispanics where they would hear their native language and encounter familiar foods and some version of their own customs. But we, during the decade of the forties, were challenged to establish relationships with neighbors who spoke English in the world we shared but spoke Greek, Italian, Yiddish, Polish, and German in the intimacy of their kitchens, where I, as a guest, learned to more or less follow their conversation, enjoy the taste of their foods, and consider the various circumstances that had brought them to the United States. Those classmates visited me and also learned in my house what the city taught all of us, that the life we had lost in "the old country" remembered by our families—whether for political reasons, war, religious persecution, poverty, or lack of opportunity—could be made up for. It could not be substituted, because some things cannot be substituted, but at least it could be imitated to a point, if one could manage to enlarge the meaning of the word "family" and by that means also enlarge one's own being, one's identity.

It seems—or at least, this is what my experience suggests—that identity is not a thing, not a static and unchanging quality, but a process that takes place from the cradle to the grave. A series of transformations, or rather a constant and gradual transformation of the intimate self of each person. But—and this is most important for the immigrant—it is a mutual transformation between persons, and also between the person and his surroundings. If it is true that the riverbed guides the current, it is equally true that the current, in the long run, forms the riverbed by here depositing silt and there undermining the banks.

The proof of that is all around us in the streets of those big cities that we find inhospitable at first but that now invite the immigrant with the fruits, the root vegetables, the sweets that we once left behind. Those things have followed us here not only to the ubiquitous bodegas but also to the restaurants and to private homes. Music, the visual arts, and the performing arts have also followed us, as have, with increasing frequency, books. This is no longer the country that I found enormous and confusing in 1939; its identity, like mine, has been altered by mutual and daily contact between the place and its inhabitants—a contact not always easy but always inexorable. The public before whom I read my work these days includes people whose parents and grandparents would not have been interested in a bilingual reading, but now they attend because they like the sound and flavor of my first language, and they have been convinced of the roundness of the earth.

Today I live not in New York but in Newburyport, the smallest city in the state of Massachusetts, in that same New England that produced most of the early writers of this country. I am surrounded by a literary tradition that includes John Greenleaf Whittier, Anne Bradstreet, Emily Dickinson, Henry David Thoreau, Ralph Waldo Emerson, and Robert Frost. I've been granted the difficult pleasure of translating the works of Frost into Spanish and translating into English the works of Saint John of the Cross and various other Spanish and Latin American poets. The ability to do so is one of the debts I owe to my parents, who loved books and were proud of their own culture. They insisted that I retain my first language, and that has permitted me to move easily from one part of my life and my being to the other, and also to offer each of my two "families" the literary fruits of the other.

The child who disembarked onto that pier in 1939 has—today, seventy-six years later—a rich, complex identity, one not yet fully formed because her life is not yet over.

She also has two cultures, two languages, and two countries she regards with equal love and an equal sense of responsibility. She has a husband born in the Bronx to a Jewish family who emigrated from Rumania, with roots in Russia. We have children born here and grandchildren whose genealogy links them to Spain, France, Germany, England, Ireland, and Scotland, with distant cousins in Israel and in the Dominican Republic. The child I was in those days would not have known how to locate on the map so many unfamiliar countries, but something alive in those distant countries knew how to find her, and that fact, as much as her education in New York City's public schools and her days in La Vega, has formed her.

IN CHINATOWN

FICTION BY NORIS EUSEBIO-POL

Translated by Achy Obejas

My aunt Marina insists that happiness doesn't exist, but I like Professor Dora's idea better. She says she carries happiness in her pocket (that's why she never buys clothing without pockets). The first time I asked her about this, she said joy is like a piece of bread you carry with you and eat when you need it. So whenever she feels depressed, she puts her hand in her pocket and touches that joy. She brings it to her face, breathes it in, and puts it in her mouth. She feels it inside herself, and then everything's better. Putting that lesson into practice is how I got the place I moved into yesterday.

I woke up this morning on my birthday in my new home in Chinatown. I know it's the end of a cycle and that, had it not been for the Señora's help, I would never have gotten this far. I feel the need to write down all that I've learned.

About thirteen years ago, I had a dream in which a woman with a beautiful, serene face stared at me without blinking. Her gaze, which enveloped and covered me, was a mixture of tenderness and sadness. I felt something emanate from her that gripped me with powerful love. I heard her voice tell me, "I'll always be with you, daughter of mine. Always, my daughter, I'll be with you." It was like a litany or chant that assured me she loved me.

I remember that in spite of having had such a lovely vision, I awoke from the dream feeling strange. I told my mother what had happened, and she told me it was the Virgin Mary who had appeared to me. She advised that I keep her image and love forever in my heart because she would save me from all misfortune.

65

My mother and I were together all that day. It was the most beautiful Saturday of my life. She talked to me about my strengths and my weaknesses, told me stories about her childhood and about the mysteries she had learned from trees and plants. We read poetry together, as she so loved to do. I still feel her embrace around my body, her hands caressing my hair and face.

The Monday following the dream, while I was at school, the principal showed up unexpectedly in my class and signaled to the teacher. He said something to her in a low voice. The girl who was nearest overheard and whispered it into the ear of the girl by her side. That girl looked at me with widening eyes and then whispered in the ear of the next girl, until it got to me.

"Ramona, your father and mother were killed in the park."

I ran and ran through the streets, and when I was close to the place, I saw the Señora in the crowd. She was looking at me in the same way she had in the dream. I stopped running, and I'm not sure what happened next. Someone took me to my aunt's house. I remember the funeral and that I felt surrounded by love.

My mother recognized her as the Virgin Mary, but I've always called her Señora. I think she likes it better that way. And as my mother said, whenever I've been in need, she's been there to help me.

It's been five months since I arrived in the city of Santo Domingo to live with one of my father's sisters whom I didn't know. She's fifty-seven years old and, according to what I've been able to find out, she left town during a falling-out with her parents and never returned. She agreed to let me live with her in Villa Francisca for a few months if I paid her a little something and helped with household chores.

From the moment I climbed the stairs to Aunt Marina's second-floor apartment, I sensed trouble. The stairs were narrow and dirty. Radios, TVs, and speakers were blasting as we ascended. Dora and I just looked at each other.

"It'll be fine," she said.

Aunt Marina opened the door, and I was taken aback—she had a face like my father's, only crossed by pain in some way I couldn't quite comprehend. She smiled without revealing the least bit of joy.

"Ramona?"

"Yes," I said, a little scared.

"Welcome, this is your home. Oh, dear niece, we will be very good friends. You can count on your aunt."

I was somewhat relieved but still felt something tight inside. I looked at Professor Dora, searching for I don't know what—maybe approval? Dora smiled. Aunt Marina studied her from head to toe, shook her hand, but didn't ask her in.

"You can leave those things there, we can put them away later. Your teacher must be very tired from the trip and no doubt wants to get back home."

Professor Dora nodded, hugged me, said, "We'll talk later," and left. I would have liked for her to stay a while and check out the place where I was going to be living from then on.

It turned out that Aunt Marina's place was very small, smaller than my grandparents' place in the country. The neighborhood is noisy. There's a lot of traffic and street vendors selling various products—clothing, hats, and pirated CDs, among other things. The CD vendors are the worst because they blast music all day long to attract customers. At night, the bars open with their own thundering sounds. It's a terrible place to live, study, and rest.

My teacher couldn't take me in because she lives with her own children and her sick mother, but she recommended me to some friends. My grandparents, who are very Christian people, didn't let me move in with them because they believed I'd be better off with my aunt, who's family. I had accepted their terms so I could leave in peace.

I arrived on a June afternoon, and since it was daytime, after I put all my things in the corner my aunt had assigned me, I went for a walk to get to know the area. A few blocks away I found Duarte Avenue, and, walking with traffic, I arrived at a giant arch that marks the entrance to Chinatown. It was really impressive with its two white lions and their giant paws. I felt as if I were entering a mysterious world, and I walked with great care. I came upon six bronze statues, one dedicated to Chinese immigrants and five representing characters from ancient China—a god of contentment named Tsai Shen Yeh, a high-ranking military figure, a man of a thousand masks from the Chinese theater, a princess who inspires hope and promotes self-help, and a Buddhist monk. They looked like people who had been suddenly frozen, bewitched in a single moment for all of time.

Two blocks later I found another arch, this one guarded by gray lions. I walked slowly to get a sense of the area. Various places emitted a smell like new plastic flowers or dolls recently released from their packaging. There were also smells of herbs unknown to me and the delicious aroma of just-cooked soup. When I looked at the display windows, there was a great variety of products—food, watches, toys, clothing, trinkets. In one store there was a plum-flavored wine with a round fruit in the bottle that made me want to taste it.

I liked the neighborhood so much that I decided to come back the next day and look for a job. I dressed up, and after visiting various stores I went to the Mei Gui Restaurant. There a very sweet Asian woman told me that Wah Hing Supermarket, just around the corner, was looking for a cashier because their regular one was about to give birth. I started my training that very same day.

Finding that job was my lifesaver, just like Professor Dora and her teachings had been, especially because life at Aunt Marina's house was pure hell. My aunt is antisocial and ill-humored; she seems to have suffered a lot. After the first few days, she stopped treating me well.

One day she got a phone call from her son, who lives in the United States, telling her he couldn't send her the usual allowance. She hung up violently and, all of a sudden, started screaming at me about how the apartment was dirty and how I must have thought I was a queen who deserved everything, and so on. We had agreed on the housework I would do, and I'd always tried to do the best I could, especially considering my job at the supermarket and my classes at the university.

On another occasion, a rainy night, she approached me with her usual arrogance.

"After the end of this month, you have to pay me more. Everything's going up, and you're too expensive. Besides, my son is not doing well in the United States."

"Auntie, after I pay rent, I barely have anything left to cover my school costs. And please remember that you frequently ask me for loans which you never repay or subtract from my rent."

She made an ugly face and slapped me. My head twisted back violently. I felt the hollow sound vibrate in my skull. In a matter of seconds, all sorts of ideas crossed my mind, including hitting her back and many things I could say, but they got stuck in my throat. I ended up simply letting loose a scream from the deepest part of me. Nobody had ever done anything like that to me before.

I ran out to the street and walked in the rain, crying. I entered Chinatown and sat on a bench until I calmed down. When I came back two hours later, my aunt wouldn't open the door. I had no place to go. My orphanhood hurt me like never before. A neighbor who felt bad for me let me sleep in a rocking chair in her living room that night.

Sometimes I couldn't handle what was going on. I tried to ignore it, but I felt, little by little, that my aunt, her ambience, and her allies were all leaving their legacy of pain within me. I cried so much in that place. The tears seemed to quench the fires of my pain. I asked the Señora to get me out of there so many times. I prayed and prayed, and my body swayed as if I were in a rocking chair. I felt as if I were entering a place of refuge to hide from everything around me. I fell asleep so many nights in that protected state and awoke with enough strength to face the new day.

The night before last I heard my aunt out on the balcony, talking to her friend next door, saying she was sick of me. I crept up as close as I could without being seen. I needed to hear what she was saying. It felt really urgent.

"Doing this favor is really causing me problems. It pisses me off that this shitty girl complains so much. She doesn't seem to understand she's a guest," I heard her say over a loud commercial playing on the TV.

"But doesn't the little bitch pay you?"

"Well, she pays a little something and helps, but she should accept the fact I'm the owner here."

"A little something!" I whispered behind the door. "She takes practically everything I make."

"The problem is she thinks she's a big deal," the neighbor said. "But she's very young and doesn't realize yet that life is really fucked."

"She'd be better off learning to accept what is, rather than wanting everything her way," my aunt said. "She's not going to find a husband that way, with all that lazy dreaming. She comes talking about her teacher or her godmother. What the fuck do I care what those lucky bitches think about life? Mine's been tough, fucked for sure. I don't need advice from anybody. I tried, and whatever I tried, I got burned for it."

The shouting from the couple arguing on the TV soap opera and the bachata playing on the neighbor's radio made it impossible for me to hear her stories. I had a sickening feeling, and I still had to study for school.

"People are just no good, Marina . . ."

The bachata and the soap opera went on, as loud as ever, and I couldn't catch anything else the neighbor said. I tried hard to focus my hearing.

"That's how it is, starting with my own parents, who never gave me what I deserved. If my grandmother Concha hadn't died, my life would be very different. She really loved me. She's the only one who really knew what I was worth, and she would have given me much more than my parents did, because they only bothered with me when it came time to mess with me, to punish me, to impose their so-called 'discipline,' which they never gave to my siblings. Me always working, and them such hypocrites. My mother and father died without forgiving me, guaranteeing I'll go straight to hell. I tell you, I was fucked at birth."

"Oh, Marina, and what are you going to do with the girl?"

"God damn it, I don't know why I agreed to do this favor and let this freeloader move into my house. If my brother hadn't died, and she hadn't been orphaned . . . I felt so bad when my aunt Camelia called, it made me soft. It had been a long time since I'd heard from her."

And so those two bitter women continued on. I couldn't study after I eavesdropped on them. My mother never talked like that. My maternal grandparents don't know my aunt Marina very well and don't know the rage that corrodes her soul.

"Oh, Mother, I need you so much."

I put a pair of cotton balls in my ears so I wouldn't hear any more of the conversation, and then I cried until my eyes went dry. I wrote to get things off my chest, prayed like my mother taught me, and fell asleep hugging my notebook.

When I woke up yesterday, I remembered the Señora had visited me again in my dreams. Her lips had moved but I couldn't hear what she said. Nonetheless, the way her arms and hands had danced had filled me with inner strength. She seemed to create or alter reality in an invisible dimension. I knew then and there that something important was about to happen, and I was overcome with a feeling that lifted me out of my misery. If the conversation the night before had condemned me to a dead end, the dream had pointed a way out. I was able to recall Professor Dora's pocket trick and practice it.

Later, at the supermarket, feeling the exhaustion of living all those months in my aunt's hell, I put my right hand in my pocket and closed my eyes for a few seconds. I felt my hand touching happiness and understood that I had to get myself out of my aunt's house. God had given me both life and joy, but also will and intelligence. I had the tools and the resources. I breathed deep, gave thanks for the guidance, and for the rest of the day asked all the customers who came through the supermarket if they might know of a pretty and well-lit room for rent in the home of some good people.

That day seemed really long. I asked so many times and got so many reactions. Some people only smiled and shook their heads; some didn't even pay attention to me; others were interested but asked exorbitant prices or offered places too far from Chinatown; still others gave me telephone numbers or asked for mine, promising that someone would call.

A man did call me, but the tone of his voice made my flesh crawl. A woman looked me up and down a few times, studied me with disdain, and asked how much I earned. When I told her, she became even more disdainful; she turned and walked out. A young woman asked for a cosigner. I told her I didn't have one. I didn't want to ask my teacher, and I don't have any family near Santo Domingo who could vouch for me. The young woman told me she was very sorry, but she couldn't rent without one.

I started to feel sad. The strength with which I'd begun my task was waning when, around four o'clock, a woman with a loving mother's face told me she could rent me a room in her apartment. Her children live in the United States, and she is alone with a granddaughter. I brimmed over with joy. I took her hands and squeezed them. She smiled nervously, as if it had been a long time since she'd been touched. My godmother says that people who aren't loved wander around in fear.

Really happy, I called Professor Dora to tell her what had happened. She congratulated me and offered to come that evening to help me move my things to my new place. She said opportunities such as these must be taken advantage of immediately. So I made the arrangements, but it wasn't easy.

I went back to Aunt Marina's, and, to put the difficult moment behind us right away, I immediately told her I'd be moving that very night to a place that was closer to work. Her first reaction was confusion; she hadn't anticipated that.

"I'm sorry, I can't allow it," she said once she got hold of herself. "I have an agreement with your grandparents and Aunt Camelia."

"Auntie, I'm old enough to make my own decisions," I said, staying calm. "Although my grandparents sent me to your house, I can't stay here anymore. You don't want me here, you treat me terribly, and I don't want to keep feeling bad about this situation."

"I treat you badly? Ingrate, wretch."

It went on like that until I started packing, and then she would unpack everything I'd done. She hit me and screamed terrible things, insisting that I couldn't leave. Hearing the uproar, a neighbor came over and tried to mediate. She told my aunt she could get in trouble with the police if she continued to treat me like that.

I was crying, desperate, putting my things in various bags in a chaotic and furious way. I called Professor Dora, screaming.

Things seemed to be getting worse in spite of the neighbor's presence.

My teacher arrived, and my aunt turned her wrath on her, hurling every insult she knew. My teacher tried to talk to her but realized that the only wise thing to do was to flee. She grabbed my things, pulled me by the arm, and together we ran out of that hellhole while my aunt continued screaming all sorts of insults.

We climbed into my teacher's car. She started it and accelerated, as if we were in a scene from an action movie, escaping from a nuclear explosion that was expanding all over the universe at the speed of light.

When we passed through the arch to Chinatown on Duarte and México Avenues, she stopped the car, parked, and stared at me. I cried and shook like a leaf in a storm. I looked at her. Her face began to hint at a smile, and her gaze had a certain spark. After a few seconds we both burst out laughing. We went on like that for a while. She hugged me, I cried, I giggled, cried, and laughed again until the horror of it all passed and I was left panting like an animal that has gone through a terrible scare and finally realizes it's survived.

We took my things to the new place on José Martí Street between Benito González and México. I arranged things as well as I could in my new room. It felt spacious and quiet. In the meantime my teacher talked with Doña Miriam, the owner of the apartment. When I finished, we went to my favorite restaurant to eat and celebrate.

At Mei Gui, after greeting everyone and ordering our food, my teacher took my hands in hers.

"Ramona, I want to talk to you today as the wise woman you are. Today I'm not your teacher, as you call me, nor an older friend, nor a mother substitute. Today I want to talk to you as a woman from the same tribe who has lived longer than you and comes to offer help in your rite of passage. Can I do that?"

"A woman from my tribe?"

"Yes, think outside the box," she said. She can be a bit brusque when she thinks I'm wasting time.

"Okay," I said, and she began talking in a voice very different from the one she'd used before.

"What happened in your life yesterday and today is incredibly important," she said, looking straight at me. "So much so that to live through it as if it were just any other time would be a waste. If you had to summarize in a single phrase everything that's happened in the last two days, what would that be?"

"That it feels like the end of an era?"

"That's very true, Ramona, that's how I see it, too. Thirteen years ago, you were orphaned, and your dreams went up in smoke. One day, you had things, the next, everything was taken away. Your siblings treated you badly . . ."

"Professor, thinking about that makes me cry."

"Remember, we're from the same tribe. I want you to call me Dora. It makes me cry too. I think it would anyone who heard the story. But seeing it, making it part of you, will free you. Forgetting it won't help you. May I go on?"

"Yes, Dora," I said, now sure the tribe's wise woman was before me.

"One day, your siblings abandoned you, left you without recourse. You lost your family inheritance. Surprise, abandonment, betrayal. Do you remember what you felt back then?"

"Oh, Dora, I used to cry all the time. My grandmother thought I was ill. She made me eat, and I'd vomit. They took me to the priest so he could bless me with holy oil. One day, sitting under a tree and looking at the crest of a hill, the beauty of the land filled me with peace. I remembered my mother and the Señora and her gaze. That day, I regained my senses and began to write. I wrote for days, and as if a thick curtain were parting, my world came into view, and I saw what I wanted."

"You were lost in a labyrinth, and that day a door opened and you escaped to sanity."

"That's how it happened. I made plans to keep studying, I moved to San Juan de la Maguana, I went to the university and met you," I said and burst out crying. I told her how much she'd helped me. She thanked me but wouldn't let me change the subject.

"In San Juan you took the reins again, decided to move to Santo Domingo, and then suffered contempt and indifference at your aunt Marina's house. That ended today, and now we're finally celebrating. What would you like to do?"

"I want to dance, to jump. I'd love to have a big bag of candies and walk down the street and give them away to whomever I meet."

"Why candies?"

"They're sweets, and my life just got sweet."

"Okay. Getting back to the rite of passage, I recommend you do this tomorrow, Saturday. Get up early and say a prayer of thanks. Whatever you do, be aware and do it deliberately and consciously. Live intensely, now that you have a new life. Before you go back to the store, go to the plaza in front of your new home and breathe in the neighborhood. To know your place is a symbolic act of power. And, more important yet, write about what you lived through at the end of this era. You'll find the right ending. I can't be with you tomorrow. You know I have to work in San Juan."

My first night's sleep in the new place was peaceful and deep. From the moment I awoke, I followed Dora's advice. My body felt light and willing. I went out to the sidewalk and the November morning embraced me as if the light were dancing around me. The day brought with it cool air that seemed to announce winter's impeding arrival. Summer was terrible this year, but now everything was freshening for me.

I crossed the street to the little plaza. A sign said it was the Zodiac Plaza. I found some cute statues of animals dressed in aristocratic clothing. I walked until I got to a glass chapel with a very large statue inside. When I saw it, my heart leapt.

"It's the Señora. A statue of the Señora," I said aloud, and then looked about to see if anyone could tell me who she was.

"What's going on?" I asked, now more calm. "I've been working just meters from this plaza for five months, and I've never seen this on my walks. Who is the goddess this statue represents?"

I stayed a while, a little dazed, staring at the image of the Señora. I was taken aback by her beauty. The line of her eyes, eyebrows, nose, and jaw had a lilting grace, as if they'd been drawn in slow motion. What did the sculptor feel as he unearthed the form in the rock?

How astonished I was to have come such a long way to find her. What Dora said was true—this encounter marked the end of an era.

Sitting before the Señora this morning, I wrote my impressions and reflected on what I'd experienced since last night. From the time I left my grandparents' home in the hills of El Cercado, I wrote down everything I had seen and all that had occurred to me, what I dreamt and what I thought about. If people knew the real value of a notebook, there wouldn't be any left in the stores.

Hugging my journal, I walked to the supermarket, which was just opening its doors. I arrived smiling, as if in ecstasy, and Mr. Chen looked at me questioningly. Excited, I asked him about the statue, and he said it was Dama Kwan Yin, the merciful mother, and that the twelve animals around her were those who had attended the Buddha as he lay dying.

I thought it was such a beautiful story that I asked more questions. In his tentative Spanish he said, "Later," and he gestured for me to prep the cash register and attend to the customers who were already moving around in the store.

Later that afternoon, as I was leaving the supermarket, I bought a new notebook. I walked to the heart of Chinatown, on Duarte Avenue. The neighborhood is very curious, a place full of stories waiting to be discovered, though it's not easy to do because Chinese people aren't very talkative. I wanted to visit the statues I liked so much. Sometimes I'd talk to them, and they told me about a world I'd only imagined.

I came to my favorite statue, the Immigrant. I called him Chang Fei. Anyone with that name grows up free and peaceful. He came from Canton many years ago. He's about five feet tall, thin, and made of bronze. He stands in front of the Scotiabank facing north, where he gazes with a look I can't really describe, a look of tragic realization. Perhaps he's overwhelmed by the idea that he won't be returning to his home country. He looks out on the neighborhood and his people here, and he knows this is his place now.

I continued walking until I got to my favorite park bench. Chinatown has so many things I like—the arches, the little plazas, the shops, its suggestive statues, the Mei Gui Restaurant and its owner Doña Rosa. And to top off my list of favorites, today I found out the Señora also lives here.

I went back to the plaza of the Señora so I could be with her. As if it were a sacred act, I started writing this story right there. I'm writing it for closure but also to cast my gift of wisdom to the winds. Perhaps someday someone will read this and discover that pain is a great teacher and that, at the other side of it, there's beauty and joy.

I sigh as the sun sets and take note of this treasure I've found, this peaceful place inside me, a fresh and secret cave filled with the call of many little lights. This has been such a beautiful day. I died last night, but I was reborn at dawn today.

I know I have my hill down south off a highway, but for now Chinatown is my refuge and my home. What I've found here is a world that's a mixture of beauty, work, entertainment, pain, legend, stories of faraway places, and, sometimes, a feeling of nevermore. Here I've become the woman I want to be, a woman who carries happiness in her pocket.

THE YIELDING PATHS

NONFICTION BY ÁNGELA HERNÁNDEZ

Translated by Achy Obejas

LIMITS

I was born in Buena Vista, a tiny valley in the Cordillera Central, which is located in the middle of the island we share with Haiti. Except for the occasional religious text, there were no books there, but there was plenty to provoke the imagination. One night just before Christmas, a luminous ball about five times the size of the full moon emerged from the north. The news ran swiftly through the rows of houses. Immediately, people of all ages were out on the town's only street. With necks craned, we watched the lighted orb pulse to the beat of an unknown rhythm until it blurred into the firmament. We never found out what it was.

In this region of voluptuous and dual-natured waters—both a caress and a threat—dawn was always marked by flocks of white herons and avian chatter. The hours were defined by shadows projected from the houses, and, lacking news broadcasts, folks would gather in the evening to comment on the day's rumors that were a mix of news brought in by travelers, recycled tales from popular memory, and the delicious extremes of imagination—all spurred by a sometimes voyeuristic interest or pure hope. Sometimes, out of the blue, local events would connect with the rest of the world. For example, in the fifties the dictator Trujillo had ordered the construction of an airfield for the military. The effects on the locals were quite notable. Foreign technicians and workers impregnated young girls and, once their mission was completed, left forever. For the first time, there was a group of kids who were children of no one, a new kind of orphan.

The first plane landed before the asphalt had been laid, enveloped by a huge cloud of dust that kept hundreds of peasants scattered in the nearby hills from capturing the details of the flying machine, which took off again before their opened mouths could even say "Oh!" Later, after much staggering in the air with smoke trailing from its tail, a plane performed an emergency landing. That was all that happened on that airfield, which was plowed up a little later to prevent landings of aircraft filled with exiled guerrillas coming to overthrow the dictatorship. Still, people gazed up at the skies expectantly.

There were no books in Buena Vista, but there was plenty of reality to be read. There were thundering hailstorms and hurricanes that flattened houses. The dictator would come to celebrate weddings at the Montaña Hotel, and it was said that if he was taken with the bride, the groom's cadaver would later be found in the misty rainforest by peasants. During the 1965 revolution, there were families whose children were on opposing sides when they were in the capital, and then while times were turbulent in the city they'd come back and hang around their hometown. There were revered family names that produced angels and accursed surnames whose offspring were muggers and sluts. There was a house that we crossed the street to avoid, where the father had hanged himself and the mother—so they said—raised toads and snakes, and the children, a bunch of boys, roved about the town revealing at every turn their maladjusted and malicious nature. There were boys and girls who hadn't been weaned yet, boys and girls who shit green diarrhea, children of God who never grew up because they were children of God. There were many lodges for tourists erected along verdant stretches where dogs with fiery red fur and fine saddle horses would promenade. There were sick people who kept their coffins—bought with their life savings so as not to burden the living poor—under their beds. The miraculous virgin visited a different family each evening. A guitarist died of sorrow after offering serenades to all the single women without finding favor with any. Manuelico, who was about a hundred years old, cured cowhides for shoe soles and peddled them on foot throughout the villages in the hills. A girl played baseball better than all the boys. A despairing man drank Eternal Darkness hair dye, and a despairing woman ate ground glass. There were dreams, and a hot thread ran through all their memories.

ENCOUNTER

There were no books in Buena Vista. That's the reason I loved them with such an anticipatory fervor. They encapsulated light and a sweet nostalgia (for what?).

I encountered my first book when I was five years old. I was waiting for my mother on a wooden bench facing two young women who were flipping through the tome. Every once in a while they'd look at me sideways and then turn back to their diversion. I stretched my neck and managed to make out the figure of a boy. Gold and aquamarine colors jumped out at me. I didn't dare try to join them. Then my mother came back, accompanied by the town mayor, who was supposedly going to cure me of the conjunctivitis that would afflict me every two or three months and fill my eyes with bloody threads. Annoyed, Atilano Concepción (that was his name) grabbed the book from the girls and, without a word, went straight to the cupboard. He carefully put it in a wooden box filled with cotton wool as if he were handling some sort of relic. "Bethlehem glass," whispered my mother, intrigued. It was understood that Bethlehem glass was the most fragile thing on earth, that it could shatter with a sigh. This was the first idea I got about books—a material so delicate, almost from the other side.

Only a few months ago Atilano, in his position of authority, had led government troops through the mountains in pursuit of guerrillas—"bearded ones" as they were known then—who'd arrived in the country with the pipe dream of toppling the dictatorship.

After their capture, the mayor—a trusted friend of the military—had the opportunity to meet the elusive warriors up close and talk with some of them before they were sacrificed. One of them was very young. It struck the mayor as a contradiction that the scrawny boy with a woman's face should have carried a gun, a pack full of munitions, and a spirit for combat. "Shitty peasant, how many times did I have you in my crosshairs and choose not to shoot at the guards so I didn't kill you," the boy said, disgusted.

"They're going to execute you," the mayor responded.

As he drank coffee, the guerilla spoke to him with condescension. "Don't worry. It's not your fault." The boy asked if he could keep the book he had in his pack. He wanted it turned over to the peasant after he was executed. It was José Martí's *The Golden Age* with a one-line dedication written in crimson ink.

Much later, in 1997 during the first International Book Fair in Santo Domingo, my son gave me *The Golden Age* with the dedication "To the most beautiful mother in the world, and with the clearest mind of all, Giordano Sosa." Right there, in that instant, in the dog days of summer at high noon, my memory flashed back a bunch of years to the Constanza River, the cupboard, the cotton-filled box, and the young guerrilla's book. I pictured the one-line dedication and realized it had been written by the mother, for the most beautiful son in the world, with the clearest mind of all. Both that book and that life would be buried in the fresh green mountains of Constanza.

When I turned ten, in one of the many places I lived, I was given a copy of *Universal Geography*, fruit of a punishment the nuns had imposed on the daughter of an active general. I remember the bright earth-blue color and a drawing of the solar system on its hard cover. After rhapsodizing over its mere presence, I opened it to find the Milky Way, the constellations, mountain ranges, fiery canyons, ocean floors, deserts that overflowed the page, mighty cataracts, delicate cascades—dizzying details that awed me. Did all of this exist? Where could these wonders be found?

In the home that had taken me in near the air force base in San Isidro, there was a Bible. It was a gift to the family from a Marine, a charming Puerto Rican who played ranchera music for the girls living near the enlisted men's housing and at the same time took part in attacks on the rebels. These "cleansings" of the Constitutionalists, by the way, were blessed by the Dominican Air Force chaplain, a trembling old Spanish priest with the rank of colonel who'd been a member of Franco's Falange and who liked to pinch little girls. "For there to be peace," the priest would preach, "there must be war."

When I was left alone to take care of the house, I'd dive into the Bible. A cascade of letters. A labyrinth of years. I rushed through Genesis. What a story. I read the second and third books, and then I got "sick" the next few days so I wouldn't have to go to school. I became enraptured with Abraham, Solomon, Ruth, David, Esther, the prophets, Moses, Job, Bathsheba, and that terrible God of trials and tributes who gave as much as He took away. Page after page, with tears in my eyes, I'd follow the worry and wonderment of a people questioning the heavens to decipher the wishes of their only God, so implacable and selective. I'd go over and over the overflowing texts of the Old Testament—the radiant desert landscapes, a sea parted by the force of a phrase, the faith that caused food to rain down, the beautiful woman who danced for the head of an evangelist, a fifteen-year-old girl surprised by an archangel who informs her that she will give birth to God, a Jesus Christ in love with a multi-hued and suffering humanity, King Solomon's seven hundred concubines. I'd soon beat the nuns in knowledge of the Bible's contents, which won me more than a few special considerations.

In the next place I lived, I came in contact at the end of the school year with a young woman who was a fan of romance novels. That's why I started reading dozens of works by Corín Tellado and Caridad Bravo Adams. They were a pernicious—and delicious—influence on my emotional education. I'm still afflicted with them. If I could free my sisters from these readings, I would, because as Simone de Beauvoir said, "Women will be free when they learn to love with their strengths and not their weaknesses." Somewhere in that dark and stormy mess, I came upon Leo Tolstoy's *Anna Karenina*, a book that nullified arithmetic and grammar for me.

In my first year of high school, elsewhere on my country's map, I made friends with a neighboring shoemaker, a former Air Force corporal. A tremendous scar linked his mouth and right ear. He lived in an apartment stuffed with pulp novels about cowboys. I went to his little hovel every day to watch him cut and sew soles, and after a while I'd leave with a pulp in my hands. Not much later, I began to think the shoemaker was a Marcial Lafuente Estefanía character because he had eyes like slits, and you could see that his hipbone was accustomed to carrying a gun. He'd been in various duels and rescued many blondes, who were always the most beautiful and most helpless in their respective neighborhoods. Still, the frank way the shoemaker chatted and laughed with me made me have my doubts, especially because the leading men in American westerns were always ugly and tough, and not a one of them would have taken the time to talk to a girl who looked like she was nine years old.

If it weren't for the fact that I could soon predict the whole plot of these Old West stories from the first ten pages, they would have corrupted me so thoroughly as to kill my finer sensibilities.

Luckily, at school there was a kind nun who taught us algebra and would take off her glasses to reveal clear black eyes, and another nun, a Canadian, slight and ancient, who'd have us sing "Silent Night" in English. Between the two of them, they'd put together a display case that included *The Diary of Anne Frank*, *Little Women*, *Alice in Wonderland*, biographies of saints, and two or three books by Dominican authors.

Something happened that seared my conscience, and I learned the power of words. A cyclone fence cut off the military housing areas, and the school for the children of the military as well. The rhythm of life there was determined by typical soldierly routines and domestic doings. At the same time, in the city of Santo Domingo just twenty kilometers away, there was social protest, political repression, and confrontations in the streets. One day during an event to celebrate our national independence, a group of youths in their last year presented a choral poem called "There's a Country in the World" by Pedro Mir. The students clapped enthusiastically. The nuns and the others in the room went mute, horrified. It was a political poem, a communist poem, a subversive text, a provocation. They wouldn't acknowledge that a chorus of military sons and daughters had just presented "There's a Country in the World" while, at the air base, a certain general threatened to hang by the testicles anyone found with so much as one of those pamphlets that were going around. After the presentation, there were interrogations, admonitions, fear on both sides. Words possessed an enigmatic power, I deduced.

The following year, I went back to my hometown, and my family decided to settle down in Jarabacoa so that my sisters and I could continue our high school education. Not only did I get to live in the same place for two years, but these were the most beautiful and liveliest years of my life—I had a group of pals my age. We ducked each other in the rivers until we almost drowned, stole flowers from ostentatious summer homes. I read like crazy from the offerings in our high school's modest library; I learned a theorem a day to keep the trigonometry teacher away; I ate enough for three.

My new friends and I liked to feel the cold, so we agreed to meet in the park at three in the morning with the pretext of needing to prepare for exams. We played drums, and our singing woke everyone. The music teacher drafted us into the band. Just behind the musicians, we'd lead all the important parades, in uniform. During that time, I delighted in the company of the most beautiful, purest, and kindest soul on earth. Her name was Nena. One morning, she woke up to a bloody flow. She was dead in three days.

Months later, I moved to Santo Domingo. I managed to get a place in Villa Consuelo, in a rooming house run by a most hardworking woman. It was frighteningly hot. The night air smelled of frying food. A film of dirty grease covered the blinds in the room, my nostrils, and my skin. In class at the university, the heat kept us in an eternal stupor. Water was scarce. Many times, we had to wash using a bucket of bug-ridden water. At night I'd wander our one very long hallway, listening to the parties of our neighbors, who lived off their "friends." One day, one of those girls died very suddenly from an abortion. In the little park in front of the house, there were undercover cops who kept watch all night.

In the rooming house where I lived with my sister Lourdes, there were ten men—salesmen, students, and civil servants—including a seventy-five-year-old man with colon cancer. He ate cow brains. He would sit at one end of the table with the head of a steer on his plate, and I would sit at the other, rice and beans before me—I got into vegetarianism right about then—and we'd have a lively chat. Don Carlos was pale, growing whiter every day. He had one thing of value, a wardrobe filled with novels that he shared only with one of his daughters and me. Thanks to him I had access to Alexander Dumas, Fyodor Dostoevsky, Victor Hugo, Jean Jacques Rousseau, José Enrique Rodó, José Eustaquio Rivera, Honoré de Balzac, François-René de Chateaubriand, Leo Tolstoy. I turned seventeen around then.

The heat oppressed our spirits, which were used to fog, the fragrance of pines, and rushing waters. But Don Carlos's books were there, as well as Doña Niña's support and that of the cook, a tiny woman, evangelical and quiet, who brought "the girls"—as she called Lourdes and me—lady-finger bananas and oatmeal cookies, spending on us the centavos that her own family surely needed, especially because she was raising three grandchildren.

In college I was called "compañera" and "comrade." It was common then. Somebody would hand me a flag, and that was enough to get me running, holding it on high, protesting against Balaguerist repression, against the Neo-Trujillista forces, and against the criminal chief of police. Paramilitary groups devastated neighborhoods, beat up, disappeared, and murdered students,

unionists, drivers. We marched in solidarity with Vietnam, with Cuba, with
Allende, against the murders of dockworkers, against imperialism. The police
and the military hated us. They were offended by the mere fact that we were
students and even more by our regal and baseless arrogance. In contrast,
the people loved us extravagantly. Drivers charged us less than the rest of
the population. Private cars would offer us rides—all you had to do was show
a T-square and a few books under your arm. When we were chased, doors
opened, and complete strangers would suddenly become guardian angels. I
liked all that, and that they called me "compañera."

The bad part was that everything had to serve the people, and if it didn't
serve the people then it was worthless. A small group determined who the
people were and what was useful and what was frivolous. One day while I was
reading *Crime and Punishment*, a surprised comrade said, "That's ideological
bullshit." He'd never held a book of literature in his hands, but he had a hole
in his skull, the result of being tortured in prison after he'd gone to the countryside just at the moment when some on the left had decided to follow the
Great Leader Mao's dictum to "surround the cities from the country" and
ordered the best of them into rural areas. And since this comrade was the
very best, he went straight to the countryside, where he was soon captured.
In prison they kept him awake twenty-four hours a day by shining lights on
him. They hit him on the head with rifle butts. And there I was, with no glory
other than being a student, ashamed, devouring *Crime and Punishment*, in
other words ideological bullshit.

During my first year in college I read stories by Juan Bosch and Virgilio
Díaz Grullón and the novel *The Blood* by Tulio M. Cestereo (about the Lilís
dictatorship), *You Can Cross the Massacre by Foot* by Freddy Prestol Castillo
(about the slaughter of the Haitians), and *Over* by Ramón Marrero Aristy
(about exploitation at the sugar refineries), gaining from those writings an
understanding of what was hidden and precarious in the Dominican soul.

That's where I was when I had to choose a career. So it wasn't strange
that I let myself be guided by two simple though opposing principles. First,
the least amount of doubt—the career with the fewest existential questions,
given that we were already overwhelmed with uncertainties living in a country that announced a new coup d'etat every week and where white hands were
painted on tombstones, evidence first of the caprice of the left and then of the
scourge of the paramilitary. Second, usefulness to the people—a career that
would help us toward technological and scientific independence (to emulate
Cuba; we couldn't even imagine the situation with the Soviet Union). In other
words, we had to lean toward precision and development. The word "steel"
then had a special weight. I found myself enrolling in chemical engineering
because it had the most difficult classes, those that required the greatest intellectual effort. It was a real challenge, and since challenges forge character,

I was there, openly dueling with technology, with hard science, with precise formulas.

I found myself consumed by techno-scientific and political literature. A constant discourse about importance and utility made up for my lack of motivation. And now that I'm on the subject, allow me to illustrate my stoic revolutionary discipline: *Thermodynamics, What Is to Be Done?* (Lenin), *Physical Chemistry, Dialects of Nature* (Engels), *Reactor Design, The 18th Brumaire of Louis Napoleon* (Marx), *Unifying Industrial Operations, A Report from Beneath the Scaffold,* all five books by Mao Tse-tung, *Balancing Material and Energy, The History of PCUS, Spectrometry, The Origin of the Family, Private Property and the State* (Engels)... It got so I had passionate raptures over differential equations, quantum physics, and crystallography, though it wasn't the same with social theory and political economy (notes on Nikitin, and Martha Harneker with notes from Das Kapital), drinks that were not very gentle on my iffy stomach. During my risky first pregnancy I had some time without responsibilities, and so I went through an entire volume of an encyclopedia dedicated to literature. It was a modest transgression in the midst of all that committed and compromising reading.

The César Vallejo literary workshop at the university met Saturday afternoons. Many times I sat outside on the sidewalk to listen to the lectures and discussions. They criticized the postwar Dominican generation, the Generation of '65; they praised the Neruda of *Residence on Earth* and depreciated the Neruda of *Canto General*; they were irreverent about poets and writers who used poetry as "a weapon loaded with the future"; they read Georges Bataille and Jean Baudrillard. They were searching for something new. A few of those conversations really captivated me. In others, I perceived a certain presumptuousness. They pontificated and passed judgment. It was from those dialogues that some of our best poets and writers, both men and women, emerged, later known as the Generation of the '80s.

When I accepted that the language of my spirit did not mesh with any of two hundred political terms and even less with scientific formulas, I was able to transcend the notions of utility and science. Uncomfortable doubts and furtive flights of imagination didn't constitute a decision but a fact. It wasn't about good and evil but about each person's individual nature. I needed to admit my genuine inclinations and figure out where my bull-headed stubbornness would take me. I found my way back, a little blindly, to poetry and fiction. I engaged in new complicities in creative matters with new friends. We'd write poems as a group. We read Borges, Franklin Mieses Burgos, Luis Alfredo Torres, Zacarías Espinal, Juan Sánchez Lamouth, René del Risco, Dante, Vicente Aleixandre, Rimbaud, Breton, Huidobro. Going town to town, we would get together for poetry readings that went on until dawn.

It was during this time that I was fortunate enough to read women writers whose works were far from the rosy books produced by Corín Tellado and Caridad Bravo Adams. Doris Lessing, María Zambrano, Monserrat Roig, Simone de Beauvoir, Marguerite Yourcenar, Clarice Lispector, Marguerite Duras, Isabel Allende, Jeannette Miller, Aída Cartagena. They took me to dazzling extremes. When I confirmed that women really wrote, I understood how much my creative development had been arrested. This realization came at precisely the right moment. I'd never again spurn a light on the truth, no matter how strange, useless, or subjective it might be.

NEXUS

From the nexus with books I arrived at some conclusions about my interests, and I hope that they connect equally with yours.

Writing, letters, is in our blood; ancestral notions that go to that part of memory visible on pictograms, codices, parchments, and volumes. Links and resonances that come alive and are confirmed by reading.

Books possess the attribute of democracy, perhaps the only one still preserved as a spiritual kaleidoscope from which to begin on our inner paths, a point of connection that is combinable with what's outside us. Certainly authoritarian and doctrinaire regimes proscribe reading. But books move mysteriously and can come to anyone's hand by winding paths. Artaud, Camus, Beckett, Ionesco, and Genet were revealed to Gao Xingjian, the Chinese Nobel laureate, in a desk drawer, left there by a French translator. Without saying a word, the young Chinese man and the translator began an exchange. Maybe this was the seed that was planted for the vocation that led to *Soul Mountain*.

I know about literary workshops in my country that take place in one square kilometer populated by one hundred thousand people. The tyranny of poverty produces all kinds of privations, and yet some of the boys and girls who make up those workshops have read better literature and poetry than most of our public officials, just to mention one sector with purchasing power. Used books are passed around hand to hand. When I started writing, one of those kids turned me on to Nikos Kazantzakis and Seneca. His eyes shone when he recited Angelos Sikelianos, John Keats, and Milton. Unfortunately, in adverse situations like those around such literary workshops, that certain euphoria is limited. Nonetheless, one or two of the workshop participants will gather the courage and resistance to take the leap required by their growing sense of hope.

Books foster friendships and strange encounters; they gather and impart the writer's own vibes. They manifest, get dislodged, and make suggestions.

Even those volumes that are burned through intolerance and terror still echo in our collective memory.

Books rout fundamentalist temptations, diminish fears, and raise awareness. To know what's inside the Bible, the Koran, the Popol Vuh, the Bhagavad-Gita, the I-Ching makes us more open-minded and frequently confirms our own faith, because once we access the results of so many quests, we will recognize the error introduced by prejudice and desire to dominate. We will know that the truth is woven precisely at the wavering moment when the language of paradox emerges, when there are no definitive lines. Interpretations should attempt to include generosity, coexistence, and the infinite connections among all that exists. The more flexible and firm the character, the more vigorous and brave the humility it forges.

All autodidacts have before them, as curse and as blessing, the presence of limits. As for myself, I recognize the emerging borders of those limits as dark and provocative landscapes that combine imagination and thought.

What drew me to literature wasn't a love of art, or aesthetic or stylistic pretensions, but an intuition about lively complicities, abrupt ruptures and absences, a thirst for connections and fresh air, a difficult taste for the truth. The book, I came to understand, is food of a mysterious material and, at the same time, a table made up of freedom, conversations, and windows.

EXCERPT FROM FEASTING ON SANCOCHO BEFORE NIGHT FALLS, A MEDITATION

NONFICTION BY NELLY ROSARIO

SETTING THE TABLE
WITH G. G. MÁRQUEZ

On the one-year anniversary of his 1982 Nobel Prize in Literature, Gabriel García Márquez had a single obsession: to celebrate with a sancocho stew at the edge of a river in his native village of Aracataca, Colombia. Why so humble a meal for such a world-class achievement?

Solitude and sancocho are polar opposites. Cooking and consuming in solitude an integrative dish like sancocho is to be a come-solo, Domini-speak for an "eat-alone." So who better to crave sancocho than the author of *One Hundred Years of Solitude*? This meat-vegetable stew embodies abundance, celebration, communion. It's an antidote to the solitude writ large by Márquez in his Nobel lecture "The Solitude of Latin America."

> [Latin Americans] have had to ask but little of imagination, for our crucial problem has been a lack of conventional means to render our lives believable. This, my friends, is the crux of our solitude. . . . Why is the originality so readily granted us in literature so mistrustfully denied us in our difficult attempts at social change? . . . We, the inventors of tales, who will believe anything, feel entitled to believe that it is not yet too late to engage in the creation of the opposite utopia.

The preparation and sharing of sancocho might actually be our attempt at some utopia, however writ small in a world of eat-alones. A pot of sancocho is an anti-bomb, a weapon of mass attraction that blasts apart the American concept of nuclear family. A pot of sancocho serves up the briefest taste of a national unity.

The history of sancocho, also regional slang for "pig slop," is about raising the ordinary to the extraordinary or—for good Marquezian measure—dystopic to utopic. The African Diaspora has always done what it could with whatever's at hand, transmuting base metals into gold, be it resurfacing rice stuck to the pot bottom as concón or throwing together locrio when meat is scarce and rice plenty. At the very least, Dominicans season our efforts well. It's how we've alchemized into a national dish the hodgepodge stew also enjoyed throughout Latin America and the Caribbean. Our bowl may be humble, but it brims.

ENTRÉE 1: ORIGINAL FICTION

Feasting on the Goat before Night Falls

> . . . did he realize that with a certain regularity they were giving
> him a bowl of soup with pieces of yucca, a slice of bread, and jugs of
> water into which the jailers spat as they passed them to him.
>
> —*The Feast of the Goat: A Novel*, MARIO VARGAS LLOSA

> Sancocho weighed about three hundred pounds, he was a sort of human
> balloon: his greatest concern in life was the preparation of that food, which he
> concocted with such passion that he became the soul of that [jail's] mess hall.
>
> —*Before Night Falls: A Memoir*, REINALDO ARENAS

Samara Potina held a secret sancocho. I only attended to fulfill the invitation of a neighbor of a friend of a cousin. What we were celebrating, who knew. All I know is that illegal assembly beats toasting alone to the evening news. Look, I wasn't the only one breaking the penal code. Not giving up names, either. I'm only a rat when hungry.

That night the neighborhood's center of gravity converged at her place. An anti-bomb, that table. An explosion of people detonated by the crude stewpot over her electric stove. Rumor has it the stewpot's a cannonball from the days of the Spanish, that Samara Potina could turn the wrought-iron thing to gold by rubbing it with magnets. There's gunpowder in her peppermill. In her kitchen she has an altar to San Cocho, Venezuela's Patron Saint of the Lost Billfish. Her age? Zero to infinity, what the hell do I know. Read the *New York Crimes* for more dirt: "White-listed by the Federal Bureau of Instigation for pacifist activities that threaten rational obscurity." Some say Samara Potina was raised in Santo Domingo, praised by the Divided Nations for malnutrition in children. I'm cooperating the best I can.

So I put my lips to the rotten pot. If you condemn Eve, condemn Adam. Liquor today, criminal yesterday. And yesterday, I ate sancocho. Prohibition makes us full of empty spirits. I miss sitting around the dinner table. My parents were workaholics. . . .

The bootleg? Pure revival. Condemn me. I had already been condemned the night before, having warmed expired Goya soup in its own can. To eat alone is to eat like a dog. But to sit at a table, no matter how small, in the company of others . . . to feel the thick broth make its way down to your own center of gravity, where it lights a flame, is to live.

I saw Samara Potina with my own eyes. She stopped to admire the house of clean chicken and cow bones I'd built on my napkin.

She sucked her teeth, quoted an Aunt Clara Something-or-Other: "Dominicans are unapologetic carnivores." Her voice is the loveliest of contraltos. She honored me by sitting in the next chair to sip stew from a large gourd. No napkin, no spoon. Her face, the meeting of civilizations, rearranged itself into a half-smile when the rum tongues began their praises.

"This woman, she gets Brugal, Barceló, Bermudez, and Bacardi to sit at this table and get wasted on each other's rums."

"A man, he's haunted one morning by a scent. Leaves work at lunchtime, books a plane from Miami to Santo Domingo, flies without luggage, and three hours later is sitting at Potina's table. Finds himself in the arms of the son he'd disinherited. I'm a rich man now."

"The couple upstairs, they stop fistfighting at the whiff of Samara Potina's sancocho."

"Her kitchen, it gets her in hot water with the divide and conquerors. They burn her crops, poison her cattle. She shrugs, says, 'Just salt in the sancocho.' Wraps up her stewpot and a couple spoons in a tablecloth. Hops on a raft to Puerto Rico, then leaves to Panama, then to Colombia, then settles here, loneliest city in the world. Hell of a tour of duty."

"Leave magical realism to the politicos," said Samara Potina. She put down her gourd, wiped her lips. "Guilty or not, you've all just committed a feast of the goat."

Those chewing on goat bones put them down.

By then, I had washed my hands.

My conscience is clean. Today I only remember four of the ten points to her manifesto.

"One. Always cook meats separately. Take them out when three-quarters cooked, then finish them with the vegetables and spices so all flavors meld.

"Two. If the meat's too tough, add rum. Leave a metal spoon in the stew while it cooks, or dip in a piece of wood charcoal.

"Three. If the broth is too thin, stir it with a wooden spoon.

"Four. Add cilantro last, otherwise it overwhelms the pot."

What this means is alphabet soup to me. Decoding the chatter is your job. Not mine. Unless, of course, you promise to get me out of this can.

Nutrition Facts: Soup in a Can

Goya Sancocho Criollo, 15 oz.

Pacific Island Market LLC's asiamex.com

Serving Size	1 cup (246g)	
Servings Per Container	approx. 2	

AMOUNT PER SERVING

Calories 140　　From Fat 5

% DAILY VALUE*

Total Fat	.5 g	1%
Saturated Fat	0 g	0%
Cholesterol	0 mg	0%
Sodium	980 mg	41%
Total Carbohydrate	30 g	10%
Dietary Fiber	2 mg	6%
Sugars	0 g	0%
Protein	–	3%
Vitamin A	–	0%
Vitamin C	–	6%
Calcium	–	6%
Iron	–	6%
Vitamin D	–	–

*Percent Daily Values are based on a 2,000 calorie diet.

ENTRÉE 2: "DUMB SOUP" AT THE SUPERMARKET

"Who the hell puts sancocho in a can?" My cousin sucks her teeth. She's visiting from the D.R. At the supermarket, we spot the bright red can in the "ethnic foods" section. "I mean, when you make a sancocho, you get excited about what to include, what everyone can contribute. Sancocho in a can . . . that's disgusting." Her lips bunch up as if tasting pig swill. "Vegetables cubed exactly the same ain't the same as biting into home-cut chunks. And then all this old meat stuffed in there . . ."

Meat, however, is not listed in Goya's sancocho ingredients—it is what's called a sopa boba or "dumb soup," a vegetarian's sancocho. The missing ingredient in canned goods is the creative process. Canned sancocho, my mother says, is for the lazy, for the empty nostalgic. For those lacking Marquez's "secret energy of daily life." Canned sancocho is a mata vida, or "life killer," to the homemade levanta muertos that brings Lazarus palates back from the dead.

A sopa boba is the thin, meatless broth that functions as the multiplication of fish and loaves. You may not have much meat or rice, but put them together, add water, and you get a bit of everything in one meal. Vegetarianism can be by circumstance in a country on the United Nations' list of twenty-eight "high priority" nations; the leading UN 2006 Millennium Development Goal was to halve the proportion of people suffering from hunger.

Hard math where rotten politicians contribute to the high percentage of malnutrition. Replayed are the same poor political and economic administration that plagued the country during the era of Dominican colonial history also known as La España Boba, or the Era of Foolish Spain (1809–21).

Today the foolishness of politics also seasons our language: vivir de la sopa boba. "To live off the foolish soup" is used to deride idle civil servants and moochers in general. It describes the making of an easy living on the backs of taxpayers. In the United States, we know it as feeding at the public trough or riding the gravy train.

To the die-hard cook, passengers of the gravy train frequent restaurants and cook/consume prepackaged, overprocessed foods—"gringo" foods. This distrust gave rise, at one time, to rumors of worm-infested American poultry. The rumors, as described by Gilbert M. Joseph and Catherine LeGrand in *Close Encounters of Empire*, caused "Dominicans to stop consuming that which they felt was consuming them. . . . It's much better to eat a pollo criollo in a sancocho at home, than to consume gringo chicken in a fast-food Pica Pollo."

Internet junkie and amateur cook Clara González collects Dominican recipes on her blog, Aunt Clara's Kitchen. She explains the importance of process to cooking sancocho: "Its preparation is long and it contains many ingredients. However, the time it takes to prepare is the time best enjoyed with friends, while drinking a little rum or a cold beer."

Cooking from scratch offers freedom of choice. Cooking styles are as varied as ingredients and reveal the soul of the maker, explains seventeen-year-old Dominican high school student Hector Orchardson: "My mom cooks it. My dad also cooks it. My favorite is my mom's."

ENTRÉE 3: CALLING THE KETTLE BLACK IN AUNT CLARA'S KITCHEN

Aunt Clara's Sancocho de Siete Carnes (Seven Meat Hearty Stew)
Prep time: 1 hour
Cook time: 1 hour
Total time: 2 hours
Serves: 8 generous servings

INGREDIENTS:

1 pound beef for stews (flank, chuck, or round)
1 pound goat meat
1 pound pork sausage (longaniza)
1 pound pork for stews (belly or chump end)
1 pound chicken
1 pound pork ribs
1 pound bones from a smoked ham
Juice of two limes
1 teaspoon chopped cilantro or parsley
½ teaspoon powdered oregano
1 tablespoon mashed garlic
1½ teaspoons salt
4 tablespoons oil (corn, peanut, or canola)
2½ quarts water
½ pound ñame (yam), cut into 1-inch pieces
½ pound auyama (West Indies pumpkin), cut into 1-inch pieces
½ pound yautía (taro), cut into 1-inch pieces
3 unripe plantains, 2 cut into 1-inch pieces
½ pound yuca (cassava), cut into 1-inch pieces
2 corn cobs, cut into ½-inch slices (optional)

INSTRUCTIONS:

1. Cut all the meat into small pieces.
2. Coat the meat (except the pork sausage) with the lime juice.
3. Place all the meat in a large bowl and add the cilantro, oregano, garlic, and half a teaspoon of salt. Rub meat to cover with the seasonings. Marinate for at least 30 minutes.
4. In a large pot heat the oil over medium heat, add the beef and stir (be careful with hot oil splattering). Cover and simmer for 10 minutes. Add a few tablespoons of water if it looks like it might burn.
5. Add the pork and simmer for 15 minutes, adjusting water when necessary. Add the rest of the meat (except for the chicken) and simmer for another 15 minutes, adding tablespoons of water as needed to prevent it from burning.
6. Add the chicken and simmer for another 5 minutes, adding tablespoons of water as needed to prevent it from burning.
7. Add 2 quarts of water to the pot and bring to a boil. Add the ñame, auyama, yautía, and the cut-up plantains. Simmer covered for 15 minutes.
8. Grate or scrape with a knife the remaining plantain to make it into a pulp, and add to the pot along with the yuca and corn. Add water as necessary to maintain the same level. Stir regularly to avoid excessive sticking.

9. Simmer until the last ingredients you added are cooked through.

10. Season with salt to taste. Serve hot with white rice and slices of avocado, and garnish with hot sauce or agrio de naranja.

Note: The trick to this dish is adding the meat from the longest-cooking to the shortest-cooking, so please pay attention to the order in which meat is added into the cooking pot.

ENTRÉE 4: COLORING IN GRAYSCALE WITH SANCOCHO PRIETO AND SANCOCHO BLANCO

The diversity of ingredients in a typical sancocho opens up a myriad of possible versions. The many styles include sancocho prieto (see Aunt Clara's recipe above) and sancocho blanco. Sancocho blanco is made with white meats—that is, fish, chicken, or pork. Though heavier than the vegetarian sopa boba, sancocho blanco, well, pales in comparison to its "black" counterpart, the sancocho prieto.

I'd like to think "prieto" is meant to be complimentary, that it suggests more than just the viscous color the stew acquires after hours of cooking. But in the D.R., the word is far from complimentary, bitter to many. The stew carries the genes of a culture that warns one to stay away from the sun; recipes, too, warn against mixing sancocho with metal utensils, as these tend to darken the stew. Blogger Ebony Lafontaine expands on the sancocho prieto as a mishmash of Dominican attitudes on race:

> The racial question in our country is not an issue of the moment; it's an everyday matter. . . . We are in the country of the "sancocho prieto": the pot calls the kettle black, it feels white; whites don't want to mix with blacks, they'd feel black; blacks with white children don't want them to mix with blacks, they want white grandchildren; whites with black children dress them up in name brands and expensive schools so that the status will reverse their color; blacks with status and black children dress them up in name brands and expensive schools so that the status will offer them acceptance.

Sancocho prieto is customarily served with white rice and avocado slices. Preferences vary. I, for one, don't like adding rice to my stew bowl or drizzling stew over my rice plate, preferring to enjoy the essence of each. The result of mixing is an impromptu asopao, a soupy rice (or ricey soup), and asopao has its own art.

Mixture and variety underpin Dominican racial and cultural identity, a self-identification that finds advocates even in theology. In *Introducing Latino/a Theologies*, religious scholars Miguel de la Torre and Edwin Aponte insist that the "Hispanic stew, whether it is called an *ajiaco* or a *sancocho*, is and should be unapologetically the Latinas'/os' authentic reality, their *locus theologicus* (theological milieu), from which Hispanics approach the larger world."

Implicit in an identity centered on hybridity, however, is the convenience of neither having to prove whiteness nor acknowledge blackness. Our Sancho Panzan desire to reap the benefits (for whatever they're worth) of both "blackness" and "whiteness" was noted by the United Nations Development Program. According to the program's 2005 report, Dominicans' sense of self hinges on the "mixture of ethnic groups that generates considerable social tensions, among definitions, conflicts and acceptance of diversity, the impact of Haitian immigration, Dominican emigration abroad, and foreign tourists, all of which are pushing Dominicans to adopt 'cosmopolitan' components within their cultural identity." Our colonial origins and the subsequent history of political instability, parade of dictatorships, and neoliberal agendas make us predisposed to what the report calls "externality" or "the perception that the behavior of the people, and the events that occur to [us], are determined by external elements."

Externality predisposes us to entrust our future to forces that are beyond our control. The solution to the dilemmas of externality emerges as an aspiring to be "another" or at least "seem to be another." Globalization furthers the dilemma by generalizing consumption patterns and lifestyles around the notion of "being developed."

In Cuba, the ajiaco as metaphor for national identity appears more entrenched in internality, or the investment in the study of the elements that make up one's own culture. The work of Cuban ethnographer Fernando Ortiz exemplifies this sense of national internality. Ortiz is in fact regarded as Cuba's "Third Discoverer" for the extent of his studies of the island and for his efforts to define *cubanidad*, or "Cubanness." It was Ortiz who coined the term "AfroCuban." The term "AfroDominican," on the other hand, seems to embody a certain externality. Outside of the work of black nationalist Blas Jiménez, the term does not have as much traction in the Dominican Republic as it does among "dominicanos ausentes" living in the United States.

The above menu items may induce some teeth sucking and the proverbial "Everyone has to put their spoon in our sancocho." But all good stews must be put to the fire, uncovered, and stirred. Frown at those who leave the table to sip their sancocho alone, pinkies turned up. From Santo Domingo to Aracataca, service is with a smile.

AN HEIRESS FROM ARROYO HONDO

FICTION BY LISSETTE ROJAS

Translated by Achy Obejas

You get to the beauty salon, and everyone looks at you like they're trying to figure you out. You understand you're like a rare kind of bat there, an unusual mammal. You're out of your element, but you act like you belong because belonging is power, and you can afford to give yourself the pleasure of patronizing a place even as overpriced and ostentatious as this. You carefully place your Prada bag on the minimalist white sofa as you sit with extreme care and cross your legs with absolute certainty that each movement is correct. You've seen this a thousand times on the soap operas, and you've rehearsed it. Still, you can't help but pick at your nails with a nervous gesture.

Hello, dear, says the stylist, your friend Yosi, with a white grin on her black face. And you respond with your hello, with your own white grin on your own black face, which is actually more poetic, though it's the same thing.

A curious voice beside you asks, Is she your sister?

No, my best friend, Yosi answers, proud that you're a professional woman, not understanding the question's subtext: a black employee and a black woman in a salon for rich white women must be family. Maybe that's why the woman beside you stares so openly at you in the mirror.

What are you looking at, Paleface? you ask her in your mind, though you never drop your dignified expression. Yosi sees your discomfort and calls out, laughing, that you can complain if they're being too rude, but you say, no, they're treating you just fine, because you don't want to rant like you used to back in the barrio, because that's not refined, and you want to act right, with class.

Your story could be like Yosi's, but it's not, because the distance between you and her involves eight years of high school and college. What brings you together is the neighborhood and the secret adventures you had out on the hills gathering guavas, mameys, mangos, and cherries back in the nineties, when that part of Arroyo Hondo was half woodland and an hour could go by without a car or person passing to interrupt your games.

Back then, you'd get lost for hours in the hills, eating your fill from the fruit trees while the distant mansions looked on indifferently. Yosi would swear that if you dug through the garbage there'd always be something worthwhile. No, no way—I'm not going to get sick because of some piece of junk, you'd say as an excuse, because you weren't into dumpster diving. You didn't need much to survive, and you never went hungry, even if you sometimes ate your lunch a little late.

"Hunting" was the most beautiful verb. You were girls and lived with so little. You'd run through the grass, and thorns would catch your short pants, or they'd hurt your legs and leave long scratches like playful scars.

How old were we then? as the song says. You were maybe nine years old, and Rosalía, the oldest in the group—a tomboy and a major mischief maker—showed you how to climb the loquat tree infested with termites. It didn't matter that you picked the leaves off each other because your mothers figured out where you'd been by the smell. You reek of chimiquí, they'd pretend to scold you, because they understood, transported to their own childhoods by the green scent of recently broken branches.

It's as if you're dreaming, anchored in that purgatory between past and present, when what's real vanishes with yesterday's perfume. You hear a question from far away you can barely make out. Are you going to have a shampoo? It's impatiently repeated. Are you going to have a shampoo? the voice asks.

Yes, yes, you respond and wipe the memory away with a wave of your hand as you get up and go toward the hair-washing station at the other end of the salon.

You're still trying to behave like a person of means when another client comes in, one of those people who talk so much everybody knows their business. This thirty-something woman insists you do both her nails and toenails. I'm going to a wedding at the Hilton right now, she says, and you're stunned, stock-still, your hair dripping Sebastian leave-in conditioner as time seems to go by at a turtle's pace. So slooooowly.

You look at her disdainfully and declare I-am-a-client, with imperious emphasis. Then she excuses herself and says, I thought you were the new girl. You comfort the little white dimwit: No, no, it's not important, it's no big deal. But you know why in a roomful of women she directed herself to you and no one else, because in a salon in Arroyo Hondo a black woman with idle hands must surely be a pretentious and impudent employee, not just someone who doesn't like to work but a woman who dares to wash her kinky hair at a shampooing station designed for la crème de la crème of this exclusive sector—because this is not a barrio—of the Dominican capital.

When they start putting rollers in your hair, it feels like the mocking laughs provoked by the Revlon Number 7 blonde's misunderstanding have finally started to subside. The same way you feel the pins on your skull, you feel a thousand eyes on your back, and you peek at the mirror, surprising nine pairs of eyes, which quickly and simultaneously shift, slightly embarrassed.

You want them to stop watching you. You're not a freak, dammit. It pisses you off, no joke, but they're looking at you as if you have shit on your face. What are you looking at? Do I owe you something, or you like what you see?

A bug. Yes, a bug under a microscope, now you understand. You feel solidarity with recently discovered microbes and start to hate the indiscreet little pupils that watch you while pretending to be thinking about something else—a nailfile, perhaps, to throw you off, to make it seem as if your presence doesn't upset them or brutally burst their stereotypes.

You consider whether maybe you're getting a complex or have low self-esteem, and that's why you imagine everyone's looking at you or talking about you. You keep your gaze fixed on a French magazine you picked up on purpose so that they'd see you're not some poor black woman, but someone who's studied, who's risen up, even if you, yourself, are not so convinced of your success.

You seem to go on reading, but you're actually thinking. Suddenly you hear the flabby blonde talking in English, saying you don't belong in such a place. She doesn't belong here, she's black, Haitian, and poor, she declares, as if English were a secret language exclusive to the rich that provides some kind of impunity when criticizing the lower classes because they wouldn't understand.

You lower the magazine and shoot her a look in the mirror. You and your dark lineage want to tell her so many things, to fire at her and hit her with words from the barrio until she's left socially crippled.

Yeah, blondie, I'm here, just like you, because I came to get my hair done and make myself beautiful and then go out on the street with my swinging step, you got that? And your blond husband's gonna honk his horn when I walk by, as if he was saying, black girl, you sure look good, and he's gonna drool, and the car will flood from it until you can't find where to sit your blonde ass, understand?

You continue to fix her with your hard stare, because, after all, what's wrong with being poor and black? If you're black and read French, then you must be Haitian, right? And if you were Haitian, so what? Would that make you a lesser person? That stupid bitch could only dream of having the heart and grace of the Haitian women you know, who are gems. The truth is she doesn't deserve you wasting your spit on a reply.

Then the woman who insulted you realizes you understand and flushes red, not like a tomato but like a strawberry, or like any other spongy fruit like her, flaccid, just flaccid. Not like you, who's got that taut ass that could be insured for a few million dollars, at least if you were famous like Jennifer Lopez.

But you weren't born like a squash, with a blossom on your butt, remember? Check out how screwed up life can be, little black girl, cuz you were born in Arroyo Hondo, the other one, the poor one, the isolated barrio, the miserable patch left over after your grandparents sold off the land for pennies. And now there's poverty, overcrowding, corruption in an island barrio surrounded by riches and by high walls that hide shiny zinc roofs, roofs that call to the skies claiming reparations for God knows what injustice.

The least poor of the area cook herring, which fills the neighbors' houses with its telltale smell. There is silent envy next door, where three children eat rice with fried egg and a mother says she will eat hers plain white because, she pretends, that's the way she likes it.

You remember how, on your side of the wall, potbellied naked kids dragged around improvised cars made from bottle caps and cardboard while on the other side they celebrated a birthday with clowns, candy, and lots of food.

Multicolored balloons floating in the wind. Balloons know nothing of private property and fly over shacks while your small relatives play at trying to catch them, but they're too high up, unreachable, like happiness when there's nothing to eat.

The kids rejoice anyway, and the mothers come out, mouths agape, teeth missing, with babies pegged to their waists. They watch the sky and laugh at the kids who pretend to have wings, jumping without looking at the ground. They're like a flock of birds gliding around a tree.

The mothers let them run-fly, because they don't know when they'll see a vejiga loose like that and see them laugh like that again. You explain, like a real professional, to your first cousin's wife, your old neighbor, that it's not called a vejiga but a balloon. And she responds, I know it's a balloon, but I don't call it that because I don't want people to think I'm putting on airs.

They say these lots are worth quite a bit, that the millionaire neighbors want to buy them so they won't have us so close, because we're rowdy and dangerous and listen to bachata real loud, drink too much, laugh uproariously, and use any excuse to party.

Every now and again, a lawyer or other legal rep shows up with a new offer, but if the children or the grandchildren of the first owners of these last lots sold, where would all these people go? Would there be enough money to settle them all in decent homes?

Your biggest fear is that there'll come a day when these kids will have to go out on the streets to fight with stray dogs over food, like the little ones who live near the Ozama River, those kids who spend all day, from the crack of dawn, turning over dumpsters looking for something to eat. They come back home to the barrio only to sleep in their little huts, half cardboard and half zinc, which seem to encrust the slope and the riverbank with resentment.

Almost instinctually, you rub your belly thinking of the children that won't come. When you see the ones from Ozama, you fear for their future and think of yours, the ones from the barrio. There's nothing you can do for them except help them with food. They're not like you were. They have nothing but rocks to entertain them—rocks to throw at birds, rocks to throw at dogs, rocks to throw at zinc roofs, and, when they get too bored, rocks to throw at each other.

Suddenly you hear a beeping that frightens you because you'd half dozed off under the dryer, and you hadn't noticed your neuron-frying half hour was up. I was intoxicated by the sweet smell of so many hair products, you tell yourself. Sweat has crossed the towel boundary around your shoulders, and a warm trickle runs down your spine like a troop of ants, tickling you instead of eating their way through everything as they do in Africa.

You glance around and see that the paleface is being blow-dried, that she doesn't use rollers cuz she has good hair. With that hair and this body, I'd be unstoppable, you tell yourself as you help the stylist pull the rollers from your head. Someone's left a very expensive phone in the box of rollers. The mirrors infinitely reflect a trio of beauty artists, the stylists dressed in white who stretch out three heads of hair with hot blowers.

Your hair is reluctant to grow and coarse—pimientica, your Spanish-descent paternal grandmother would say. Hair like your family's, your maternal grandmother would say, and your aunt would censor her from the kitchen, disagreeing through her thin and twisted lips, whispering under her breath, not like ours, I don't know where this girl got that nap.

Everybody knows hair and nap aren't the same thing. You can comb through hair but nap . . . well, nap needs relaxer, lots of relaxer (one with lye is best) every two months just to see it hang down a little, just to hide the blackness all Dominicans have behind their ears.

They hide those licks of bad hair behind your ears to camouflage them. Please, don't pull so hard, you plead, but dignified. The stylist reminds you of your Aunt Amalia, the one who'd pull on your bad hair to make you pretty, she'd say, so you could wear a Sunday dress.

Certainly, when they're finally done with you, you agree that the stylist really fought it out with your mop. She heated it up with the blower and flattened it out until she left it for dead, so she tells you. And you, either grateful or a fool, leave a generous tip for the whole staff, so the rich women will know who you really are.

You lift your head high. You look at yourself in the mirror and start to apply makeup to your prominent cheeks, your flat nose, and, lastly, to your thick lips—the target (red target) of the originality and obscenity behind the flattery of Dominican men. And you remember that day on your way to the convent, when you were still a girl, and a guy came up to you and asked blandly, and what's that mouth for, mamma? And you, barely twelve years old, answered him, annoyed and innocent, what's your mamma's mouth for, huh?

You laugh in the mirror at your youthful naivety. And that gives you an excuse to laugh with delight in front of your adversaries, who don't even understand you because they don't care. By contrast, you say goodbye to your allies, the stylists, with your mouth and your hands, as if you were Miss Congeniality. In the parking lot, you climb into your super car, the one the company assigned you a month ago.

You speed toward the neighborhood. The little gray houses—marvels of the architecture of poverty—cling to the hillside with fierce desperation. Kites fly in the wind, far away, high above the zinc roofs, while a group of boys plot mischief under the almond tree. The colmados in their perpetual celebration play lively bachata.

You're on your way to get your father, who's practically deaf and has an appointment with the cardiologist. When you pick him up at your former home, the old man still sees you as a child and, though he's not completely senile, repeats stories and seems to be remembering things as you head down Camino Chiquito. The tall condo buildings slip away in the opposite direction from where you're going.

Do you see that property? he asks. That used to belong to the Camilos. We used to have hundreds of acres of land. Only the Arvelos, who owned half of Arroyo Hondo, had more land than we did. And you see those buildings way over there? That belonged to the Campusanos, your mother's family. Thousands of acres, yes sir.

But you're not up for absurd inventories. This being and not being hurts enough. You want to say, enough with the lack of belonging, with the painful rejection that accumulates inside you like a lagoon that clouds up with each new drop, each new aggravation, like today at the salon. You feel humiliated, because what happened this morning at the salon was the drop that caused your soul to overflow. Enough with the bullshit, Papi, you mutter.

What? he screams.

And you respond, knowing he can't hear you, enough with the bullshit of how I should be proud of being an Arroyo Hondo native, or sixth generation, or how they'll bury me in the Arroyo Hondo cemetery when I die—even though they couldn't fit another body in there, even standing—because that does me no good at all. I can't even wipe my . . . clean my wounds with that, I should say.

Don't come telling me that being from here is some kind of lineage, because hey, what good has it done me to be a native of Arroyo Hondo? Do you
have any idea how they looked at me at the university when I said I was from
such an exclusive community and then had to borrow money to make copies
because I couldn't afford to buy the whole book? Did I ever tell you how many
times I had to borrow from my friends so I'd have enough to pay bus fare?
Have you ever felt the fear of someone who has to get up at five-thirty in the
morning because you have class at seven and you have to walk to the Rotunda
to catch a carrito because there's no service in Arroyo Hondo?

Papi, don't talk to me anymore about Arroyo Hondo. We're no different
than those people who took over and built La Puya, no matter how proud you
may be that grandfather bought our vast lands for seven pesos and a small
hog. I'm ashamed of getting ahead. Because I'm not from here and I'm not
from there. The rich can't stand me and the poor don't know me. The fact
that I didn't choke on my own poverty means my friends from here don't treat
me the same or even remember when we used to fish for betas and tadpoles
in the creek, which was fast and clear back then, and I'd pretend to be the
mother of all the fish I collected in the mayonnaise jar—I swear to you those
fish spoke to me and told me that I'd be rich someday, just like the white ladies who went to the church, remember? The ones who used to sit in the front
pew for Father Marcial's masses and on Christmas, always on Christmas, gave
us sweets or socks. Those ladies were so generous. And their perfumes were
wonderful.

One thing I never told you, Papi, because I almost never tell it. Seventeen years ago, when I was ten, I almost drowned in that creek, and I barely
saved myself, I swear, by grabbing a tree on the shore whose trunk was full
of thorns. I started to bleed from the palms of my hands. And Otto said, don't
cry, it's no big deal, and he carried me across to the other side on his shoulders. But Otto's gone, I've lost track of him, and now there's no one to help
me cross, on either side of the water. I'm not blaming you for anything, Papi,
I know you did the best you could for us. All I'm asking is don't go on with
all that bullshit about being from Arroyo Hondo and just leave me in peace
to pay for the apartment I bought (on one of our former holdings?) on my
twenty-year plan, if I live that long, because I don't want to live in constant
regret or be rending my garments over a past that, no matter how you insist
otherwise, was never mine to begin with.

ON BEING A
(LATINA) JOURNALIST

NONFICTION BY
JULEYKA LANTIGUA-WILLIAMS

During the first ten years of my career in publishing and media, I worked as a magazine editor, book editor, journalist, and syndicated columnist. I wrote about a wide range of topics, from the environment to education to women's advancement to pop culture to pregnancy. I also edited writers covering equally varied subjects, many of whom focused much of their work on Latinos in the United States. My own work often concerned the state of Latinos in the country at the time, the first decade of the twenty-first century.

At my first journalism job—as an editor at *Urban Latino*, a magazine written for, and mostly by, Latinos in the United States—my sense of duty toward our readers was often accompanied by nagging uncertainty about how much information was too much information. I was not the only one; my colleagues also struggled with striking a balance between offering our readers upbeat and positive news and information about our communities and covering less attractive aspects of being Latino in the States.

Once, I encouraged the magazine to run an article on the tension-ridden relationship between Haiti and the Dominican Republic. At first the editorial team was excited about igniting a debate on an issue that had at the time been getting a lot of attention in the world press. As I began working with the writer, I started having second thoughts. What would fellow Dominicans think? Would I be airing our secrets? Did other Latinos need to know about this? As the assigning editor, I could have pulled the story but decided to run it, since any reaction—and I fully expected there to be plenty—would be a step in the right direction. (A couple of letters did reach our offices, and we did print them.)

Some years later, I pitched a national op-ed to my editors at the Progressive Media Project, a syndication service that creates, edits, and disseminates opinion editorials on timely national and international issues. I wanted to write about the impact some cultural practices and moral codes could have on the spread of HIV/AIDS among Latinos, especially women. My contention was that the generalized acceptance of infidelity among Latino men was leading to more women who were married or in other presumably monogamous relationships getting infected. Much of the research I conducted as I wrote the op-ed supported my thesis.

Before contacting my editor, I agonized about the idea for days. My first fear was that I would somehow come across as condemning cultural practices accepted by many Latinos. Another fear was that my article might be seen as "explaining" some cultural aspects of our heritage to a general audience. The idea of doing either made me very nervous. After much consideration, I resolved that shedding light on the matter, even if the article only reached a small group of people, would be worth any potential grief I might face from readers. In the end the op-ed was well received, and I did not hear any negative feedback.

My decision was based largely on the belief that it's fitting to discuss how cultural beliefs, practices, and attitudes—and the misinformation they can sometimes lead to—affect our health. At *Urban Latino* we wrote about a woman in Chicago who adamantly refused to believe that her husband had given her an STD. She was convinced of his faithfulness. In the meantime a counselor got him to admit that he had ventured from the marital bed. In another story we explored how our elderly, as a matter of personal choice or necessity, frequent healers, spiritualists, and clairvoyants when they should be examined by medical doctors.

Without undermining the cultural role such practices play in our lives, any reporter—Latino or not—should feel that part of our professional responsibility involves exposing how such practices might be hurting us. As (Latino) journalists, we should not feel like we're airing family secrets when we report on a santera's inability to cure a serious medical condition.

Often when I think about seldom-covered topics, I feel an obligation to pierce the veil of nostalgia through which many Latinos see ourselves in the United States and to crack the crystallized image we have of our native lands. I believe we hold on to stagnant memories that keep many of us from embracing ourselves and our home countries as we/they truly are.

Perhaps it was the brazenness of youth that propelled us to seek out stories at *Urban Latino* that other Latino publications didn't. For example, we dared our readers to learn about slums in Nicaragua, where girls are forced into prostitution from age ten. We also reminded those who point fingers at foreign perpetrators that many of the tens of thousands of Colombian women prostituting themselves throughout the world were sent away with their families' blessings. And we celebrated the rich African legacy of Honduras's Garifuna people, while highlighting their struggle for land and equality.

Journalists—regardless of race, gender, religion, or other identity characteristics—have an obligation to the truth. We record events we witness or gather from sources. In many ways, reporters are present-day historians, creating a record of life as it happens.

However, do some reporters, because of who they are, what they look like, or where they come from, have a responsibility to report another kind of truth, a responsibility that can allow them to take sides on certain issues? In light of the blatant prejudice that often passes for news, should Latino journalists, for example, exclusively report on our communities in order to ensure more balanced and accurate coverage?

No.

Latinos do not bear a special burden to cover our own communities. Are journalists who are also parents obligated to report on children's issues? Are Baptist reporters confined to covering events that affect fellow practitioners?

Furthermore, if a Latina wants to cover the science beat or the technology beat or the environment beat, she is in no way mandated to go and find the Latino medical researcher or the Latino executive at Apple or the Latina marine biologist studying the life cycles of coral reefs. If she happens to find any of them, and writes about them, so be it. But her first and only obligation is to report with accuracy and a balanced perspective, giving equal time to all sides of an issue.

Another burden Latino journalists should not bear is the burden of educating "mainstream" (read: white) America about us. Instead, our responsibility is to arm ourselves with knowledge to combat the deluge of ignorance that floods magazines, daily papers, and the Internet. We must seek out the good and the bad. And we must be willing to report on both.

As an editor at a magazine for Latinos, I also took very seriously the task of reminding readers that many of us have become comfortable—some to the point of complacency—with the notion that the umbrella term "Latino" means we're a monolithic group. When we speak among ourselves, no one questions that Chicanos, Cubanos, Dominicanos, and Argentinos are quite different from one another. But as soon as conversations open to include white participants or references, we obediently form a cultural chorus line that dances to a forced tune.

This response often misleads non-Latinos into thinking that we are in fact monolithic and that any one of us, or any one group, can speak for all of us. There is no real benefit for us in this reaction; we simply do it as a defense mechanism to protect what very little economic, political, social, cultural, and physical space we have in this society.

Following the 2000 National Puerto Rican Day Parade in New York, several young women were attacked by revelers in Central Park. *Urban Latino* published a conversation we had with two prominent leaders. We titled this exchange "Breaking Our Code." When these attacks were first seen on television in snippets of homemade video, we asked ourselves what we should do about it. Do we make a public statement? Do we seek out some of the people involved? Do we examine the mainstream/white media's coverage? We knew we had to do something, but at first we couldn't figure out exactly what.

Then we started listening very carefully and realized that we—the editors and staff—were afraid to speak openly and truthfully even to each other. I suspect it was because of heightened cultural sensitivity, since among our editors were a Colombian, a Puerto Rican, and a Dominican (me). That's when the only productive course of action became obvious—we had to talk to respected individuals who could spark a dialogue with and among our readers.

The reaction was astonishing. Our interviewees—then CNN correspondent Maria Hinojosa and former Young Lord Richie Pérez—were so forthcoming and honest, it was a painful task to edit their comments to meet length requirements. Our readers were very grateful, women especially. They congratulated us for broaching the subject in a critical way. We were pleased to have set this precedent for ourselves. Issue after issue, we continued to seek similar opportunities to initiate this kind of open dialogue.

After many years of writing about all sorts of topics—many that specifically affect Latinos, many more that don't—I have accepted the fact that my obligation is first and foremost to my craft and my profession. I must use the tools and skills I have acquired to do my very best reporting and writing. I must strive to tell the most accurate story. If, in the process, I shed some special light on an issue that affects my fellow Dominicans, my fellow Latinos, or my fellow (insert category here), then I have reason to feel especially good about that particular story.

By the time it comes off the presses and arrives in people's hands, I've already moved on to the next one, feeling the same clarity and commitment I bring to every story.

THAT'S
NOT ME
ANYMORE

THE INTERVENTION

FICTION BY SOFIA QUINTERO

The first thing I see when I regain consciousness is a spot. Then another. Then many. Black splotches orbiting stains of brown. Whatever they injected into me drains from my blood, allowing my vision to focus. Leopard spots. I'm on my back across a bed, hands cuffed to the metal post, ankles bound with straps of fire, and mouth stuffed with a rag ya ape'tando de moja'o because of my own spit.

I blink at the ceiling. Is that a leopard skin rug? No, that whiteness is too waxy to be skin or fur. That's . . . paper. The flimsy, shiny kind used in magazines. That's . . . me. Me in a leopard skin monokini crawling across the sand and snarling at the camera. And next to that is the photo of me in a silver lamé halter top with matching pún pún shorts and go-go boots leaning against a graffiti-covered security gate. And the one with me in the purple lace thong and camisole, sitting on my haunches with my back to the lens, glancing over my shoulder and sucking on my pinky. Every photo from *Smooth*, *The Source*, *XXL* has been taped to the ceiling, all of them, as if the kidnappers wanted me to know the second I came to, "Bitch, this is why you here."

They're in the next room blasting Lauryn Hill. "That thing, that thing, that thiiing . . ."

Maybe they do it so that I can't hear them or in case I get this toalla out of my mouth and scream. No matter. I strain my ears to snatch pieces of conversation. There are definitely two of them, at least. One loud, angry, in charge. Female. A sista talking, "Education. Inculcate. . ." Damn, haven't heard that word since Sarah Lawrence.

Another female voice. Softer and hesitant. Nuyorican, no doubt. "Friday." Not Brooklyn. Uptown. Way uptown. The Bronx.

Then footsteps. I close my eyes to let them think I'm still out. The door creaks open. Warm fingers wriggle between the ropes around my ankles and the chafed skin. I fight to not flinch. A tug at my ankles. "These are way too tight, B." Definitely the Nuyorican.

"Don't. Use. Names." The sista is definitely from Brooklyn. Definitely in charge.

"But Lo . . ." A third woman. Can't place the voice. No race, no age, no geography.

Now four hands jerk at the ropes at my ankles, loosening their grip yet scraping away the skin with every pull, and I pray that they can't see the tears creeping under my lids. Teeth sucking, then a pinch to my side, and my eyes fly open like lights when switched on. "She's up," says the brunette, who I call in my mind La Morena.

I give her a nasty look, surprised by how pretty she is. Soft even, with lush lips and long lashes. I expected Madea and get Meagan Good, and I want to smack her for that, too.

"How are you feeling?" says Miss Indistinct with clueless features to match the voice. Wiry hair, eyes brown bordering on gray and pinched at the corners. Got a Mediterranean hint to her skin, pointy nose, thin lips. She could be white. She could be Asian. Maybe even Latina. Probably mixed. I have no fuckin' idea, so I just squint. Without words, she asks La Morena permission to remove la toalla from my mouth. La Morena rolls her eyes, and Miss Indistinct takes that as yes and pulls the rag out of my mouth. "How are you feeling?"

Miss Large-and-In-Charge gives her a dirty look, like what the fuck she care how I feel? Like this isn't about me. Like I'm not the point of this twisted slumber party.

Magnetic, the word "feeling" draws sensations from all over my body. My stomach wails, and my bladder stretches. Wrists and ankles numb, legs tingling all over, head pounding. "I need to pee," I say. "And I'm fuckin' starving."

La Morena's answer is to tighten a blindfold around my head and grab at the rope around one of my ankles. I whimper in pain, and Miss Indistinct cries, "Let me. Please."

La Morena falls back, and I feel another pair of gentle hands around my other foot as La Boricua helps La Que Sea untie me. Miss Indistinct leads me blindfolded across flat carpeting, wooden floorboards, and finally cold ceramic tiles. I can hear her breathing as I pee, then wash my hands. She brings me back to the room. La Morena takes off my blindfold and warns me to not "act the fool." I get on the mattress, and she allows the other two to rope my feet to the metal bedpost and only handcuff one wrist. Satisfied with their work and my good behavior, La Boricua says, "We'll bring you something to eat soon."

La Morena leads them out the room. The door closes, and the lock catches.

I wait until the footsteps fade, and then I scream. I scream and I scream and I scream, waiting for the thunder of footsteps. Only Lauryn answers. "You just lost one," she tells me at level forty. "You just lost one . . ."

As I wait for them to feed me, I figure out what I need to do. There may be three, but their unit is weak. Already with the side eyes and exasperated tones, and right in front of me, no less. Trios be like that, especially among females. Growing up in the Heights, I only had to learn that lesson once and ain't never let two bitches turn on me like that again. When three chicks form a trio, one assumes the lead, and the other two follow, resenting her the whole time, like, who died and made you queen? You'd think two would be easier to manipulate, but that shit's not true. If you don't win over the stronger of the two, it's a wrap. When, how, why these three came together to do me like this, I don't know, but right now this crew ain't that tight. Yeah, three is a magic number. Choose and turn the right one, and I get the other just like that. The two-for-one sale of my life right here. If I can jog one of them nuts loose, the whole machine falls apart.

But which one?

No question about it, La Morena runs shit. Don't they always, though? If I change her mind, the other two automatically fall back. But she also has no love for me. None whatsoever. Even if it were possible to win that bitch over, I don't have time. They said something about Friday.

Now the Nuyorican, she got some concern. Just don't know who it's for, where her interests lie. She was the one who screamed when whoever decked me in the face in the back seat of the town car. La Boricua talks to La Morena, talks back even. They got the push-pull thing going, so getting the Puerto Rican's ear might work to my advantage. It all depends just how up under La Morena she truly is and how much sway she has.

Miss Indistinct? So far she's a cipher. She wants to take care of me, though. I can dive into that unknown and swim to safety. Or I can drown.

Bottom line, one of them is my ticket out of here, and I have until Friday to figure it out.

The biracial chick, or whatever she is, comes back alone and sets a tray of rabbit food on my lap. With my free hand, I point at the mound of mush that looks like some parsley and tomatoes beat the yellow out of un mofongo. "What is that?"

"It's couscous salad." La Mulata pushes the bowl of orangey soup toward me. "And this is dal. I made it with lentils, steamed carrots. It's completely vegan."

"Vi-¿qué?"

Esa rubia con los ojos hincha'o me dice, "No meat, no dairy, no animal product whatsoever."

Yeah, these bitches trying to kill me. My stomach is gnawing on itself, and the soup thing does smell nice, so I have a spoonful. It's thick and spicy. "That's not bad."

"You see." La Que Sea sits at the edge of the bed, grinning at me as I scarf down the food. "If I can convince those two to eat clean," she says, tilting her head toward the door. "Trust me, you won't miss any of it."

Trust her. Right. "I don't eat that much beef or pork anyway." Maybe that'll win me some points.

"I mean everything. Beef, pork, chicken, fish . . ."

Give up paella y arenque, too? Now I know she's not Latina. Strike one. Then again, maybe not. I whiff a martyr streak. I'm about to ask her what the hell she care what I eat, seeing as she and her people done snatched me off the street and are holding me against my will. But I check myself 'cause she's obviously not the one to come at that way. "You care if I'm healthy?"

La Que Sea looks at me with gentle eyes. "I know it hardly seems like this, Yadira, but we want to help you. This is an intervention."

"An intervention? I don't need a fuckin' intervention! I don't drink. I don't do drugs. I don't even smoke."

"There are other ways to harm yourself." Miss Indistinct points to my photos on the ceiling. "Like conceding to your objectification." Before I can ask her what the hell she's talking about she says, "I mean, you majored in English with a minor in journalism. Summa cum laude, no less. Why didn't you pursue a career in that?"

I get it. The three of them are PhDs in me. They know more about me than can ever be found on the sticky pages of *Don Diva*.

Because journalism is a joke, I almost say. Where has she been? Los blanquitos barely practice journalism in this country anymore, so what makes her think they're trying to have a brown-skinned Latina up in their mix? The closer a nation is to the United States, the less Americans want to know about it. And the few americanos who give a damn about Latin America ain't trying to hear shit about Latins *in* America, as if only the cute shit—the food, the music, the language—gets imported. Does La Boricua ever school her?

Better question. Do I tell La Que Sea all this? Will it impress her that I actually gave the shit some thought? That I've got substantive opinions about shit besides hip-hop, entertainment, and all that stuff? What if it makes me seem more rather than less of a threat? I don't know enough about her, though, to risk revealing this.

And yet it feels too soon to ask her what the fuck she is, exactly. If I come out and ask her straight up, "You black? White? Latina? What?" that may show my hand. And what do I say if she asks me why I care? What if the mere question pisses her off? I've dealt with these ambiguous chicks before, and it's a crapshoot with them. Some take pride in keeping you guessing, especially if you're a dude. Bat their eyelashes talking about, "What do you think I am?" Or even more annoying, reciting the fuckin' census. "My great grandmother on my mother's side was Irish. . . ." Fuck out of here with that. But the ones with something to prove can be worse. "My mom's white, but that don't mean I'm not black!" Yeah, bitch, but I'm blacker than you, so where's *my* medal? Not that the wannabes don't piss me off, too. Daddy's whiteness didn't bleach you none, so stop frontin'. How you gonna be born and raised here and not know the one-drop rule is still in effect? I was barely off the plane when I got hip to that shit, so I don't get that.

Sensing that it is too soon to try to cross that minefield, I just say, "I couldn't get a job in journalism after graduating from college, so when a class-mate of mine got work on a music video—"

"Yes, yes, yes, I know," La Que Sea interrupts me, her face hanging with sympathy. She places her hand on my bound ankle. "I've been where you are, Yadira, just giving myself to anyone who would have me in order to escape the doubt that I truly mattered at all. But thanks to—" She stops herself before saying their names. "With their help, I got to the core of my issues, and we're going to help you do the same. We'll make you understand why you commod-ify your body this way and realize that you're more valuable than that."

Bitch makes me feel so gutter that I want to chuck this spoon at her face. Think she has me all figured out, but don't she know that for every job I've gotten, I've lost two because I wouldn't let the director get into my pants? Ese pendejo Radhames Castillo thought I owed him some just because he's a third cousin five times removed and now is on a mission to sully my name in the industry. And here this one comes talking sideways about me like I'm some one-woman sex trade. This body ain't no tourist trap, hater! This right here is a five-star resort, and I reserve the right to refuse service. *You* the bland one. You're Motel 6. Econolodge. Best Western. No matter what the hell you're made of, you still had so little flavor, you had to give it away, and once they had a taste they didn't want it anymore. They got what they paid for, and it wasn't worth it. But you want to save me? Okay.

Bitch reminds me of my sister. Who I love to death, I really do. She's the only one in the family who looks me in the eye when she speaks to me, like she hasn't forgotten that I'm more than the body sprawled across the center-fold. She reminds Mami and Papi of that when they want to use my schedule as an excuse to not invite me in the first place. She keeps me in the family, and I love my sister for that, but I also pay a huge fuckin' price for it. When she makes indirectas about my life, I have to eat them because I can't risk losing her too. I have to pretend that I feel shame in what I do and that I'm looking for another way. Most of all, I have to hide that I know that my choices finally made her the favored daughter and that she revels in that shit. If I keep modeling, then she's the good one with her government job and co-op apartment, and if I stop, she's the one who "saved" me from myself. I can never tell my sister that she only got to be somebody in our family because of me unless I want to have no one at all.

La Que Sea has on this plastic grin as she pats my ankle. "It's okay, Yadira. Once we're done here, you'll be a whole new person. You're going to love who she is." Then she skips to her feet toward the door. She opens it, looks at me, and winks. "By the way, don't let the light skin fool ya." Then she leaves to brag to the others about her "breakthrough," no doubt.

I get myself together. Think this through, Yadi. This is no time for emotions. I don't know what the fuck she meant by that light-skin line, but if there's a rescuer on the set, it's her. La Mulata-Blanquita-La Que Sea is on a mission to save me. If I can stand her projection, I might be able to use her to save myself from the mindfuck they have in store for me. But I don't know if I want that chick running loose in my head.

I wake up the next morning to the smell of coffee. My back aches from sleeping upright while leaning against the metal bedpost. La Boricua removes the tray from my lap and places it on the floor. She pulls a cafecito out of a brown paper bag and removes the lid. She blows on the coffee, then brings it to my lips.

Then La Boricua reaches into the bag for a tostada. She holds it close enough to my mouth so that I can sink my teeth into it and tear off a piece. The familiar mixture of hot butter and sugary milk in my mouth gives me a fleeting sense of safety. I'm thinking maybe La Boricua is less like La Morena and more like La Que Sea, so I put her to a test. "Is that from Marisol's on Dyckman?"

She offers me another sip of coffee, but says, "Yeah, like I'ma tell you that."

I can't help but smile at her. This one isn't stupid. Respect, ma. "¿Eres boricua?"

She hesitates, then nods.

"¿Pero naciste aquí, verdad? ¿Y en que parte de la isla nacieron tus padres?"

She blinks at me like a headlight on a car stalled by the road. She didn't understand a word I said. Just when I fear I can't bond with her that way, I realize that she's ashamed. *That* I can take advantage of. "Oh, you don't speak Spanish, my bad," I say real gentle and nonjudgmental like. And there it is again. Got her back all up, neck all tense. Tread carefully, Yadira. "That's all right. Why should you? You were born here."

"But you were only four when you came here," she says. That's right. These chicks have been studying me. And La Boricua's voice is so full of resentment, as if I took something that once belonged to her. The language thing is a real sore spot for her. A weakness. An opening. "I don't see the difference."

Remembering what La Mulata said, I think of something critical to say that they might not already know. "Yeah, but I had to learn Spanish all over again." Never told anyone that. Never had to. People always assume, long before Pitbull shouted me out on that record. "Y como adoro Yadira. Mira tan bella, como habla mas fina, como parece la reina 'lla misma." That song made me big time. I swear, I'm thinking that for females in hip-hop, it just might be better to be a chick dudes rhyme about than to be one who rhymes herself. For real, all the love without any of the drama. That song took my game to a whole other level. Couldn't go anywhere without someone spitting that lyric at me. Black, hispano, Asian, blanco, they were coming at me from all quarters. 'Cept that stupid production manager on the video shoot in Punta Cana with his little indirectas about my "abominable" Spanish. Snotty little Cuban all surprised because debris didn't fly out my mouth when I opened it! So I've got some idea how La Boricua feels. "I took Spanish all through school."

"So what? So did I," she says, her voice quivering between an argument and a plea. "I took it in high school. I took it in college. I even went to the Dominican Republic to take an immersion course, but nothing sticks."

"Why would you go to the D.R. to learn Spanish when you're Puerto Rican?" Even as I ask, I sense the reason. I watched the Puerto Ricans for years to learn what *not* to do. Los pobres . . . they care too much. Try too hard. Give up so much just for the mere promise. It hurt to watch sometimes. Scary even. Their patria, their language, sus barrios . . . just forked it over to los blancos, y con los negros shared too freakin' much just for the asking and not demanding enough credit in return. So much talk about Puerto Rican pride y pa' qué? All they have left is a parade hawked by po-po and flags small enough to hang from their rearview mirrors. It's too late to holler ¡Presente! now, love. I hope Dominicans never go out like that, but damn, it's hard 'cause these americanos are so fickle. Ni importa si son blanco o si son negro. As much as they be beefin' with each other, that's one way they be the same— making it hard to figure out when to mute your colors or preserve your exotic. I have that shit on lock, but I'm just one person.

La Boricua bends down to pick up the tray. "That's a long story." She lays the tray across my lap and places the lukewarm cafe y tostada on it. Then out of nowhere she says, "I fuckin' hate it when people jump to conclusions, you know. Assuming that I don't want to know Spanish or that I'm not proud to be Latina . . ."

Before I can figure out if her sudden outburst is good or bad for me, she runs out the door. "¡Esperate! ¡No te vayas!" But La Boricua is gone. Damn, that's not a good look.

I've been screaming for hours in the dark for food. The sun is gone, I have to go to the bathroom, and no one brought me lunch. Finally, the door flies open.

"All right, already," says her shadow. The light flicks on, y ahí está La Morena holding a paper plate in one hand and a can of soda in the other. "Here," she says, taking the sandwich off the plate and handing it to me. Bitch just slapped some spiced ham and cheese from a bodega onto Wonder Bread. To' seco sin mostaza, no mayonnaise, no nothing. Brought Pepsi instead of Coke. Did that shit on purpose. She knows I love me some Coke 'cause I made a big deal about it in that interview with *Vibe* when I landed that endorsement deal. Mami's right. I talk too much. She always said that to me. You talk too much. Too loud. Too fast. ¡Callete ya!

"What did you say to my friend?" Says it like she already knows and is trying to catch me in a lie.

"Which friend?"

"You know which one." La Morena chooses her words before answering. "The one you made cry."

I didn't realize La Boricua had cried. Were they angry tears or sad tears? Either way I knew that wasn't a good look. "I didn't make anybody cry! She did that to herself. I was nothing but nice to her."

"Why do I find that hard to believe?"

"I don't know." And I don't fuckin' care what she believes. I shouldn't be coming at her like this, but La Morena just takes me there. "What I know is you fuckin' bitches is crazy! You don't think anyone's going to miss me?"

"Miss you?" La Morena laughs all contemptuous and shit. "You're more delusional than I thought, Yadira." I hate the way she says it with the Y all hard and the R too soft. I can't stand it because I just know she knows better. "Like the fact that your book was a bestseller had nothing to do with all the *men's* names you dropped." She folds her arms across her chest and smirks at me. "You actually believe you matter that much."

"I was important enough for you bitches to snatch me up off the street, though, wasn't I?" She actually thinks I was talking about industry motherfuckers? When they overtook my town car, I had just walked off the air on 'BLS toda enfogoná because that bitch Wendy Williams tried to play me on the air like I knew she would. But my manager all but threatened to drop me if I didn't do the show. Dique how can you write a hip-hop book and not promote it on Wendy Williams? Wendy came for me 'cause my shit did better than anything she ever did. She stayed in her little black ghetto, but Yadira crossed over. Black, white, hispano, women, niggas who don't even read put my shit on the *New York Times* bestseller list. When those bitches jumped me, I was slaying the industry left and right like my iPhone was Excalibur and shit. First, I ripped my manager a new asshole. Then El Javao texted me, talking about how he wants me for his next video. What I say? Fuck that nigga. He's over, and his peoples are grimy. Delete. This industry dude hollering at me, that one kicking game, a third trying to play one. Delete, delete, delete, deleted them all except Araceli calling to confirm our interview and my sister hoping I wasn't flaking out on our heart-to-heart. Araceli might think I just blew her off, but my sister's going to worry. What makes La Morena think I ain't got no one waiting for me to come home? I don't care how much researching and plotting and scheming they did, they don't know everything about me 'cause I don't fuckin' reveal *everything*.

"With all the women out there who do what I do, why y'all coming down so hard on me?" Yeah, I dropped names in my jawn, but I didn't suck 'em all off like Karrine Steffans did. Why didn't they drop squad her ass? La Que Sea wants to ask me why I "commodified" myself by becoming a model instead of a journalist as if Kim Osorio didn't fuck Fiddy one way and Eminem another, all in the name of the Source. Parlayed that shit into a book deal, too, so why didn't they come for her? They want to snatch up women off the street in serious need of an intervention, all they had to do was roll up to the office of 51 Minds the next time those motherfuckers are holding auditions for their next VH1 "reality" show.

La Morena walks over to a desk and pulls open a file drawer. She rummages through it and eventually pulls out an issue of *Fuego*. Damn, that must be a collector's item or some shit because they only ran, like, three issues. It pissed me off, too. Finally, a men's magazine geared toward Latinos who loved their women. I'd never been prouder to be on a photo shoot. The photographer, the stylist, everybody was mad nice to me, wanting to keep it hot but tasteful. Even Araceli, who interviewed me, was about it. No hint of hatin' there. Once we got past the sex talk, the description of my ideal man, and all that usual BS, she asked me some relevant shit. Like instead of asking me would I fuck Junot Díaz, she wanted to know if I related more to the work of Julia Alvarez or Angie Cruz. Seemed genuinely happy that I showed love for Kat DeLuna and Zoë Saldaña instead of trashing them like Jennifer López did to Cameron Diaz and Salma Hayek back in '88. That's why I wasn't mad at her when she asked me if I ever worried if my modeling work might encourage American men to fly to the D.R. to participate in sex tourism, and I thought at the time I gave her a good answer.

But before going to print, they erased all my depth. At least Araceli was woman enough to call and give me a heads up. Said that her editor loved it, but the publisher overrode him and slashed the copy, leaving in all the spice and cutting all the substance. Half the staff and freelancers walked because they didn't cosign to recreate *King* in brownface. Yeah, they wanted the mag to be sexy, but they also wanted it to have significance. Araceli wanted to meet with me again and talk further with the hopes of selling a longer piece to another magazine. In fact, she's waiting for me at El Malecón this very moment.

My feature in the magazine is marked by a fluorescent tag, y La Morena flips to it and reads. "When asked what she makes of her overnight dominance in the hip-hop industry, Yadira is at once pragmatic and philosophical. 'The reality is that the industry is run by men, mostly black and white guys who really want the same thing. They desire someone who is at once exotic and familiar. They want to leave home but still feel at home, you feel me? Being Latina—especially Dominicana—I fit the profile . . .'"

I yell, "I was misquoted."

"Oh, were you now?"

"Yeah, I didn't mean it like that at all. I was just describing things the way they are. It's not like I cosign."

"Oh, but you do cosign. Even though you know it's wrong, you take full advantage of it. Every time you get in front of a camera like that," she yells, pointing at the ceiling, "you say, 'Look at me, I'm just black enough!'"

La Morena slaps the magazine onto the desk and puts her hands on her hips. I see her standing there like that, and the memories rush at me like water from a fire hose. All those years my father had my sister and me on lockdown because he was so worried that we'd keep getting beaten up by las moyetas. Or so he said, but that wasn't what really had him shook. No, the worst thing that could've happened to his negritas would be for the black girls to invite us into their fold. Oh yeah, given the choice, Papi would rather they beat the shit out of us than become our friends. Right now he'd be real fuckin' happy.

I start to cry as if La Morena had slapped me. I'm not the fuckin' enemy. If she thinks that, she don't know me. The more I try to stop them, the harder the sobs come. She don't know me, but I know her. Every night I looked through the security bars down at the stoop across the street for my daily lesson in americana, and there was Keisha holding court with her girls. Rocking her platinum chain and bowler hat, rhyming along to *Hard Knock Life* and doing the Harlem Shake, she was a complete curriculum in what to do. I never took anything away from Keisha or her friends but the example, and now here I am.

La Morena shakes her head at me, believing these are crocodile tears. "You think because you went to college—"

"I went to a *good* fuckin' college!" I yell, hating how pathetic I sound.

"—and never worked the pole—"

"I'm supposed to apologize for that?"

"—you're going to be the exception to the rule, Yadira? You're not. And you're not walking out of here till you understand that."

"What you gonna do to me, then? You on some *Scared Straight* shit here?"

La Morena bursts out laughing.

"What the fuck's so funny?" I'm losing it, but I can't help myself, and that just makes it worse.

"I like that. Couldn't have put it better myself," she says. Then La Morena taunts me, wagging her finger in my face and putting all this crunk in her voice. "Because you're the chickenhead come home to roost."

I smell the shea butter on her, and it all comes back to me. The way the town car screeched to a halt, slamming me against the windowpane. How I barely got it together when the back door swung open. A sound bite of cars zipping on the highway. Stressed voices whispering. A flash of face, soft and brown. La Morena. Her four knuckles slamming into my face. The weight over my body. The hint of shea butter, a pinch in my arm and then darkness.

"Th-th-this is s-so f-f-fucked up!" I sob. "I didn't create the game. No fuckin' woman did! If you wanted to make someone pay for that, why didn't you kidnap someone like Diddy or Jay-Z or some other industry nigga?"

And just like that, with that single word, I slap her back. It's not how I meant it, but that's how it comes off. Given her hatred for me, there's no other way she could've heard it. I throw up my free arm to fend off the blows, still gripping the spiced ham and cheese sandwich. But nothing happens. I slowly lower my arm to find La Morena staring at me with a Mona Lisa smile. She says, "You were accessible." And with that smile still on her lips, La Morena strolls out the door.

The next day I wake up to find the three of them hovering over me. I stare up at them; fragments of my body splayed across the ceiling peek through the spaces between their faces. I debated with myself all night over who I should target, and I finally made my choice. And just as if some force wants to confirm that I made the right decision, she is the first one to speak.

"Yadira, have you decided to cooperate with us?"

I look her straight in the eye. "Yes." And to avoid any suspicion, I glance at the other two. "Yes."

They unbind me and take me into the next room for my first session.

THE QUEEN OF CHÁ

FICTION BY MARIVELL CONTRERAS

Translated by Achy Obejas

I gotta be respected, you hear me. I deserve respect. I'm a person who keeps her distance and her position so she'll be respected.

So I'm gonna tell you a little something. Don't cross the line with me, dammit, because if you cross that line with me, you won't see what's coming, lover. I'm not as dumb as you think. I'm no ornament at this club. I'm no ashtray. I'm no match.

You don't know me. Even if you see me here shooting the shit, that don't mean a thing. Just like you, I used to have a home, dammit, a respectable home, just so you know. I'm not nobody. I'm not some shit you think you can just mess with, or taunt, or put through whatever BS you like. I don't know you either, or what you're capable of, but I'm not gonna put up with that, bud— uh uh, you gotta respect me, respect me and don't fuck me up tonight.

You can't come at me with that—I haven't been up for that in a very long time. You saw me, right? You saw what I really am, right? I don't hafta say squat to you. You're a grown man, and you know what you're doing. Cuz of what I am, I don't hafta take shit from nobody.

You saw me, right? You saw me good. You were in the middle of the Malecón when I got there, and you saw that the discotheque's neon sign— pink, sweetheart—is a mere gas lamp compared to me. When I walk, even bitches bark.

When I got outta the taxi, the bitches there musta seen a vision cuz they went crazy. The cab driver asked me, whatcha do to those bitches? and I didn't wanna say nothing, but I looked at him and said, same thing I could do to you ... Daddy. The guy got scared and took off without charging me, so that was worthwhile. I'm still laughing about it.

I'm no crazy old woman. You saw me. That's the only thing that gives me peace of mind, that you saw me tonight. Away from Chá, I'm a special, hand-made, made-to-order doll. But here, I am what I am, and I don't hafta explain nothing to you. You saw those fools out there clapping and yelling bow wow wow over and over. Just so you understand, that whole thing about the bitches and the barking, that's no insult here but the highest compliment ever.

You know what bitches do, the four-legged kind? They let all the dogs kill themselves over them and then, when they decide on which one they want, they fuck him and never look at him again. I'm not saying I'm like that, because where I use my powers is on the stage.

I'm fabulously bitchy, a real bitch, a true and respectable bitch, and that's cuz wherever I go, nobody does it better. I look around, and the dykes and fags cruise along, and those who haven't made it in a long time, their eyes just pop out of their heads and follow any new piece of ass, and people like you, who won't do what you have to do but won't let someone else do it. You see them dancing, women with women, men with men, loving the party, but not everybody's as aware of every little move. If you're not one of us, then what are you looking for here? And to top it off, now it's my fault. But no, it's not my fault. I won't take that shit from nobody.

Although, to be honest with you, I wasn't always this way. For a long time, I was nothing more than a confused and fearful person. I trembled when anyone spoke harshly, insulted me, kicked my ass, made faces, or taunted me in any way. But no more, my love, no way. That's not me anymore.

My mother and father suffered a lot because of this bullshit. At my house, I was my parents' firstborn, just so you know. They got married legally and in the church, and I'm no "premature" baby.

At my house, everything was done on the level—school, homework, school uniforms, toys. Nobody could ever complain about me at home because they never had to tell me nothing twice. And that's why, at the end of the day, the owner of this place respects me. I don't talk about what's not true, and if I can't do something, I just say so. If I say I'll do it, then I'm the best.

Did you see? La Lupe's a rag doll next to me ... "What I asked of you / that it not be just trusting understanding / that you know that in this life / there's no love like my love ..." You saw, you heard. I know this really well.

And don't think I'm out to fool anyone. I never do that, never. What I can tell you is that, here and anywhere, I get respect.

You saw, no one can tell there's an extra something on me. Look how I open my thighs. Do you see anything? No, right? You stand some woman next to me, and she has to be a hell of a woman to make anyone have second thoughts about me. Listen to my voice, look at my face, my body. There's no woman who can compare with me one on one.

You wanted to come here, to get me, and then leave me flat. You saw the conga, not even Gloria Estefan in her finest moment does it better than me. I've seen how to do it. I learned all her routines off her videos. That's why I'm called the Queen of Chá, because whatever I do, I do very well.

And not just on the stage—which is my life—because I have a lot to do besides that. I'm a makeup artist, but not the kind that just smears stuff on your face, no, never. I do makeup on real artists, on those who make a living at it and sing or talk on TV. I'm the one who paints everyone up for all those musicals they put on at the National Theater.

From *Cassandra* to *Cats*—I did those cat faces all by myself, lover. Since I've had my hands on so many faces, you can imagine how well I know my own. I know it very, very well. That's why you can see that all kinds of people come here and that, dammit, they respect me, cuz this stuff is not just fooling around.

You saw the eighties show—I'm not from the eighties, I'm from just the other day, but I know the songs and the choreography. I can do an Amanda Miguel that will kill you, and just so you see how good I am, I can also do a Miriam Cruz, a Yuri, or a Vickiana. Any of the girls can be absent and the show won't fall apart, because I'm here, with a repertoire of possible voices, all very feminine. La Cape, my love, which is no small feat and demands respect—a lot of respect.

I came all the way from Máximo Gómez shaking my tits. I took the Malecón, crossed the palm-lined street, right by the sluts and their pimps who hang out at the corner two blocks from here, and I made everything perfectly clear. I came through the door wearing a canary yellow dress, with my hair done up at the salon, my tits where they're supposed to be, and my ass just right. My clothes are exclusives, and if you see anybody else wearing what I'm wearing, you tell me, cuz no one has what I have.

That's one thing you don't know—that I make my own clothes and that I've never worn the same dress twice. No, love, I make and remake them. I transform them all, and nothing I wear looks the same way twice. I don't even use the same perfume twice. Any bottle that's used up, I switch to another, the wildest, like the new Carolina Herrera, for example. I'm crazy about CH, Chavo, Chapulín, and my best childhood memories, and those big Chanel bags, the bright red ones in which I can fit my whole life.

I came here because you sent for me. Go, cuz he wants to talk to you. I asked La Charo about it, and she said, sweetheart, go, you're not going to lose a thing. He was the one with the champagne, right? Go.

I don't always care about that bullshit, but I hadn't finished the show and you were there, looking me right in the face—you weren't taking your eyes off me—and even though I didn't like you at first, I gotta confess that once I put my mind to something, that shit works.

And it did work. All these faggots saw you giving me the eye. And you came so far, even up in this corner with me, for you to tell me now to move over, that you have a woman and that I'm crazy.

Dammit, I'm not crazy. You asked for me. You sent me champagne to get me going, sometime between Michael Jackson and El Varón's "a ripe banana won't go green again / time that's lost won't come back / . . . I'm the man." But what kind of fucking man can I be, given I'm such a faggot. And there I was doing contortions, doing splits, and glorying in how it was all done with class, even as the bubbles were starting to get to me.

Man, I even danced to Candy, and I sang it seeing myself in your eyes, you wanting me. The only things missing were my curls and my innocence "shining at my window." Listen, dammit, I was singing Candy in a group of faggots drinking vodka and cranberry with the same gusto as a little kid drinking red pop at a birthday party.

Oh God, and me fighting, cuz those fags wanted to drink the champagne as if it was water, and I said no, that's for me, because you wanted to get me ready, cuz "my night is ready for you."

And now you come with this shit. Faggot, faggot, fucking faggot. Respect me. If you have a woman, if they're gonna talk about you, then why bother doing all this shit? You said I was the prettiest thing you'd ever seen, that you were dying to kiss me and to finally have someone who completely understood you.

Dammit, that's me, the same woman who was driving you crazy two hours ago. Don't talk to me about your family or your Jeep or your office. What the fuck are you doing here? I didn't go to you, you came here, to my place, to this disco full of strange people, people who just want to be accepted, loved, respected. That's why we love, why we're artists well beyond this ghetto where we don't even know anymore if you confined us or if we came for refuge. And to top it off, we have a bunch of fags who are really interesting. Some accept themselves, and others don't know how to live with what you straight people call a defect. There are those who come here because they know this is their place and others who pretend they come for fun. But that's a lie, dammit, because nobody comes here by accident or willingly exposes themselves to this scene where you have to stand with your back against the wall so you can put up with the rest of it.

When we're here, we don't just win your applause, we also kill time and put off any offense that might come from outside. We spend our whole lives rehearsing for any show that will end before we get used to the scenery because here we do have our say.

I'm a very talented girl, a helluva fucking talented girl. I helped decorate the disco. Do you see that giant crown on the stage? That was my idea. Let's put a crown there, lover, so we crown the bitchiest queen, the queen of the bitches. And that's me. Didn't you see how they hugged me and congratulated me as I made my way to your table?

And you were my other crown today, my love. I'm just telling you the truth. I've never crossed the line with nobody. No one's ever seen me cross-dressed in my neighborhood. I live alone now, but my house is respected. I've never brought a man home because I respect myself. I'm someone whose parents taught her how to respect herself. It's true that it took blood and fire, but they did it.

I don't know why I'm talking about them now. They also disrespected my love, and you know what happened? They never saw hide nor hair of me again. I send them a little something now and again cuz my sister lets me know when they're going through hard times, but I never go see them, cuz the last thing they would have wanted is for me to turn into this crap.

You don't know what it's like to be stared at in your own home like you're a weirdo from the time you're a little kid. Then the others kids in the neighborhood start fucking with you, they say, this kid's a bit of a flit, look how loose in the loafers he is, he practically flies off the ground. I prayed the longest rosary, starting at six in the evening until six in the morning, from the time I was seven until I left home at fourteen.

You don't know how much my father beat me. Straighten up and uncross your legs. Can't you see how men do it? When have you ever seen me messed up in women's things? The trouble would start right there, and my mother always got sucked in. He always sucked everybody in. Even my mother's prayerful friends would get a piece of that vulgar man's mind if they dared defend me.

My mother isn't to blame for anything. But he convinced her I turned out this way because she was churchgoing and had the house full of women praying and doing their thing. Can't you see that your son should be what I sired, a MAN. And from that day on, his response was to throw glasses, cups, whatever, to the floor. The praying women would flee in terror. He tried to straighten me out in all sorts of ways, but, love, it's like what Willie Colón says, the tree that first grows crooked never straightens its trunk.

Holy Mother of God—oh, my poor mother got herself punched every time, and I couldn't do a thing, because I also got mine. That's why I won't pray even if it kills me.

I've been around more than a wheel on a carrito.

I know you're not interested in my life, but what I want you to understand is that you're not talking to just any ol' fag. I'm a girl you gotta respect, who learned how to take care of herself and respect herself on the streets. I've never been found in an alley with anybody, and I don't deal in furtive love.

When I'm in a relationship, I'm committed, and that's a luxury in this world, when each and every night you get an offer too tempting to pass up.

I still don't get how I was wrong about you. I thought you were different. I said, that one's mine. That guy's not afraid, he's not ashamed to tell the world he likes me, he's dying to kiss me and not on the fifth stop on the metro, but right here.

How'd you fool me like this, sweet-talking me in front of the whole world just to leave me flat in front of the whole world? No, nobody does that to me. You even told me to grab my bag. Did you see how pretty my Chanel bag is? That CH isn't made in China, sweetheart. I have few things, but they're fine, and they're designer.

I abandoned my own womanly sense of modesty. You think I have no modesty? Well, I do. I'm not one of those girls who can be sweet-talked in front of everybody and just be left sitting here like nothing and then take a cab home at four in the morning or get on a gypsy bus.

No, no, you're not being fair. Now you're trying to tell me that you're not into me, and I can't be into you, and that you're not taking no risk for nobody, that you've got a good woman. What, I'm bad? No, I'm not bad, and I deserve respect. So do me a favor and calm down, cuz you don't hafta put on a show here. You decided against it, that's fine. That can happen to anybody after a coupla drinks too many who lets himself be led by his desire and all that crap. That's fine, but to the owner of Chá—who is like me, a very respectable woman, you saw how pretty she is, she really does look like Candy, with her big blue eyes and blond hair—I can't be left flat in front of her like some kinda slut. Do you know where you are? This is no brothel, my love. We're all adults here, and we all know we don't come here to hook up, but if something comes up, we deal with it discreetly.

We're here to have fun, so you don't have to pay nothing, not to me or the house. But, c'mon, we can't have all those people who saw me with you see me now all alone and pissed on. No, no, lover. Take me home in your car. I'm not talking to you anymore. I'll show you the way, that's all, just get me outta here right now. Cuz I'm not gonna lose my crown cuz of you. As far as everyone else is concerned, tomorrow I'll still be the bitch, the damndest bitch. In other words, the prettiest and bitchiest, the Queen of Chá.

THE SLANDERED

FICTION BY JEANNETTE MILLER

Translated by Achy Obejas

I felt bad listening to him cry like that. "I'm no good for anything anymore. Tell your mother that since I married her, I've never so much as looked at another woman. But at my age . . ." He sobbed. He was sixty-five years old, and the calendar is unforgiving with men.

"A woman can still have sex at a hundred. But men rarely make it past fifty. They have to drink and tell themselves stories in order to have a glorious little morning," my grandmother told me. She said virility was a deposit that was depleted with use; in other words, the more women a man had, the faster his potency would vanish. That's why, whenever there were rumors during coffee hour that a husband had been cheated on, she invariably said, "Those are the ravages of a bad life. He's paying for all the terrible things he did to that girl who married him without ever having had so much as a boyfriend."

The other day, a weeping Luisita had confessed that, after seven years of married life, she'd never had an orgasm. But now it was my father who was crying like a baby, and I felt bad watching him wracked by sobs, drooling and snot-nosed, bereft of dignity, and asked to perform at an age when he rarely got an erection. And when he did, he mostly felt fear at the thought of not being able to maintain that miracle so often denied him by the laws of gravity. On the other hand, he was probably sick of my mother, who had been a beautiful woman but whose nine children had physically and temperamentally drained her. Where before she was gay and fond of singing, she was now a sergeant giving orders so as to maintain the house on her husband's salary, which was too small for so many mouths to feed, so many feet to shoe, and so many bodies to dress. She had to send the boys out to see what they could find in the neighborhood. The meals had to be carefully planned not for their nutritional and caloric content but rather for the ration size. Stuffed dumplings, spaghetti with plantains, rice dishes with herring or sausage so the boys would drink lots of water and feel full. Even so, they were thin as needles, and when it came time to get dressed, shirts and pants were passed down from older to younger sibling until the youngest complained that the fabrics were see-through from so many washes.

But the boys were happy. They'd learned the important thing was to be together, be truthful, and share the good and the bad with joy. This was the first big crisis, when my mother, who was still "lively," as she frequently said of herself, grew more jealous as she jotted down every time she had a silent night. She kept track in a notebook she also used to record her daily purchases at the corner store. The number of nights passed one hundred, with my father asleep in front of the TV before nine o'clock.

A hidden hope for his virility made her think my father no longer needed her because he was sleeping with another woman. And since my father was the kind of man who went from home to work and from work to home, her only hope lay with the secretary he had in the dreary office where he worked as the director of the local post office. The poor secretary was not only ugly but also cross-eyed. When I reminded her of this in an attempt to calm the blind rage that possessed her, she surprised me by saying that cross-eyed women were known for their sexiness, which I heard for the first time from her lips and then later checked out with the guys at the university. I still don't remember exactly why, but they explained that more than a few great men had confessed their attraction to cross-eyed girls, including Teófilo, the group's sexologist, who confirmed the theory.

The thing was, my father just kept crying every time he had to defend himself from my mother's wrath. He took refuge in me. I was the only one who'd gone to college, and he wanted me to explain to my mother that it wasn't that he didn't want to but that he couldn't. He'd get anxious, touching his straight hair, which was still black, until I'd distract him with a guava and cream cheese treat and a big glass of water and start talking to him about politics to change the subject.

I was the only girl. I had eight male siblings, four older and four younger. We were all so different that I often thought, and sometimes still do, that I might have been adopted because my mother had had an attack of hysteria when she saw that life brought only males and not a one was going to help around the house, and even less so in her old age, because men go off and belong to the family of the woman they're sleeping with.

My eight brothers were lazy, dirty, and stupid. None of them had wanted to study, and they all worked temporary jobs to earn enough for beer, cigarettes, and women. Every now and then they'd go to the cockfights or to a ball game to see the local players beat the foreigners and yell and drink. The next day, the bathroom would have to be hosed down to wash away all the pee that didn't make it into the toilet, the occasional vomit, and stinky little gifts the rest of us would sometimes find in the morning when they'd forget to flush.

One of my few pleasures was to be done early on Saturdays with helping my mother clean the house, though it looked more like a pigsty than a house, so that, even if only for a few hours, the bathrooms would smell of pine and the sheets like sunshine and cuaba soap after having boiled them in an empty oil can for half an hour, which was the only way to get rid of the stink they carried. I'd finish up quietly and, practically hiding, get dressed in silence, then take a carrito down to the theater to see the movie I'd chosen for the week. Today, though, I was a little distraught because I'd seen in the listings that the Diana was showing a movie I hadn't been able to catch at the Palacio del Cine the week before, but the Diana was in a neighborhood that represented the boundary between decent girls and sluts. It was surrounded by a good number of Chinese restaurants that rented rooms, and I was afraid that if someone saw me they could think I was up to something other than just watching a movie. In spite of that, I decided to go. I was sick and tired of having only a few moments of pleasure.

Of course, if my father had found out, he would have gone nuts yelling at me because he'd made it plain I wasn't supposed to go anywhere near places like that. Even when my cousin and her husband accompanied me, he hadn't allowed me to go to the end-of-month sales at the Duarte department stores. My father lived with old-fashioned dignity and values, a sense of honor and shame, a rein on where girls could go because anything could stain their reputation, and, above all, absolute honesty. I can't fathom what he would have thought if he'd heard the tough guys talking at the university, the things they said and the stories they told in all their naked glory. I pretended I didn't hear, but sometimes I couldn't help myself and laughed. The truth is that I learned more from them than from books on sex education. I especially learned what big talkers and cheaters men can be. There wasn't a single one who was true to his wife or girlfriend, and they warned me that if I saw them with another girl, I wasn't supposed to say anything. If I did, they wouldn't let me borrow their textbooks or look at their notes from the days I had no choice but to miss classes because my mom got hysterical and threw a fit that made my father cry.

The carrito left me in front of the movie theater. When I stepped off, I looked both ways and made straight for the box office. After I got my ticket, I bought a Nestlé bar with almonds and a Coca-Cola, which were just as expensive as at the Palacio del Cine, and I went and sat down in the right corner of the last row, careful to place my purse and sweater on the seat next to me to make it seem like it was taken and thus avoiding having someone sit next to me. That's the first thing my father had told me to do the first time he let me go to the movies by myself. "Don't let any man sit next to you, and don't go to the bathroom, no matter how badly you have to go, because there are lots of sickos at the movies."

When the lights went down, I relaxed. Everything was black until they started playing the trailers. Two women came and sat in the seats by the aisle, which comforted me because this meant no tough guy exhibitionist would sit there. One of them ate popcorn while the other explained everything that was happening on the screen to her. God, they weren't going to let me watch the movie in peace. I shushed them when the titles came up, rather vehemently, and they looked at me with surprise, but they shut up.

Almost immediately, a couple came looking for a place to sit and went down the row in front of me. When they sat down, I realized it was my father and a woman I'd never met. He put his arm very casually around her shoulders. I thought I was going to die. My heart was beating hard, and I couldn't breathe. I was terrified he'd see me, but I was also blind with rage, and I wanted to slap him on the head and make a scene right then and there. As I held back tears, I managed to see the woman's face and realized it was the cross-eyed secretary from the post office. My mother had been right! I couldn't watch the film, intent as I was on my father's behavior with that woman. He gave her candy, took her hand, whispered in her ear. I could barely keep from sobbing and had to close my eyes with all my might to control myself. As soon as I could, I grabbed my purse and sweater and ran out without saying excuse me to the two women so my father wouldn't recognize my voice.

When I left the theater, all the signs on the stores and bars were lit. I felt dizzy and confused. I went down to Mercedes, but instead of taking a carrito back I just kept walking in the direction of my house, my chest hurting from the betrayal. I hated my father for every tear of his I'd dried, for every treat I'd ever given him, for every errand I'd ever run for him, for the refuge he made me believe he found in me when all he was doing was hiding his lies. I remembered when Martina, the neighbor, said that men were only good to have fun and to get you pregnant but never to marry, nor to give your life to. Then I remembered when Iván, my cousin's husband, offered to take me home and on the way invited me for a beer, and I had to play dumb. But I especially remembered Teófilo, the group's sexologist, who told me once at school, "Little sister, don't be stupid. We men aren't born to be true. It goes against our nature. Fidelity is just a story the Church tells us to keep leading us by the nose. You see, I'm married, and I fulfill my duties with my house and with my wife. All my playing around is during the day, and she's happy. What she doesn't know can't hurt her."

After much crying and walking, I decided I wouldn't tell anyone what I'd seen. No, my mother would never know that my father, that great hypocrite, was a cheater just exactly as she proclaimed, while he cried and made her seem crazy. No, my mother would never know. But I was going to get back at him by doing exactly the same thing he was doing. Little excuses so as not to deal with him. I'd forget about the guava treats. I'd not pay attention when he talked to me about politics. I'd stop listening when he came playing the martyr. Maybe drop a few hints that I knew the game he was playing and, if he asked, deny everything in a mocking tone. That and so many other things, until his life turned into the hell I was living. After all, he'd just shown me his life was based on lies and that the only way I could defend myself from him was to never again tell him the truth.

PAPI

FICTION BY LEONOR SUAREZ

"Come on, Elena, you have to come this time." There's urgency in Raquel's voice. "He's very sick, and we can't ignore him."

She's been trying to make me go visit you for years. You live under your dead brother's house, hiding away like a mouse in that hole—a small bedroom with a single bed and an old blanket that smells like mothballs and cigarettes. And in the corner you call a kitchen, a shaky table with a hot pot, a plate, a fork, a spoon, and a mug. You have to use your sister-in-law's latrine. In the mornings, you go up the little hill to the house with a small jarro, a tooth-brush, and a towel. Her bathroom doesn't have any running water; you have to brush your teeth with a cup of water from la tinaja and bathe from a bucket. It's the only time they see you up there.

"I have everything I need" is what you said to Raquel the first time she went to visit you. After so many years, you turned into a hermit, shutting the world out; it's a self-imposed isolation. No one knows why, after being the woman-izer who drove Mami away, after your outings with friends and all the drink-ing, you lock yourself up alone.

The Eighteen-Year-Old—that was her name in my mind—left you after she had two kids. The others you brought to the house left you, too. Your other children don't come around. Everyone is gone. You're alone. Defeated and old, you moved into that tiny room under your brother's house. You're barely a shadow of who you were.

"He's going to die one day, Elenita, and you're going to regret not seeing him."

"Raquel, I don't care if he's sick, he doesn't deserve it. Did he ask about me when you went last time?" We're at her house folding a mountain of clothes, me overworked from my shift at the hospital and she overstressed. She has three children with a husband who doesn't want her to work.

"Ay, don't you feel sorry for him? His other kids don't visit him. Amalia and I are going next week. We have to. Mami would have wanted it that way."

Raquel is right; Mami insisted on us being in contact with you. "I have taught you girls better, don't be like him. Besides, God wants us to forgive," she told us many times.

We left when I was thirteen because Mami was very sick and needed us by her side, yet you gave us such a hard time, as if by letting us go you were losing your own imaginary war. "Don't come back here needing my help. ¡Malagradecidas! You abandon me, that's how you thank me? She was the one to leave you here, don't ever forget that."

I can still see you sitting on your favorite couch as we were packing. One of your women tended to you like always, lighting your cigarette and bringing you a batida de lechoza, your favorite. You coughed so hard as you talked, your wheezing echoed throughout the house. Mami was dying of the poison you exuded out of your pores. She was dying of cancer, and you didn't want your pride bruised. Cancer was the only way you let us go. Until then, you held us hostage, knowing that Mami was suffering without us. She had to come visit from La Vega and see the circus we lived in. You were the ringmaster, with a smirk on your face as she hugged us tight with pity and despair.

"Amalia's coming over, and we're gonna make the plans for the trip."

We hear a knock at the door. Raquel opens it, and Amalia walks in, taking a deep breath, exhaling the outside smog and cool seven-o'clock air. She's sweating from riding a jam-packed bus from the water works department in the center of Santo Domingo, where she has a job as a secretary. I always joke with her that she works so hard and yet there's still a water problem all over the country.

"Ay déjame tranquila, I work to pay bills, waiting for a man to save me from this everyday stuff." This is her usual answer. She blinks away the outside and focuses on the people in the room.

"¿Ya? Are you coming with us?" Amalia says as she comes over to give me a kiss on the cheek. With a sigh, she sits down in front of me and the mountain of clothes, which seems to have gotten bigger. She snatches a shirt away from me. "¡Deja eso! Leave it, have Mrs. Housewife over here fold her own clothes. Aren't you tired, girl?"

Raquel ignores Amalia's comment but does not press me.

Amalia is right. Being a nurse, I'm on my feet all day; I can barely think straight. I spend my days dealing with doctors and their egos. Patients come to the clinic without money, and we never have enough equipment or materials to treat everyone. I don't know if I was folding or balling the clothes.

Raquel had called, insisting I come over, so after work I took a taxi and can't remember when I started folding.

"And you haven't given her food? Geez, Raquel. Let me see if I can find something." Amalia disappears into the kitchen and shouts over the sound of clanging pots. "So I was thinking we leave Saturday early and spend the day with Papi, see how he's doing, and come back by seven. What do you say, Elenita?"

It wasn't always like this. For a while you were my Papi. You used to make me laugh when you played with your belly, pretending you were pregnant, moving it around as if a baby was shifting inside. You did it to make me giggle. While you were under the mango tree reading the paper, I'd sneak over to surprise you, then I'd hug your belly. "Do it, Papi." You'd take me and tickle me until I begged you to stop. "Please, Papi," I'd say in between chuckles. You then laughed, showing all your teeth, and made your belly dance. I hugged it tight, giggling some more.

Amalia comes back with hot chocolate and bread for all of us. "Don't worry, hermanita, I'll protect you from mean Papi." She pokes my side and starts laughing. To her, the world is very simple. "He's very sick, Elenita. Come and keep me company, you know I'd do the same for you." Both of them look at me, waiting for an answer.

When friends visited you, and one of them jokingly asked how many children you had, you'd answer over your nicotine laugh, "Who knows, like thirty!" You boasted about your many children, yet now none of them goes to see you, only the girls you don't ask about, the ones from your only marriage. We never found out the exact number, but I remember vividly when the first one came. Her sudden arrival in our lives pushed me over a precipice I didn't know existed.

Raquel saw the figure of a girl standing in the hot afternoon sun and eyed her like a street dog guarding food. The dark, round figure was etched against the dust rising in the yard. I had seen her walk by, first across the street and then as she went around the outside fence, where she stopped and looked in. Our dog was barking, ready to jump over, following her every step. When she stopped, Bobo's snout squeezed between the bars, trying to get at her. The girl ignored him. Her eyes scanned everything, as if memorizing each tree, the pattern of our lawn, how many different types of flowers were planted around the yard. She gaped in as if she was at the door of a bakery, salivating, letting the sweet smell flood her lungs. She stopped in front of Amalia and me, hips at least twenty inches bigger than her waist; it made her seem like two different people stuck in one body.

"I'm here to talk to my father," she said. Her voice was raspy, as if she had just woken up.

Amalia and I sat by the gate, not moving to open it. Bobo stood guard, barking and showing his teeth through the bars. Raquel was under the mango tree, arms folded around her chest, and because she was the oldest, she was the first to speak. "Then go home and talk to your father," Raquel yelled over our heads. She was fifteen and tried to take care of us, helping us in the morning with our hair. "I don't want you guys to look sloppy, Mami wouldn't want it that way," she said while inspecting our uniforms before we left the house. Sometimes she even took us to school, although her classes didn't start until after twelve.

"I want to talk to my father, Emilio Manuel De León."

She said your name. When I heard her, I felt hot and dizzy; the earth was spinning underneath, ready to take me in. I looked back at Amalia, then at Raquel. We'd always heard about them; we'd never met one. Raquel seemed to blink more than usual. I almost threw up right then and there.

"Well, he's not home." Raquel tightened her arms around herself.

Bobo would not stop barking; Amalia and I were paralyzed.

"You better open, I'm not leaving until he gets here." She shifted her weight. The girl looked about Raquel's age but seemed older, with lines and dark circles under her eyes. "My mother doesn't have a job or money." She looked over our heads to Raquel, put her hands on her hips, and added, "It's about time Papi did something for us."

Amalia, Raquel, and I looked at each other; we didn't know what to do. My two older sisters were too young to make any decisions, and the eighteen-year-old you brought home, the one you said to call "Mami," was out. Raquel cocked her head at me; I took a hold of Bobo's collar, walked farther into the yard, and tied him to the avocado tree. Amalia opened the gate. The girl came in as if this was her house and went into the living room to wait for you to get home from work.

"Yep, that's it. When Papi gets here, I'll tell him that I'm staying, and that's it."

She slumped into a shaky chair. On her left she set down a rice sack that had only two corners tied with a tattered rope, and on her right she placed a yellow plastic bag from the store La Sirena. Both were full of clothes. The colors seeped out of her bags, an arrangement of dull pink, dull green, dull blue. They sat there, two mounds of overflowing housedresses and old pants, and in between, a massive mountain of a girl padded with cellulite. She was the color of the mud in our backyard after a rainy day, the kind that stayed on our shoes after running into the house. Her matted hair seemed to hang on top of her head out of boredom; it was the dusty brown cloud that cars leave behind on dirt roads. Her clothes clung to her dull and dirty, like the old underwear fabric Mami used to tie our ponytails. She had on skin-tight orange jeans, same as the ones the Eighteen-Year-Old wore around the house, the kind Mami said women in bars used. From my place in the corner, her pants and dimpled legs were melted lava oozing down to the pattern of the floor.

She said her name was Lili De León. She called you Papi. My heart felt heavy on my chest, and my eyes were teary again. Papi, just like that, as if she'd been calling you that all her life, like us. I started shaking. "Papi" became a heavy word. It bounced in my head back and forth; it felt almost like those words I'm not supposed to say out loud or else Mami smacked me. "Papi," a word I had been using all of my life, was now coming out of her lips, knocking me over and making me dizzy. Your face was fading with her words.

"What's your name?" I asked in a whisper, hoping that she'd give me a different answer this time. I felt her eyes cut my face.

"It's Lili De León," she said, peering at an opened bedroom door.

I looked down, tearing up even more. Your last name, my last name. I was nauseous again.

"Y Papi ennegreciendo la sangre," Amalia said with a look of disgust on her face. She sometimes had trouble keeping her mouth shut, and Mami had to taparle la boca because she got so fresh sometimes. No one was here to slap her mouth.

In my corner of the floor, I tried to figure out how anyone could "blacken blood" as if it were paint. There, next to the red couch a neighbor had thrown out and you had picked up because we needed one, shapeless tiles melded into one another. I liked wedging into the corner of rooms, feeling the coldness of the ground against my skin, exploring the cracks on the tiles. These were my places in the house, and even more so since the Eighteen-Year-Old moved in. The corners were my hideouts; the floors were a world just for me. The Eighteen-Year-Old's favorite punishment was to send me under the bed, Mami's bed, for hours sometimes. She didn't know that those times, though scary, were magical for me. The first time she sent me there, I was afraid of El Cuco that my sisters insisted lived there.

"Make sure you don't move a muscle, or else . . ." they had teased. Thirty minutes later, Amalia and Raquel came into the room to ask if I was still alive, if El Cuco had bitten me, or if it had grabbed my legs and pulled me down to its underworld. This was when the images began to appear more often, on the floor and soon after in the shades of trees, on the branches, on sand, on all the negative spaces of the world. It was a world that came to me as I sat there. It was my eye game, looking at patterns on our floor. White and gray squares danced before me, coming together and falling apart. Dwarfs and lions appeared, and a castle of sugar loomed in the background. You just thought I was a strange and lonely child and let me be.

Lili was your daughter because she had your last name; it's what she said. Her face had a hint of you, the shape of her dark eyes and nose. There was a trace of you in her. I looked back down at the spot I was poring over before. The dwarfs and lions were not there anymore; only marmolite stared back.

"There go those De León girls," people always said in church, "with their 'good' hair and 'clear' eyes." People whispered about the three of us wearing matching white dresses, and the New York white kneesocks our aunt sent us with mini pom-poms hanging on the side. Me with a sorry excuse for Shirley Temple curls, which Raquel slaved over at six in the morning so that I looked the way Mami liked to see me on Sundays. Halfway through mass, the curls always unraveled, my lazy hair refusing to be bound.

"Those De León kids, no pueden negar su sangre. They have strong blood; they stand out anywhere," said Doña Tata, our neighbor across the street who had a kiosk in her yard. She let me have sweet bread without paying right away, knowing that I would pay for it later. As soon as you got in the shower, I'd sneak into your pants, which reeked of cheap perfume and Winston cigarettes, and steal five cents. I don't know if Doña Tata did it on purpose, but sometimes I heard her talk about you and your outings to her customers.

"You can go to the interior part of the island, and if there are any De Leóns around, you'd be able to spot them. That is some good blood." This was Doña Tata's favorite saying about our family. She pronounced these words as if they were honey in her mouth, as if saying them often enough could soften her own family's dark features. As if her daughters could wake up the next day with "good" hair, the kind that you ran your fingers through, like my real mother's silky hair.

Sometimes, when I went to her kiosk to buy bananas, she ran her hand through my uneven bangs with an air of pity and envy all around. "That man has no shame. Going around chasing skirts! And he's been chasing younger ones," she said while peeling a plantain for her daughter to fry later. Albita, Doña Tata's oldest, stood in front of her with her crusty brown eyes, holding a big empty olive oil can that they now used as a pot. The few customers outside the kiosk were her audience. "Mira, those poor girls. I almost cry when I think of their mother, you could go to the other side of town or any corner of this island and see the same eyes, those eyebrows, those Spanish genes. That woman, I don't know how she's been able to stay with that man for so long. The Pope himself would forgive her if he knew the torment that man has put her through." Doña Tata sometimes talked about my real mother as I've heard priests talk about the saints in church.

"Ay, dios mío, that's her cross to bear for the rest of her life. Eso fué Dios, it was from God." Doña Tata waved an unpeeled plantain in the air, then with a threatening gesture toward Albita, who already seemed to feel the weight of the plantains in the bucket, she added, "You better not end up with a man like that, give yourself respect, and make your man respect you. There are many of those bad men on this godforsaken island." Albita blinked her crusts away.

The gray-white goo from my corner oozed over to Lili De León, who had become one with the bags and the floor. The colors were bleeding into one another before me. Raquel busied herself trying to make our TV antenna show us something from *El Show del Gordo*, pretending that Lili wasn't there but catching glimpses of her once in a while. Amalia disappeared into the room and came back with a mariquita doll she had gotten in exchange for three beer bottles you drank that she saved for the bottle man. I stayed in my corner. We waited impatiently for you.

Three months earlier, in my history class, Sister Rosario reviewed the Spanish colonization. "In 1492, the conquistadors invaded the island of Hispañola. They killed the natives, a peaceful people, for gold and other goods.

"Their intent was to take advantage of the indigenous women and the land," Sister Rosario continued. "The Spanish colonization is responsible for the different shades of mestizos in the Dominican Republic, the different shades of the beautiful brown mixed people in our blessed land."

She walked around the room looking at the sea of us, but at none of us. "The Spanish came, bedded the indigenous women and the black slaves from the other side of the island, but kept their blood pure by legitimizing under God and the Throne only children with their Spanish wives. If a child was outside of the family, and if the baby was light enough, then perhaps they could be recognized as kin and given the family's last name. This practice continued for many years." She looked around the room with a smile and the calmness only nuns can give. I don't know if I was imagining things, but as the class went on, I think I saw some of the kids looking at me, no side glances but straight at me. Brown faces and brown eyes stared.

"But remember, children, we are all the same in the eyes of God. Now stand up for our goodbye prayers . . ." Sister Rosario's sweet voice echoed in the classroom of different shades of brown. We all seemed to be thinking about what she said. I saw some kids compare the inside of their arms because it's the lighter side. If you were light you had more Spanish blood, you were purer, closer to the Spanish conquistadors, you were legitimate, better than the darker mestizos and even better than the black slaves. If you were white on this island, your family had money, as it has always been since the beginning. You were white, you owned things, you were higher than the indios claros or indios oscuros. I had a hard time breathing the heavy air in the room. The afternoon sun seemed to melt everything that surrounded me— the blackboard, the metal windowpanes, the concrete in the playing yard. The world around me trembled following the heat's order; sharp edges became rounder, walls quivered, desks melted. The chalk dust, the whispers, the remarks of those brown mouths all competed for space against the Caribbean sun.

"God, what kind of Spanish white girl are you? You don't even have money."

"What happened, the Indians took all your family's stolen money?"

"I heard my mother say that your father is a modern-day conquistador."

"Your grandfather was a conquistador, now your father is a conquistador, raping choco-women."

"Go back to Spain, white girl."

But I was like everybody; my skin was brown too, only a little lighter. I was Dominican like them, I've always been. I didn't know anything else and didn't want to go to Spain. I ran.

Those insults followed me all the way from the school yard, past the naked kids playing with their cracked marbles, past the Haitian mango stand two blocks away from my house, and Pedro's shoe-shining box. Images ran through my mind as I raced home, all dark, all brown, pounding and coming at me from all directions. Their dark brown eyes jumped out of the garbage piles I ran by, out of the luncheonette where the city bus drivers ate their rice and beans, out of the new park with three swings and a tilt-a-whirl. My head spun like it did the first time I rode in that tilt-a-whirl; blurry black and brown figures surrounded me. I got home with my face flushed and sore from crying. I ran to your room and hid in your closet to envelop myself in its darkness, like a blanket. This darkness didn't have a color.

I don't know how long I was in there. I cried until my head hurt, until kids' voices and mine were silent. All was quiet for a while, then things changed, noise stirred the calm. My ears were numb. The sounds came at me bits at a time. I heard them coming from outside. They traveled in between the clothes that caressed my face, hovered over my head, and entered my ears with fury. There were disoriented steps, quick and urgent, following an uneven rhythm. There was a hole in the closet door. The hole with its ray of light sneaking in was a window that wanted to show me everything. Through the hole, the shadow of a figure swayed like the bells from the church. The shadow was of my mother, who scrambled around the room; a shadow following its owner, an owner following her shadow. She seemed distant, yet her figure loomed in the room, like my classmates' insults at school that day. Soon after, another shape took over my window, a figure whose presence was heavier, darker, standing near the door. From in between the clothes, I smelled cheap perfume and Winston cigarettes. I held my breath. The window allowed in only fragments, half sentences.

" . . . can't stand this anymore . . . your cheating, the kids, it's humiliating . . . I need to leave, get away . . . ¡Que Dios me perdone!" I hid deeper in between the clothes and shoes, but the flood of words and sounds kept coming through the hole to my ears, clearer now.

"I hate you and them . . . I know everything, neighbors talk about it, the kids know, too . . . your collection of bastards around the neighborhood . . . is this a punishment from God? What have I ever done to deserve this?"

Then she stopped, silence all around. I focused on the opposite side of my window, looking for dwarfs, castles, any kind of movement, but I didn't see any. Before me, only the clothes looked back with sadness. You didn't say a word, at least none I could hear. Then waves of sounds, strange and sharp, came at me from my window, of shoving and shuffling, of fists hitting face, head hitting wall, screams. They came in and out through the hole with a constant beat. Blows swooshed in the air. Mami's heavy sandals tried to catch up with her sudden movements as she dodged your fists. The clothes around me felt rough and hairy; they tugged at me, pulled my long hair. I didn't want to be there anymore. The noises that invaded the closet, her crying and then your yelling, were nightmares in the dark. The clothes became those nightmares, piercing through my attempts to stop hearing, stop seeing.

The hole started to change form before my eyes, losing its shape. I held back tears but couldn't control them; my window became a blurry opening. It only allowed in screams and your great, booming voice. Those deafening sounds seemed endless. I covered my ears, but the screams got louder. Then, as quickly as they started, they stopped. There was a silence, heavy and charged, like the one during mass before the altar boy rings the bell when people kneel and pray for their loved ones. The shadows that were once animated and urgent now were still. I waited, but only the silence escaped from the room through the hole into the closet. The shadows did not dance. The hole was calm, unmoving, as if holding its breath. The loud silence hammered around the walls, the clothes, the smells, and colors engulfing me in my cave. I fell asleep in the closet.

It was sometime later, when the clothes and the stillness began to suffocate me, that I left my hideout. There was no one in the house. Your bed was all over the room, the blue sheets had been torn, and the pillows' insides decorated the room, giving it a white glow. The mattress sat lifelessly under the window.

That night, I cried because Mami wasn't home, and it was getting late. Raquel took me aside and told me that Mami was staying at Mamá Cheché's house in La Vega for a while. Later that week, I overheard Amalia and Raquel talking in the shade of the avocado tree about how they'd had to clean up. While I had been hiding in the closet, asleep among the clothes, Mami broke all the plates in the kitchen in a fit; she screamed at the plates and threw them across the room, repeating over and over again that they were dirty.

"I'm tired of this hell . . ."

"May God forgive me, but I can't take this man . . ."

"I can't bear to hear any more gossip, all his bastards, everywhere like stray dogs . . . To hell with him . . ."

Raquel said that after destroying the kitchen, Mami had walked to the bus stop. She wanted out and away from the dusty capital, to return to the green hills of La Vega. Who cared anymore what Doña Tata told the other rolled-up-haired women who came by every day to gossip? Who cared what those brown, scarred, round faces thought about her? She was probably tired of our complaints when we didn't have enough food and had to get it from Doña Tata, saying, "We'll pay you back later." Later had become more and more distant. Doña Tata then turning around and telling everyone.

Mami didn't want me. I wanted attention when she was busy trying to get some money out of you before you went out.

You called her a nag, ugly, old, worn out, when other women out there took care of themselves. I heard you yell at her, all the time. "You only go to church, that's all you do. Complain and go to church with the old ladies . . . just stay there, have church give you money . . ."

Mami wanted to forget.

A month after Mami left, the Eighteen-Year-Old was there when Amalia and I got home from school. Raquel said that you walked out saying we couldn't go on living without a woman in the house. You were tired of her cooking and our whining.

"Maria is the woman of the house now, I expect you to treat her with respect. It's about time a woman took care of this place." You didn't look at us. You had your favorite slippers on; you smelled of Winston cigarettes like always. To you, nothing was different.

"Elenita, don't just stand there, grab that comb and shake out my dandruff," you said to me in your normal tone, as if some strange woman was not in Mami's kitchen using Mami's pots, making us rice that we were supposed to eat just like Mami's. The Eighteen-Year-Old was there to take over; you just walked away without saying anything else. I don't know why, but I realized then that you never looked me in the eye. I don't think you had ever looked at me, as if you were afraid that I could see you. Mami was gone, and for weeks the thought had reverberated in the corners where I hid. I was a zombie going to school, doing my homework, staying out of everyone's way, and hiding. Mami left me, shadowing me with every single step of my day, at school and in that empty house. Mami was gone. And here was the Eighteen-Year-Old to take her place.

The Eighteen-Year-Old's skin was rough, and her nails were bitten to the skin under the fake red ones she bought at the variety store, where they sold shampoo for fifty cents in a small paper cup. She was the color of the milk with coffee that Mami used to give us in the morning before school. Her eyes were almost as dark as the black saints on the windows of the voodoo botanica stores that I passed on my way to school. I wasn't allowed to go into botanicas, because only Haitians went in there, and they worshiped the devil. Gladys, the girl who sat in front of me at school, said one day that if you looked at those saints for too long they ended up coming to you at night while you slept. And when Edwin, because someone dared him, asked Sister Rosario in class the name of one of those saints, she told us that they were not real Catholic saints and that we were not supposed to go near those stores. We were not even supposed to look at the statues; doing so would be admitting that we weren't good Catholics, which brought a harsh punishment to us and our families.

For days after you brought the Eighteen-Year-Old, I came home from school in my fog. I hoped that she had been a bad dream, but no, there she stood in the middle of the kitchen stirring a pot of white rice, her thick eyebrows raised in penciled-in arches with a red lipstick that seemed to be superimposed on her face. Doña Tata said that those country folks spend their days talking about the things other people have, envying and casting the "evil eye" on everyone. That's why whenever the Eighteen-Year-Old looked at me with her witch's stare, I said a "Holy Mary mother of grace" in my head so I wouldn't catch any of her envy spells. A girl at school said that animals could smell when a witch was nearby. If a dog barked out of the blue in the middle of the night, it meant a witch had flown over on her broom. Sometimes while the Eighteen-Year-Old ordered me to do some chore I concentrated on the shadows of her face and her neck looking for the scales of a witch. Every day after school on the walk home, I prayed that she would be gone, but when I walked into the yard I could smell her cheap perfume and her coconut food seasoning. Even the dog had stopped coming inside.

"You girls are so pretty. You should be careful with that woman, she probably envies your beautiful hair, and before you know it you're going to wake up one day with kinky hair like her. That's what envy can do," Doña Tata reminded me when I went to the kiosk to buy two eggs for ten cents.

"Did you see the campesina Papi brought home?" Amalia started the discussion one night before going to bed. During the day we tried not to speak aloud, too afraid that you would punish us or hit us if we did. We walked around the house trying not to bump into each other or cause any noise, trying not to breathe too loudly, to not disturb the dust and air. Mami was gone, the thought weighed down on me heavier as days turned into weeks. I spent more time under beds and in corners, looking desperately for my friends in the floor. I wandered around the yard, which had become small since Mami left and the Eighteen-Year-Old arrived. Once in a while I caught glimpses of her washing Mami's dishes, mopping Mami's floor, using Mami's cleaning rags, and I dove deeper into the fog I was living in.

The three of us slept in the same bedroom, next to yours. A steady flow of sounds came from behind the wall that separated the two bedrooms. Amalia's bed was on that side of the room. She and Raquel had their heads pressed against the wall.

"I can't believe they're doing it, knowing that Mami is at Grandma's." Amalia's face glowed in the light streaming through the window from the lamppost across the street.

"What are they doing?" I asked, even though they always ignored me.

"Be quiet, Elena, you're only nine, too young to understand anything, just go to sleep, or El Cuco will come and grab you for butting into grown-ups' business," Raquel's shadow said from one of the corners of the bed, of my stage. Only babies believed in monsters. I sunk deeper into my sleeping space, afraid, but still paying attention to the show. The green mosquito net made their shadows dance; I squinted my eyes even more. I was on the corner of my bed trying to fit my body in between the mattress and the wall. There I slept most nights somewhat enveloped by the net, mosquitoes buzzing near me. Through the mosquito net I pretended that Amalia and Raquel were puppets in my show. Their shadows paced from one side of the green net to the other, sometimes growing and getting closer to me. When this happened, they were monsters with sharp, glowing teeth. They gossiped and moved their limbs in slow motion. The shadows shaped and wavered with each fold of the net, with the breeze that escaped the night to invade our room through the window.

"And did you see how dark she is? She's not just café con leche, she's the bitter dark coffee Mami has in the morning," the monster with Amalia's voice said. "I bet he either found her in a fonda drinking rum and all drunk or picked her up from the hills. I bet he went to her house and promised to take her out of the hole she lived in with her mom, some shack with a latrine outside. He must have come right in with a charming smile and told her all about the house he has in the capital. He got himself a naïve hick from the hills." Even though Amalia was only twelve, she was always the one with the most information.

"Did you hear about all the bastards he has around the neighborhood?" the Raquel shadow asked the dark room. And then I couldn't breathe. We'd never said that out loud before. I pressed myself harder into the wall, more afraid now, as if somehow you could come through the wall. The moon glowed on her face. The Raquel monster did not look at her other companion. She asked this question to all the gossip that we had heard for years, to you who sat under the mango tree and bragged to your friends about your thirty kids. You would sit in the shade, a glass of Dominican rum in one hand, and wave it in the air as you tried to remember how many bastards with your face and green eyes were scattered around the neighborhood.

The monsters' words were drowned out by the sound of a truck outside; their shadows joined and became bigger, hairy, a creature that came in on a ship to take me away. I fell asleep with their voices still echoing in my head, with their images coming at me through the veiled darkness of the net. That night, El Cuco didn't take me to a finca where all the bad kids were sent to work without food, away from their families, like Raquel once told me. El Cuco took me to a white room where Mami sat on an iron chair. When she saw me with the monster, she refused to talk to me and looked away. I tried to pry away from the monster, but it kept a hold on me, digging its claws into my arm. Mami just turned away, shaking her head. I was not there.

Lili De León sat on our couch waiting for you, her papi. We had heard about her in one of your musings, but she had stayed far away and imaginary. She didn't exist to me. She and her mother lived in a shaggy house made out of patches of plywood on the other side of town, far away from us and you. From my corner, I heard Amalia and Raquel talk about Lili when she asked to go to the bathroom.

"Papi is bringing more dark trash into our house," Amalia said.

"And this one is worse than the first one. She's gonna have to wait for a while, Papi's working late tonight," Raquel added.

As soon as Lili came back, Amalia got up and whispered to Raquel, "Gotta go see if there is something missing in the bathroom, these people are thieves."

Lili took her place by her makeshift luggage and sighed.

"Where's your mother?" I asked, because on the marble floor two dwarfs were already cleaning the red paint off the lions, and my sugar castle had shaped away into a mound of caramel. As soon as I said this, Raquel grabbed me by my ponytail and dragged me to the closet because I was too young to butt into grown-up things.

"I told you not to ever come here." It was your unmistakable voice that I heard from the closet, through the hole. I had fallen asleep once again in my cave, in between the shoes and pants, under the empty hangers where Mami's other clothes should have been. She had taken most of them that day while I slept in the closet. She didn't even wake me up to say goodbye. Now there were only the few dresses she hadn't taken, the ones I had nestled into, smelling Mami's sweat and tears, hearing her voice singing me to sleep. I clung to them as I cried to the ringing of her voice left there in her dresses' memories.

"Didn't I give your mother enough money? All you people are so ungrateful, always wanting more . . ." Your voice rose and shook all the clothes around me. I grabbed onto them, and I smelled Mami there.

Mami wanted to forget you. She wanted to forget us. She wanted to forget me. I was her burden, I complained too much, I wanted too much. I looked the most like you; Mami didn't want to be reminded of you, that's why she didn't take me with her to Mamá Cheché. Mami had left for good. She left us. She left me. That day I knew I was rotten. Mami left me because I was not worth staying for; I was stained with your looks, with your last name. I felt tears tracing down my cheeks. In that closet, in that instant, all sounds disappeared, even the thoughts were muted, and only "Mami is gone" echoed. I couldn't hear you, what you were saying to this Lili De León. "Mami is gone" was the only thing I heard among the clothes. It was as if those words had become an evil parasite growing inside, taking root in every part of me, rotten me. I lived them every day, in every corner of the house. "Mami is gone" was my monster now taking in my every breath. "Mami is gone" echoing in the silence of my days, in my dreams, in my sisters' Cuco, in Doña Tata's comments and stares, in the emptiness of the house, in the Eighteen-Year-Old's cooking, in your empty eyes. My monster was in Lili De León.

I clung to Mami's clothes and could almost feel the monster's heart beat as my own. But suddenly I let go of Mami's dresses with eyes still closed. I felt the monster's breath coming out of me. I screamed then. I screamed at the muted words. I screamed, and my small window pushed itself open, and with eyes closed I could see them all. The monster could see them all, looming over them and laughing. I was that wickedness that was you, the bastards could all come out, all the eighteen-year-olds of your world could come out and play all they wanted. The monster would scream you all away.

I will go for Mami, not for you, Papi.

GREÑAS

FICTION BY KERSY CORPORAN

"¡Estas greñas son imposible!" Mami never called my hair "hair." She called it all sorts of things, all of them dark, difficult, and useless. "Greñas" was her favorite term. As far as I could gather, it meant something rough, uncontrollable, strawlike. Whatever the meaning, the word referred to what I had on my head, which was kinky and unmanageable. Doing my hair was always a chore for Mami, an unnecessary struggle she had to undertake, and I was somehow at fault for her trouble. She attempted to "fix" it—her hands flailed around me, and I felt my eyes pulled back as she bound the thick mass into two tight braids.

"Aaay," I cried.

She pulled me up, spun me around, looked me over, and said, "Ya, vete greñosa."

I moved away, rubbing my stinging hairline. She did not hide her annoyance or inconvenience, but I knew she cared. Her love was real. My hair just seemed to represent all that had made her life more difficult—her relationship with my father in particular. My hair was more like his than hers. She could claim me as her girl except for the hair. All I wanted was to not have this daily reminder. I wondered what life might be like if I had silky locks that required little grooming. Straight hair would be a dream to comb. Wouldn't it be wonderful if Mami took pleasure in doing my hair instead of feeling annoyed? These thoughts lingered in my aching head. I plodded out the door in search of my brother.

As I made my way outside, the bright sunlight blinded me for a moment. I shielded my eyes. I wanted my brother—my playmate and constant companion. We shared everything together, creating imaginary worlds with Barbies and GI Joes that read like telenovelas. But I remembered he was with my cousin Juan. Me being only seven and three years younger than both of them, Juan wouldn't want me to join them. He wouldn't allow a little *girl* to play with them. This increased my frustration and boredom.

I surveyed the apartment complex. The hot sun baked the asphalt, turning the air above it into waves. Flies swarmed around the rotting garbage containers; I looked past them and skirted the woods. A path cutting through the high grass led into a dark canopy. The temperature cooled there, so I followed the path a few steps, even though the dry grass scratched at my legs. My shorts were still sticky from having sat so long while Mami did my hair. I walked deeper into the shade, my senses sharpened by fear. Juan could be anywhere; he was a bully who pushed my brother and me around whenever he could. I heard voices up ahead. As I rounded a bend, my brother and Juan came into full view. They were crouched on the ground.

"What are you doing?" I asked as I approached.

Juan looked up with a frown. He stood up straight, inflating his chest, and barreled toward me. "Get outta here!"

I stumbled backwards.

My brother stood there without saying a word. His eyes pleaded me to go. Juan always ruled over my brother, even though they were the same age. Junior was Juan's favorite victim. The tíos were fond of telling the stories of Juan's cruel pranks. "Remember when Juan tied Junior to a tree and made him drink two two-liter bottles of soda?" or "Remember when he called Tío Marco a 'maricón' for wearing Speedos?" The tíos laughed at his prowess; the telling added to their own manliness. Later I found out Juan had caught a toad that day and had burned it alive in a brown paper bag.

I walked back home. When I stepped into the apartment, Mami and Tía were talking in the kitchen. A quick glance from Mami cut me off. I knew I was not wanted in the adult conversation, so I decided to watch television. After changing the channel a few times, I found *The Brady Bunch*. In each episode of the program, they solved all their problems. They were the blueprint to the real American family, a constant reminder of a mold that we never fit. Our problems were beyond those presented in Brady World. The Bradys didn't face challenges with money, alcohol, or domestic abuse. They were happy people whose problems never persisted. Their life seemed perfected, and they looked perfect. By watching TV, I knew what was beautiful. I hadn't questioned my idea of what was ugly and beautiful, I had just taken on that of my family, which was supported by the Bradys.

"¡Kiki, ven aquí!"

I bristled at the disruption but ignored it.

"¡Kiki, ven aquí!" The sternness in Mami's voice forced me to pry myself away from the Bradys.

With my eyes still locked in the direction of the TV, I walked toward the table with heavy steps. Tía grabbed my upper arm, swung me around, and undid my braids.

"Tú ves," Mami said. "¡Mira! Who can deal with this?" She waved her hands in circular, exasperated motion. "It takes at least a half hour to do in the morning." Her finger pointing at my head let me know it was ugly. My hair sprung into a mass that seemed impenetrable—it was one of the specific factors that determined ugliness. To be too dark was ugly, to have too wide a nose was ugly, and to be large was ugly. Hair was a particular obsession in my family. Having good hair guaranteed you would not be placed in the "ugly" category. Bad hair had to be dealt with, especially if you were a girl.

"Aay sí," said my aunt. "It's the only way to deal with it, trust me."

I stood there absorbing everything without much feeling. Before I knew it, I was seated on a chair, propped by pillows so that I could see my reflection in the mirror. Tía held Mami's scissors in one hand and a comb in the other. She put down the scissors and began to comb through my hair. She held my head with one hand and yanked through my knotted hair with the other. I stayed still, unable to squirm for fear of toppling from the pillows. The physical pain filled my eyes with tears and blurred my reflection. I stared at the resulting bushiness in the mirror. My heart sank with shame. By watching how my primas were measured against each other according to their appearance, I knew beauty was very important for a girl. I wasn't too young to be sized up by my tíos. The verdict: my potential was limited because of my features—my wide nose, my thick lips, and my hair. These determinations by the adults around me seemed like truth. I wanted to withdraw, to ignore my reflection.

But there was my hair, and it stared back at me. It seemed to insist on being hard and stiff, not fitting in with anything beautiful. Tía began to cut off the puffy ends. I was pleased by what I saw in the mirror. All the kinkiness was gone. My hair was transformed into a smooth yet wavy chin-length bob.

"I like it like this," I whispered to Tía.

She continued to cut. I watched my locks, now tamed, fall away from me. My dreams of redeeming "beauty" fell to the floor. I wondered how much more she would cut. As it got shorter and shorter, my reflection blurred. I was no longer myself.

"Ya," Tía said. "Now that will be easy, see how nice."

I stared at my reflection, with a sinking feeling in my chest, unable to speak. Tears began to well up in my eyes again. Then streams poured down my face, cutting warm paths, felt but unseen. Tía picked me up from the chair and lowered me to the floor, not acknowledging my breakdown. The crying boy no longer stared back at me.

"It looks nice, mi hija! Stop crying." Mami ran her fingers through what was left of my hair.

I stared at the floor as I walked to my room. I fell to my bed and broke down. A few minutes later, I heard Mami's steps at the door, but she did not come in. The door creaked open. Someone slipped inside and tiptoed toward my bed. It was Juan. He held something in his hand and brought it up to my face. I blinked and looked closely to see. It was a picture of me with my long braids and ribbons in my hair. He held it in front of my face.

"See how nice you used to look," he said, grinning.

I became aware of a growing heat inside me. I bit my lip hard and swung my fist, smashing the picture against a full-length mirror. I was on top of him, sinking my teeth into his arm.

"Maaaa," he cried as he twisted and writhed.

I would not let go as he twirled me around. I was blind, holding on, biting harder, immune to his blows. I heard Mami's voice through a fog and felt her pulling at me. I let go to come up for air. The rage began to ebb, like a tide going out.

Juan was crying. He lied about what he'd done, but the broken picture served as undeniable evidence.

"Good, you got what you deserve," Tía said in a stern voice with a satisfied smirk on her face. Her words gave me a sense of vindication; I stood up still shaking from the storm. He held his injured arm, shot an angry glare my way, and I glared back.

Juan never picked on me again. Whenever we encountered each other, I stared him straight in the eye. He knew to leave me alone.

My story became one of those told at family parties, one the tías told with zest, adding their own exclamation, "¡Para que no joda! ¡Coño!" Their telling and retelling of my story created an uproar. The riotous laughter drowned out that of their fathers, brothers, uncles, and husbands. Through their laughter, the women embraced each other in their eyes; they embraced all of me.

PERO, M'IJA, WHERE DID YOU GET THAT FROM?

NONFICTION BY
DULCE MARÍA REYES BONILLA

In early 1997 Mami became obsessed.

"M'ija, ¿y de dónde saca'te *eso*?" she muttered in disbelief. On the phone, she'd accompany the inquiry with a chuipe–Dominican teeth-sucking–followed by a pregnant pause. If we were face to face, she'd shake her head. She soon stopped, however, maybe out of frustration or forgetfulness. And frustrated she was: she must have stopped shaking her head after growing tired of her failed attempts to educate me during this period, giving me, for instance, a much-delayed lesson on the birds and the bees. To my horror, she was now telling me how much she'd liked un güevo back in her day. Or saying, with regret, que se le había ido "el tiro por la culata" with her sternness: she thought her restrictive attitude about me dating in my youth had backfired. Mami especially lamented forbidding me to see Henri, that Haitian guy in Brooklyn who she was now convinced was a real macho and would have provided a preventative cure for my "problem." Maybe she stopped shaking her head simply because she didn't remember this was one of the options for showing disapproval. Her memory was already giving intermittent signs of exhaustion three years prior to a diagnosis of early-onset Alzheimer's.

My mother's eagerness reminded me of my own as a kid. When I was little I insisted she play the game of a thousand questions with me. No, not twenty questions. A thousand. On the why of everything. She was referring to my lesbianhood–I don't say lesbianism because that sounds like a disease, a vice, a problem to be solved. To me, lesbianhood indicates a state of being. And actually, a more fitting term for me is lesbiqueerdom. But my mom doesn't understand the concept of queer, other than that of being a pervert, and can't really tell the difference. Or why I choose to combine the two words. Besides, I've called myself a lesbiana for so many years that it doesn't matter. But lesbianismo? Nah, nothing sick with it. Or with me.

My sexuality, esa pajarería, was something that my elderly, traditional, and uber-religious mother couldn't understand. Something from which she couldn't quite recover. And how could my sixty-two-year-old mother ever recover? She was una señora decente, Doña Dulce, una Maeña, raised in her madrina's small village, Navarrete, in Santiago's deep campo since she'd become an orphan at two years old. Mami was one of the six children distributed to the homes of "gente buena" in the world of my grandparents in Mao in 1936. This was in what was meant to be a mutually beneficial arrangement after my thirty-year-old grandmother's sudden death and considering my middle-aged grandfather's inability to care for the children, who ranged in age from zero to twelve; Mami was the second youngest. She had been the lucky one, ending up as ahijada of my grandmother's closest and still-single cousin. Ninina loved Mami deeply. That's probably how my mother survived and became the baby of the family, dethroning Santiaguito, the months-old sibling who had died of hunger in his own godmother's home. Mami was considered the lucky one of the group, spared from being rented out to strangers and having at least been in a classroom. But even with all this "buena suerte," she only received a third-grade education. Mami was taken out of school at age nine, in 1942, to focus on more important things: to babysit her madrina's firstborn; to pick auyamas, tomates, repollo, berenjenas, and leña; to milk cows; and to learn to ride un burro. This was the beginning of a lifelong and varied career in domestic service that would span nearly six decades, taking Mami from Navarrete to Mao to Arroyo Hondo to La Feria to El Ensanche Naco to El Mirador del Sur to Cancino to Union Square to the Bronx and to Brooklyn. My mother should have been done with paying her dues by her fourth decade. But when ese "prieto-y-feo-pero-educado-con-esos-ojazos-abigarriaos," ese Maeño, entered her life at thirty-five, a cataclysm hit her. He never got a chance to clarify that the three children in the photo he'd shown her while courting her were the oldest ones, not the only ones like he'd said. Or that his wife hadn't really abandoned him, never having gone to Curaçao "a cuerear," and that su señora was really at home about to get pregnant with his ninth child. He never got a chance to tell her the truth because at thirty-six Mami, who already had a fifteen-year-old son, got pregnant. And he never got to tell her beforehand that he didn't, under any circumstances, "permit" any woman to abort un hijo suyo. And he never got to tell her either about his other girlfriend in Villa Vázquez, the other one who was pregnant.

How could Mami recover when her only daughter, that once-five-pound baby she'd carried on a pillow, now a married woman, came out of the closet at twenty-five? Weeks before, on the phone, we'd talked about the sad state of my marriage of four years, a marriage to a great man. We chatted about the "situation" with "another person" that I had mentioned. She didn't know the other person's sex, but obviously hoped for the best. "¡Bueno, ha' lo que tenga que hace', te apoyo siempre y cuando sea con un hombre con quien tú té!"

There. I had Mami's blessing, but it wasn't unconditional. She wanted me to tell her that the mystery person was a man, some sort of real man, with a big güevo like the ones she had supposedly liked in her day. She wanted to hear me say, "Pero claro, ¿y con quién má' voy a ta'?" But I didn't say it.

When I answered that it was too bad she wasn't going to stand by me because the person I was "with" was otra mujer, Mami nearly died. She hung up on me and didn't want to talk again. Two days later she woke up, seemingly from a stupor. Had she been a drinker, I'd say hangover. "Muchacha, pero ¿de dónde tú saca'te esooo?" she asked like a muerta en vida.

Not having had any clues during my adolescence or early adulthood about what I sarcastically call my "inclinations"—which, to be honest, weren't consciously obvious to me either—Mami continued with the "uni-question" for the next year like a hopelessly scratched LP that has become immune to the healing powers of vinegar. She continued even as she adjusted to my new life. And even as she adjusted to what now had become her own new life as a result.

Almost two decades later, Mami no longer asks. But over time, a lot of folks, different kinds of folks, have asked where this comes from. Today, like yesterday, my most simple answer is that it comes from three different places: desire, opportunity, and what I like to call resistance in connection to my politics. But really, much of it is desire. And opportunity. Resistance is the sum of both, but I'll leave that story for another day.

This lesbiqueer desire is no intellectual exercise. Nope, nothing abstract here. I've long heard cis-straight-progressive women say, "Oh, being a lesbian must be fun; not dealing with males, not dealing with kids; not dealing with a household. So very cool." First off, really? I don't know a single lesbiqueer woman who doesn't have to deal with one or all of those three, just by existing in the world. And a household, especially a household, I long for the day when I don't have to deal with mine. And I'm not even on the far end of the clean-cleaner-cleanest spectrum. But I digress.

"And you, would you be willing to go down on a woman and lick nipples on the regular?" I pose to them, blushing, obviously failing at playing devil's advocate.

"Oh no, noo, I'd die."

End of story. Of course, the lesbiqueer feminist in me who sees potential in E-V-E-R-Y-O-N-E agrees that they'd die. Of pleasure, that is. If only they tried. But I don't say that. I tell them that I'd die; I'd be willing to die if I were condemned to never again touching someone who—bar the need for lifesaving surgery—has breasts and a monthly period they don't regret. It's a good thing no one is sentencing me to that. I don't want to die.

The first time I kissed and caressed a woman like that, on the third Saturday in February 1997, the year Mami became obsessed, just weeks before that fateful conversation, everything fell into place. I know for a fact that I must have been wearing an invisible veil, because as La Gringa kissed me that early evening I could see something that wasn't visible before. She really reminds me of the New-York-born-and-raised Dominican youngsters visiting Santo Domingo whom I remember from when I still lived there, before I moved to Brooklyn in April 1989 just before I turned eighteen. There was a certain no sé qué about her, a certain freedom, a certain lightness of being. This was still at a time in my life when those things were foreign to me and when most of my life references were still coming from the place where I had lived most of my life: la República Dominicana, where we called our young relatives born in the States americanitos or gringuitos. The month I met her I was celebrating nine years in the United States and had just become naturalized six months before. That's why I have no choice but to call her La Gringa. When she kissed me, there came a light that was unknown to me, something that had truly been missing, if not for decades, then forever. She filled a void whose magnitude and presence were the size of the Grand Canyon, a perspective you can't begin to appreciate from a distance.

At the time, I was married to Pedro, a Nuyorican from the Marble Hill housing projects of the Bronx. He was a feminist, a bohemian, an artist who helped me grow like tundra under torrential rain and gave me "permission" to go explore what at the time we dubbed bisexual "curiosities" and "tendencies"—those twentieth-century words that in the mid-nineties had not yet lost their titillation, their cool, but that today only embarrass us. I hadn't been dissatisfied per se. But in all honesty, he could only do so much. It'd be a lie to say that our anatomies, in relation to my desire, were a total mismatch, but it'd be a greater lie to say that our anatomies and what I craved were a total match. I desired him most when he went without a beard and when I felt his hands, softer than mine, upon me. For nearly three decades, he had endured homophobic and sexist teasing, if not outright bullying. No one should have to endure that; it's irrelevant to say that he was straight as an arrow, but it speaks to the misogyny and heteronormativity in our society. He was mocked and "suspected" for being sensitive and artistic, for a lisp he struggled to shed, for being fat, for being soft-skinned, for being infertile, for needing monthly testosterone shots for life since adolescence. This was caused by his loss of a testicle at birth, as he was forcibly removed from his non-

English-speaking mom's womb after twelve hours of neglect at the Lincoln Hospital's ER. Such was life in 1964 New York, a time when—even at a public hospital in the Bronx—Spanish didn't exist for patient care in emergency rooms or maternity wards, to prevent a primeriza, a woman in first-time, risky labor, and her fetus in distress from almost dying. Pedro was in no way a homophobe, but my presence in his life seemed to challenge his masculine identity. It was one thing that a friend, also Nuyorican, had told Pedro he was "pussy-whipped" because he always checked in with me when going out with friends. It was quite another in the early nineties, even in a marriage as modern as ours, to have his wife express interest in "getting another girl" as a birthday present "for him" and an anniversary present, the two occasions one day apart. It was my unconscious-closeted lesbiqueer luck to have married the only male on earth not interested in an FFM threesome. Or in an open marriage.

And so began the saga, and the agony, as a transfer student from BMCC in 1995. The college crushes. As my mind expanded in this new environment of Hunter College, my desire and curiosity grew incessantly. I had also gotten my first promotion at my job of three years: I was now an outreach counselor at the center for homeless youth—many of them LGBT, just like the staff. They weren't kidding when they asked me, in the first interview for the reception desk job, what I thought of people who did drugs and of homosexuality because it would be everywhere. They didn't tell me that HIV/AIDS would be too. Or death. And none of us knew that one day my family would say that it was all those people en La Cuarentidó who made me gay.

In May of 1995 it happened: my first real-serious-"ownable"-conscious crush since I'd been pondering my desires. Like me, Maria was applying to the CUNY BA Program at the Graduate Center, though she went to Queens College while living in Manhattan. Sadly, the Angela-Bassett-meet-Angela-Davis-meet-Jada-Pinkett lookalike—whom I befriended and could have sworn was constantly flirting with me—turned out to be an ardently homophobic fundamentalist Christian. She invited me and my bohemian hubby to her church a couple of Sundays in June, a month that would end in Pride weekend. The sermons were earth-shattering. To this day I've never heard the words "homosexual" and "sin" and "hell" strung together so often in one sentence. In the following months I made sure our friendship dissolved. But meeting her had been a watershed moment.

After Maria, I proceeded to fall for every other female classmate's brain; I judged this by hearing them answer questions in class. This was before I knew, or we knew, the term "sapiosexual," which today I also use to describe me in terms of what attracts me to a person. I, however, understood that I needed to be more practical. How exactly was I to approach a classmate I felt drawn to, without risking que me dieran una galleta por fresca? That would have been a justified slap for propositioning them for female-female sex without checking their credentials first. Or even without being certain of mine. After all, wasn't I a married woman? At that time, with clearly limited options, there was no confusion about the sex of my spouse. I was a cis woman married to a cis man, yet ready to proposition someone like me. Maybe my then-recently-deceased gay coworker and friend Warren had really seen something all those years he teased me as a baby dyke while I demanded with feigned demureness, in the middle of our banter, to be addressed as the Mrs. that I literally was, having traded my father's last name for Pedro's.

In the spring semester of 1996, at the beginning of my last full year of college, I thought my chance had come with the ad in the fifth-floor bathroom at Hunter. Someone had graffitied the door of one of the stalls: "Wanna eat pussy?" I accepted the invitation to call seven-one-eight and who knows what other seven digits. Maybe the girl had been pranked or maybe she got shy, because when I called and asked if she went to Hunter, she said yes, but she denied everything else. Although I tried to be diplomatic when asking about the ad, didn't even use the P word, she said she didn't know what I was talking about and just hung up. Another hope had been dashed. I took a break, but I can't say I had much choice in the matter. I focused on juggling my full life the rest of the year. There was a lot that needed my attention: my struggling marriage; my classes at Hunter and at Brooklyn College, now that I'd been accepted in the honors program and could go to multiple campuses freely; my full-time job as a counselor; my community organizing courses and their accompanying service requirements; a volunteer assignment that during the summer would turn into a side gig and eventually would lead me to a huge job nearly three years later. The crushes and the anxiety didn't stop, but I'd found plenty with which to console myself. For now.

Nearly a year later, in January of 1997, I was saved once and forever, and the timing couldn't have been better. There was a new way of learning and talking and connecting with people privately. It was called the Internet. With my new AOL account in hand and the gigantic new Mac for Pedro to work on his designs, I decided to investigate again. And as destiny would have it, it happened.

I met La Gringa, a Bronx-based Dominican-York, in a chatroom for bisexual women. To this day she is still my briefest love ever, for a long time my only one-night stand. La Gringa had been "initiated" as a teenager by another woman, an older cousin in San José de las Matas, her parents' native town in the D.R. In good Dominican homosocial and practical fashion, they'd been assigned to sleep together in the same bed, under a mosquitero. Naturally, the net was to protect La Gringa from those Nueva-York-blood-loving mosquitoes, during one of the unaccompanied-minor, summer-long vacations that every kid in the States with Dominican-born parents either relishes or hates. La

Gringa didn't hate it, but she could have done without the mosquito net. For two whole months that bed was an oven.

We immediately hit it off, turned on and surprised by our mutual ability to go back and forth between Spanish and English. And our shared rebelliousness. Our desire was fueled, in part, by the awareness of the huge taboo-breaking pair we made—in our Dominicanness, in our cross-cultural bond, in our lust for other women and for each other, across racial lines, and in our defiance of our campesina mothers. Necessity more than attraction moved us from computer to phone in no time. Internet speed in early 1997 was like the eternity you felt as a kid while waiting for El Día de los Reyes, at least when you were still getting regalos de los Reyes, if you were either young enough or perceived innocent enough to believe that the Three Magi existed. My in-person story with La Gringa started in my office cubicle, then moved onto my boss's This End Up couch in midtown, then headed uptown for a night of improv, and then to the Village for Mexican food, and ended near Prospect Park, where we almost got arrested. To residents, our two a.m. make-out session in her blue Toyota looked like transactional sex. No matter, I still got my first yeast infection out of it, courtesy of those Marlboro Lights she smoked and her unwillingness to use dental dams or Saran wrap. I almost didn't do it again. Almost. Thank goodness for Monistat. And thank goodness for friends who assure you the itch is not an STD and take you to the clinic near Central Park for HIV testing. Almost didn't do it again. Almost.

And from that encounter, from that first kiss with La Gringa, who smelled like Johnson's baby powder and tasted of nicotine, who unleashed so much in that one and only date that changed my entire life, each and every time I enter intimacy this way, no matter how brief the moment, no matter the intensity of our bond, I feel in my body, in my veins, in my hair, that I belong here. When I see myself reflected in the eyes of una mujer, I know that I was born for *this*. When I feel her hips and buttocks on mine, or when my nipples feel her insides, or when my nose smells her scent of apple peel, or when she tastes my juices and my sweat, my salty taste, I'm in an agnostic's version of heaven.

They say that hindsight is 20/20. *This* desire shouldn't have been a surprise. It's that same sensation we're left with at the end of *The Usual Suspects*. The truth was there all along, but we didn't see it because we got carried away with assumptions and stereotypes. Our own blind spots betrayed us. Once we went back in time in our minds, we saw that reality was clearly there all along, always. There were the childhood crushes in Matahambre, the ever-so-close moments, and one particular near-kiss in one of the intense teenage romantic friendships in Los Minas/Cancino. There were the nothings with two different family friends in late-eighties New York City and that flirtatious Indian coworker at my office job at the Alexander's headquarters on 34th Street who made my stomach flutter. By the time I came out, there were almost two decades of moments: missed moments, cowardly moments, unnoticeable moments, confusing moments, scary moments, unconscious moments, flirtatious moments, innocent moments. Criss-cross them all together como una trenza and show them all at once in a long flashing frame at the end, like in a film, and there's the truth. La pura verdad.

There may even have been a moment when some part of me knew, but I just thought I was a pervert. It was the moment I saw Adrianne naked, though I never saw her in person. She was there the first time I "went all the way" with a man, with Pedro. While he struggled to do his thing, I thought of her image: an oak beauty whose nipples looked like perfect chocolate kisses and whose curves I won't compare to a musical instrument for not wanting two clichés in the same sentence. No, she wasn't there. Unfortunately. But I was creative. I conjured her up from a black-and-white photo—she'd posed nude for Pedro. He had thousands of photographs of everything and everyone, developed in the makeshift darkroom that Grandpa Willie, a war photographer in World War II and his lifelong next-door neighbor, had taught him to put together. That afternoon in 1992, while I fully discovered sex, I wondered in silence why it hadn't been me, instead of him, who had enjoyed her body, her essence, and why it was him, and not her, who was there touching me. Back then, even still seeing myself as "normal," though a bit of a freak, and lacking a consciousness or a backbone, I felt that the world was unfair.

I don't know where *this* desire comes from. Ni me importa un carajo. For better or worse there's a lot of public interest in the origins of *this*, as if it were the only human sexual expression worth researching. But in a truly free and humanistic society it shouldn't matter who one is or why. Our humanity is what should matter, regardless of who we love or fuck, of how many people we love or fuck, or whether we love or fuck at all. Our right to be should stand, regardless of how we dress, how we carry ourselves, how we present our humanity, regardless of anything, regardless of everything. In that kind of society, our humanity and diversity and justice are what count. It's my right to exist and claim and proclaim that, indeed, I'm a lesbiqueer cis woman, una pájara, y me gustan, no, me encantan las mujeres con senos-vulvas-caderas, and I can love more than one at a time sin tapujos y sin vergüenza. And by the way, I'm immigrant, black, fat, prieta, activist, caco pelao, countercultural in ways people can't see. Being those things without facing any social scorn, without risk, that would really measure whether we live, whether we believe, in a free and just place for all of us. And our will to fight for that right will measure whether we deserve it. But before we have a right, before we have to fight, before it all, there is desire.

I had to wait almost five years until the kiss with La Gringa to understand that the world feels less fair when you act like an avestruz, sand all the way up to the neck, like I had done all that time, not only with my sexuality but also with my blackness, my natural hair, my large body, my big features, my opinions. Desire opened the door to freedom.

And unbeknownst to them, Mami and my tías made me free. My mother, one tía in the D.R., and the others in the U.S. struggled all their long lives. From El Cibao to New York, they milked cows, worked someone else's land, washed clothes, cleaned floors, cooked food, scrubbed walls, sewed gowns at home or on a factory floor, wiped the bottoms of babies, wiped the bottoms of elders, sold arepa, sold helados, sold dulce de coco. The sacrifices that they made, all reflected in their callused hands and their mostly sexless middle-aged lives, meant that I wouldn't have to do manual labor or depender de un hombre. Were I to pick up the phone today in 2015 and try to tell Mami this, she wouldn't see it as a compliment. She'd accuse me of wanting to start a fight and would get all ofendida, taking the metaphor to a literal-causal logic. "¡No, m'ija, yo no te di un mal ejemplo!" would be her words. Her paranoia would kick in at the thought that I'm somehow suggesting she made me "así."

She can't erase the obvious, though. It's not only because of that job en La Cuarentidó; it's not because she brought me to los Estados Unidos; it's not because I went to college; it's not because I married Pedro instead of the Haitian Mami would never have allowed me to marry; it's not because here "se' pájara tá de moda." It's because of her. So much of my lesbiqueer desire is because of her. It is rooted in admiration and respect for her. And it's now channeled into a deep love and alianza to other women, especially the ones who are poor, las campesinas, las negras, las sirvientas, las indias, las obreras, las luchadoras, las sacrificadas, "las feas," las viejas, las marcadas, las humildes pero poderosas, the courageous ones. It's a love and commitment and desire that surpasses sensuality and lust, and that comes from the lessons my mother taught me and the path she paved and the price she paid for my liberation.

And it comes from adoring Mami. If only she knew that she herself is the answer to the question.

THE
COUNTRIES
BEYOND

THE CARIBBEAN, OR
THE FEMININE FACE OF
MULTICULTURALISM

NONFICTION BY
SHEREZADA (CHIQUI) VICIOSO

I was on my way back to the Dominican Republic in a twin-engine plane from the island of St. Martin, that tiny territory shared by France and the Netherlands, a rare paradise of coexistence in today's world torn apart by ethnic wars, at the precise moment that neoliberalism calls for the end of all borders and the empire proclaims a single "universal" culture.

I was coming from the Primer Congreso Internacional de Lengua, Literatura y Educación, which took place in Puerto Rico and was sponsored by the island's Department of Education, bringing together eight hundred literature and Spanish professors. The conference kicked off with a magisterial presentation by the Chilean Antonio Skármeta ("The World as Metaphor: One Hundred Years of Pablo Neruda") and the Nicaraguan Sergio Ramírez ("Caribbean Splendor: The Centenary of Alejo Carpentier"), followed by a panel of Caribbean speakers, including Edgardo Rodríguez Juliá (Puerto Rico) and Antonio Benítez Rojo (Cuba), with a paper on Julia de Burgos.

From Puerto Rico I had continued to St. Martin to participate in its second Book Fair, which included writers from Trinidad and Tobago, Jamaica, Canada, Curaçao, Liverpool, and professors from Yale, Howard, and Brockport universities, as well as from universities in the West Indies and the Virgin Islands, joined by the best-known writers from St. Martin.

I mention these two events because both are connected to a debate best exemplified by a phrase from Julio Ortega's prologue to *Caribeños* by Edgardo Rodríguez Juliá: "After all, what is Caribbean if not the chronicle of an incessant mixture?" While in Puerto Rico the Spanish language is the bastion of na-tionality–the raised flag in its cultural resistance–in the English, French, and Dutch Caribbean the debate centers on multiculturalism and is expressed in a curricular program in primary schools where children are educated in English and French while speaking Spanish and Dutch at home.

Tired, I managed to sit by myself and nap for a while, but the voices and laughter from the Dominican folks nearby interrupted my rest.

To my left, a young woman with a short yellow afro and a silver pin in her nose, perfectly made up and dressed in a sexy outfit, was telling her story. "At fourteen, I hooked up with a man who gave me six kids. I barely got to sixth grade and there was nothing to do (laughter). He left me when the youngest was only three months old and needed food and some brand-name clothes. It's letter after letter asking for things, all expensive, all brand names. I left for Suriname, but things didn't go well, so I went to the little island of Saba, an island of gossips, undoubtedly because they're so tiny, and from there to St. Martin. I have a good man there. The women there might raffle him off, but I'm me. Now I want to rest a little bit. It's been eight years since I've seen the kids and my mother. And then I'll go to Spain."

"To Spain?" screamed the woman behind her. "Girl, that's pretty tough going. You'd be better off in Holland. Look at me. I even got citizenship."

"How'd you do it?"

"With an old Dutch man from St. Martin. They die for us . . . (laughter)."

ST. MARTIN

With a population of barely seventy thousand, St. Martin is a territory free of borders, where two nations (France and the Netherlands) criss-cross freely, and there are two ways of thinking, two daily lives. Dominicans make up the largest group of immigrants, and the vast majority of these Dominican im-migrants are women, victims of slavery, of domestic abuse, legal problems, a lack of self-esteem, and alienated from civic participation. The Dominican community works mostly in the service sector, in hotels and domestic work, beauty salons, auto repair, and construction. The "service" sector also in-cludes sex work.

In a meeting I had with the board of directors of St. Martin's Women's Desk, the members expressed great concern for Dominican women, who, according to them, are victims as well of the local women, who reject them because of their jobs and the attraction island men have for them.

The members of the Women's Desk, three of whom were surprisingly de-scendants of St. Martinians who worked in our country and so have family in Santo Domingo, wanted to know why our compatriots "have an inclination for sex work." I responded by asking them about the real prospects for jobs on the island. I also told them about the results of a study by the International Migration Organization (OIM) about Dominican women who emigrate to the smaller islands, which said they generally come from San Cristóbal, Haina, Azua, or Barahona and have had some kind of work experience in free trade zones, or in domestic work where they were victims of exploitation or sexual assault.

THE VANGUARD

"The Caribbean External Frontier" is what José Martí called Caribbean immigrants, including Hatuey and the indigenous island natives who traveled on our seas. In his most recent book, *Coming, Coming Home: Conversations II*, the great Barbadian writer George Lamming describes the women from our islands as "the most effective vanguard for realizing the true potential of regional integration, [precisely because] they will be the most wounded casualties of that dominance."

Fundamental subjects of what Lamming calls "a dialectic intelligence born of our historical experience and our contemporary realities," the women of the region have had the virtue (if you can call imposing a pragmatic view of subsistence on the conqueror's "binary" vision a virtue) of having imposed multiculturalism as praxis, multiethnicity, the dilemma of difference (which, according to Lamming, is in the end a rich source of energy for sustained growth and social dynamism) on the West's somber unidimensionality. The West here is understood to mean "a power which has resided historically in a minority of men who never considered themselves an organic part of the landscape they controlled." These are men whose visions (and capital) reside in the metropolis of their dreams, whether it is Madrid, Paris, or Miami.

MELISSA

"This is Melissa," Mayra said when she introduced me to her daughter, a very fat black girl with large eyes and long lashes, the product of her marriage to a man from St. Martin.

"How are you?" Melissa asked, using the informal *tú*, which prompted her mother to correct her immediately.

"How are you?" she said, using the Spanish formal *usted*. "Don't you see she's a lady? Be respectful!"

"Sorry, mom. That's how I talk."

"Does she speak English?" I asked.

"Of course. They teach her in school."

"And at home, what does she speak?"

"Dutch with her father and Spanish with me."

"So she speaks three languages."

"No, four, because in school they also teach French. Remember that there are two official languages here."

"How does she manage?"

"Very well. All the children in this country speak four languages."

"Four languages!"

And what if one of those children decides to be a writer and to reclaim her or his Dominicanness? Would we build a linguistic wall worse than the one in Gaza?

TRINIDAD

"When I first came to Trinidad," says Lamming, "I discovered that in every family I got to know, the only Trinidadians by birth were the children. Mothers, fathers, aunts, uncles had originated elsewhere. A concept of nation that is not defined by specific territorial boundaries, and whose peoples, scattered across a variety of latitudes within and beyond the archipelago, show loyalty to the 'nation-state' laws of their particular location without any severance of cultural contiguity to their original worlds of childhood. They have created the phenomenon of a transnational family, [a powerful element in] the economic stability of many a Caribbean family across every language of our region.

"From the middle of the nineteenth century," Lamming continues, "to the second decade of the twentieth century, Barbados provided over fifty thousand workers to Guyana and Trinidad. [And] during the first two decades of this century, more than one hundred and twenty thousand Haitians and Jamaicans became a resident force of labour in the Republic of Cuba."

However, the numbers for Jamaicans, St. Martinians, Kittitians, and Haitians who emigrated to work in the sugar industry in the Dominican Republic have yet to be calculated. If that hasn't been determined, imagine the challenge to estimate the number of women migrating from Jamaica to Haiti, from the Dominican Republic to Puerto Rico, to Curaçao, to Panama, or to the Lesser Antilles, and it is quite the undertaking to approximate the number of women merchants who have generated and continue to generate a great volume of trade in the eastern Caribbean and Guyana.

Trafficking for the sex market must be added to this calculation, and it's an activity practiced not as a "natural inclination," as some would suggest, but to maintain the women's immediate family, that is, the children but also parents and siblings of the immigrants.

The final calculation of the economic dimension of the migratory phenomenon, an anchor that keeps our islands from sinking once and for all, is the work of economists. What interests us writers is to consider the future cultural impact of a generation of Melissas, Dominican–St. Martinians who grow up speaking four "native" languages, in the creation of a new Caribbean culture, which, ideally, reinvents itself and should transform the stagnant linguistic postures of our respective insularities.

"The Caribbean intellectual," says Lamming, "has been fixed in the habit of digging up exclusively the small island enclave whose language zone corresponds to the particular metropole whose institutions have largely fixed this agenda of discourse and made him one of their own.

"It is rare," he continues, "to find a Caribbean historian or social scientist who takes the entire region as his field of enquiry and engages in a comparative study of the particularities of each. So Martinique and the region's other French colonies engage in dialogue with themselves and Paris; the Netherlands Antilles clings to a professed notion of being an equal constitutional partner within the Dutch Kingdom; the Hispanic territories responded to Spanish and wider European orthodoxies; [and] the English-speaking Caribbean . . . made its accommodation with an exclusive English tradition."

I think that if Caribbean intellectuals persist in this task—vital to our sense of importance—the women intellectuals of the Caribbean, faithful to the pragmatic tradition of survival like our women merchants, could begin by asking ourselves the following questions:

1. If language is the center of the dawn of every human conscience and is the verbal memory of our past that allows us to reflect on who we are, and every child needs to learn it as a necessary initiation into society, what are the implications of the multi-linguistic and cultural processes in an immigrant childhood?
2. What are the consequences of this multi- and inter-linguistic phenomenon for a regional integration that already transcends economic integration?
3. What concept of nation, not defined by specific territorial borders, are we talking about? And what is the impact of this "new concept" of nationhood on our literature?

I'll conclude by quoting George Beckford. "We in the Caribbean are already integrated. It is only the governments who don't know it."

SAINT MARTHA'S
DAUGHTER IN MADRID

FICTION BY RIAMNY MÉNDEZ

Translated by Achy Obejas

Amid the heavenly murmurings of the blessed Altagracia, the Spanish con-
suls hand over the visa with the smile of one floating on an orgasm. And the
gringos will even give residency to women who want to leave this little island.

That's what they say, Lisania, in the enclave where you were born, a
southern village called El Salao, or Unlucky, because its whitish and salty soil
makes the brown, black, golden skins that abound in its populace always look
opaque, worn down by dust.

The young men who still live in that enclave whisper that Altagracia is not
the devout woman their mothers describe. They're convinced she was just
one more slut, one of so many who have lived in Madrid.

How can the truth be known? I was born with a gift inherited from my
mother—a woman, like Altagracia, also from El Salao, where I spent my
childhood.

I developed my gift between the village alleyways and the irrigation canals
for the plantain fields. But I didn't know I was tied to The Mysteries until my
grandmother figured out I could predict future harvests.

One day, sitting around the hearth on our family's farm, we were preparing
a sancocho. My grandmother fanned the flames. I closed my eyes and saw
trucks filled with provisions, in spite of the drought in the canals. I described
my vision to her, and she cried with happiness. She was convinced that,
despite all the signs, there would be a plentiful harvest of plantains, which
turned out to be the case.

"You have a gift, like your mother's," she told me. I was just thirteen then and spending my first vacation from high school with her. It had been a year since I'd moved with my mother to the capital.

Since then, my ties with the spirits have caused me problems. To those southerners, I'm a witch with an attitude. To my friends in the capital, a clairvoyant who can see the past, feel the pain and joy of those who lived back then, or a fake.

But, girl, I think that because I made fun of the saints when I started at the university—I didn't believe in what I called bullshit in those days—I only see and feel fragments of reality. I can never quite capture the whole story behind a life. It was the punishment imposed on me by The Mysteries for my insolence.

In the year since I built this altar in my apartment in Gazcue, a neighborhood surrounded by gardens and old money—once I understood that my mother and grandmother were wiser than my professors and my fellow biologists—I've been praying to Saint Martha, the serpent spirit, so that I might know the truth about Altagracia.

My prayers began when I dreamt she was whispering something unknowable to me. In her voice I heard a peace that drove me to reconcile with The Mysteries. I saw my grandmother's spirit smiling as she fanned the flames of the fire. I knew it was Altagracia by the fragrance of the Lady-by-Day-Whore-by-Night flower that she left behind in the room. According to the people in the neighborhood, it's evidence of her presence.

The wise women whom I frequently visit in El Salao and in Bahoruco Province—a region blessed by God and The Mysteries with many seers—say that Altagracia intercedes with Saint Martha for women who need comfort or material goods.

I know that, like you, I'm a distant cousin of that woman who became a legend only ten years ago, right at the beginning of the millennium. I needed to know why she visited me when I had never known her, why her smell sometimes invaded my altar.

For a while I thought the whole thing was silly. The miracles performed by the saints and the blessed are always documented. Altagracia wasn't known for doing anything on a grand scale. As far as I was concerned, the doors she opened were not impossible to unlatch. Yet no one attracts as many followers as she does. Never male followers. But the women who ask for favors at her altars are always satisfied.

Lisania, a week ago I put aside my fears and answered the blessed woman's call. I renewed my altar—styled it, my microbiologist friend would say—so I could invoke her presence. Enveloped in the smoke from the rose incense I'd put under the table, I said a special prayer to communicate with Altagracia. Through images of an archangel defeating the devil and the Virgin embracing the miraculous baby Jesus, Belié Belcán, the African spirit, came slowly and invisibly between them, happy to be king of the party, to flirt with Saint Martha.

I bought red and white roses. I put them in the center of my altar, on its purple cloth. Roses for Saint Martha and Altagracia. No foul-smelling tobacco, like on common altars. No screams or kettledrums either, just a CD playing the sound of gentle drumming.

I wanted to put together an exquisite celebration for the ladies who'd be helping me discover my connection to them and what connects us to you, little one. I'm writing these lines for you, though I don't yet know you, to complete the part of the visions that made me tremble before The Mysteries. I want you to read them. I want them to accompany you on your mission. I'll only guide you for a while. And then you will be the teacher.

In the end, my gift hasn't helped humanity much. I barely guess my friends' secrets. When I go to El Salao now, nobody asks me to predict the future harvests of the few fields still in cultivation.

I tell you, Lisania, the visions began when I asked Saint Martha to appear at my altar and help me find the path Altagracia had taken.

"Come, Saint Martha, come to me, though I may be unworthy of you. With your permission, I'll come to know Altagracia's story. Tell me why I have this gift and if I'm really connected to her," I prayed to the saint, and with much effort I wrote down what I saw and felt at my altar, on which a vision of a Madrid neighborhood had begun to appear.

Just like in picture postcards, I see the gardens in Aravaca, with its traffic-clogged streets and big clay-colored houses. It's almost as if the homeowners are afraid of bright colors and can barely tolerate the green of the trees. A few pedestrians move like robots on the sidewalks. They look at the ground, afraid of making eye contact.

Altagracia walks among them like a stranger. She doesn't seem to recognize anything. I'm moved by the sadness that follows her as she makes her way to the park in Aravaca. She sits down on a bench to relive her nostalgia. It's cold here in Madrid.

In El Salao, the sun gets into people, into the dirt, into things. Sucks the moisture out. Leaves them dry. The town is full of absences, of the names of people who are no longer here, of myths of spirits and saintly women who, in the "countries beyond," became whores capable of waking the dead.

In the park in Aravaca, where Caribbean islanders stunned by European solitude sometimes create the illusion of a little island, Altagracia is alone, surrounded by Spaniards who pretend not to see her. The islanders—including those from this particular island, where they came for refuge from sad encounters and parties—have had to emigrate.

She entertains herself with the memory of her first visit to this park, and she moves her waist to the rhythm of a merengue that's playing only in her mind. She hears voices in her head, noises. A bottle of hair relaxer to straighten out unruly curls falls on the ground in the middle of the park, which in memory becomes a beauty salon and a family room for those first immigrants, these dazed, lost Caribbean islanders.

I dig deeper into Altagracia's soul, and I realize that she came to this park because it's the only corner of the city that feels a little bit hers, even though it's already been taken away from her. "We have to establish order," said the police officers who threw out the Dominican women who had worked as maids in the houses of the rich back in the eighties. The neighbors hated seeing them and were pleased when the mulattas had to move their fat asses from the elegant benches.

At nine in the morning, sitting in the park with her eyes wide open, she traverses time and the Atlantic.

I look at her shivering. She flies to a lost village in the Caribbean. There's no sea in this panorama of wood and zinc houses thrown about every which way and surrounded by dry bushes on the north side. To the south, there's a lonely and blistering highway that seems to come from the other end of the island.

In Madrid, she has wrinkles, the loose skin of a woman more than fifty years old, with drooping lids and a strange yellowish color. She's the most bundled up of the women.

In her village, she's just turned twenty-five, and she's happy. She's wearing very light clothes that cover her skin, show off her curves, and end midway down her small copper thighs. She smiles at Horacio, her husband.

It seems as if the sun wants to burn down her small home, even though it's evening. Eagerly they wait for night, Altagracia's hips swaying as she goes about making dinner, caring for her son and looking slyly at her husband—tall, strong, charming, and, in her lovestruck eyes, so unique. He always wants to caress her, to say sweet nothings, in this village where other women receive only rudeness.

From my altar, as Saint Michael demonstrates his power and Saint Martha uses my body to dance to the drumbeats, I look up at the couple.

Horacio doesn't want to miss a single movement of her hips. He sneaks into the kitchen just so he can smell that sweet flowery scent of Lady-by-Day-Whore-by-Night that comes off her moist skin.

Night finally arrives. The terrible sun is gone now. There's darkness and sex, not like in those tasteless scenes offered by Mexican soap operas, but rather like those imagined, between heat and shame, by the devout village women who have no men.

Love is still fresh tonight. It's hard to drown its sound in a world of zinc and wood, surrounded by other less happy universes. Altagracia slides down his body, zigzags between his legs, lets her face graze Horacio's glossy black, boxy belly. Every now and then she lets him set the pace so he won't get alarmed. She wants Horacio to feel that even here, where she's goddess, he has control too. When the screams are over, her small face rests on Horacio's square features, so like those of other men. In contrast, she is so different that not even the dust manages to steal the shine from her indecipherable skin, black and gold at the same time.

Morning brings back reality. Pascual, the neighbor, knocks on the door. He throws himself on a rattan chair. Without meaning to, he rattles the pieces of aluminum between the boards on the wall. The idyll is shattered.

"Don E'teban won't plant no mo'," Pascual says, looking down at the tiled floor on which Horacio spent six months' worth of savings, all the while resisting the impulse to go out and have a beer.

"What the hell, Pascual!"

Altagracia serves them coffee. "If I go to Spain, we won't have to put up with this shit," she thinks as the cups spill over.

"Woman, what's wrong with you?" Pascual asks, shooting her a disapproving look before turning his gaze back to the floor fashioned from Horacio's abstinence.

"I'm going to light a candle to Saint Martha so she'll give us a hand," she says.

"Bye, sweet black girl," Horacio says and caresses her neck.

Pascual follows him, still looking at the floor.

The two men go for a stroll in the neighborhood and buy some rum with Horacio's last hundred pesos. He doesn't come home until dawn.

With him comes their first argument, and the first physical blow to the woman who, just five minutes before in a very distant past, was the happiest in the village. A blow because he fears that that golden skin might no longer be his because he has nothing to offer, because he believes a woman so pretty will run off with the first man who can get her out of this shit, dammit. A jealous blow, because he's already jealous of the man who, according to his fears, will no doubt come.

Altagracia cries in the park in Aravaca. Her body's so feverish that I start to sweat, and I have to turn on the A/C in the living room. A very slight, barely perceptible headache reminds her she's alive in two different worlds.

In her lost village, the world is the goat pen, the repair of her house's wallboards, and the celebrations that she—Saint Martha's daughter—organizes with the santeras.

Saint Martha the Dominant One takes over her body and screams with pleasure, drunk from too much liquor, and dances divinely, dances where joy is not forbidden to decent women.

Later, the Daughter of The Mysteries makes do by counting the pesos Horacio brings home. The pesos from jobs he gets now and then in Tamayo, the big town, where he's a cabinetmaker, farmer, handyman, and a nobody. He's the only man in his family who didn't move to the capital to work in construction or buy a motorcycle so he could make a living from cycle-taxi fares.

Twenty minutes have passed in the park in Aravaca. Altagracia's headache is getting worse. Her temperature's rising, and her chest hurts.

Five years have passed deep in the Caribbean, where, in order to drink water, you have to lean over a well, and the sea is something far away that can only be seen in photos of blond tourists. Two of her neighbors with little experience of the world have followed in the footsteps of the women of Tamayo, which they see as a city, with its paved roads and many colored houses.

During market days in Tamayo, they hear that some of the townswomen have gone to Spain to mop floors, or sell their bodies, no one really knows. Thanks to the money they send, some families are building two-story homes.

The wind is so cold in Madrid. Two kids run by Altagracia, who doesn't even notice them. Her chest hurts. A very sad memory comes to her in that instant.

Breaking with the traditions of six generations of women, she reaches her limit and takes the initiative. She reaches out for her husband's body. As she prepares for love, it's pouring outside, an oddity in a place where there's always drought. But by the time the sheets are changed, the floor is dried, and the boy is calmed down, Horacio's passion has passed.

The next day, after news that the plantain fields are flooded and the tobacco is lost, Horacio comes home without hope of getting work anytime soon. No one will hire him to do anything. Evening comes, and the idea's stuck in his head.

"I'm going to Spain to work," says Altagracia, nervously reaching for her husband's hands.

"In Spain you'll be nothing but a damned slut!" screams Horacio.

"I'm a slut only with you, Horacio," she says, trying to avoid his blow.

Then there's silence.

Tired of my drumming ceremony, Saint Martha tells me everything. The journey's inevitable. At thirty, Altagracia is, as I am now, at an age where you have to take a definite stand or surrender. She'd already seen five different relatives from neighboring towns take off for Spain. They left when their fathers or husbands announced they weren't capable of supporting their families anymore. These declarations weren't made with words, but with screams, with rum, with rage. It saddens me.

Saint Martha doesn't want me to get consumed by a melancholy that is Altagracia's. I don't listen to the drumming anymore. A fast, powerful music overtakes me, intoxicates me, and makes me laugh aloud as I enter the lives of Horacio and Altagracia again.

She plans her trip. In Tamayo, they take her to Don Bartolo, who "fixes her papers" in exchange for the deed to her mother's house. He gives her a new identity, makes her a native of the capital, and rich.

In Madrid, the world has a different rhythm. It's been twenty years since the last time she saw Horacio's and her son's faces. Now she sits in the park with a plane ticket in her hands. The rich Spaniards out walking their dogs look at her strangely. She remembers many faces and the last celebration with the santeras. Saint Martha's horse screamed from pleasure, as always. The dancing, the drumming. Her skin, moist with sweat, gives off that Lady-by-Day-Whore-by-Night scent, warm like steam when it reached the neighbor women who were envious of her screams. "Horacio! Horaciooo!"

In the park in Aravaca, with a pain in her chest that's now almost unbearable, she stares at what's real right in front of her—her rugged hands, an apron she keeps in her purse, and a black-and-white photo of a smiling, young Horacio.

"Goddammit, I only enjoyed it with you, Horacio!" she says to the memory of a man who hardly ever thinks about her, busy in his world of women, poverty, children, liquor.

I can see Horacio's face, his gaze like a yellowing guasabara plant, sick of living, without even the strength to play that game of sticking us with thorns. His skin, like cinnamon before, is now ashen. He's ravaged by rum but safe in Altagracia's memory, longing for life in the eyes of his snake, in her dancing, her joy flooding El Salao.

He sees no joy in the pious woman he coupled with to make a family after Altagracia left, an obedient woman who will never go to Spain nor so much as cross the street without his permission.

Altagracia, his wife, is far away. She won't come back to the village or to the big town or even to her country's capital, that Santo Domingo she barely knows. Her papers are finally in order, and she won't come back.

Her heart can't take the memories. It stops beating in that park in Aravaca. Here, here in Madrid. In her hands, the photos of Horacio and of a young man—her son, a stranger to whom she has dedicated her life from a distance, her salary, and almost all her tears. There's a postcard of Saint Martha in her purse. It's eleven o'clock in the morning.

When Altagracia left my living room, with her Madrid and her El Salao, I fell to the floor. I thought I would die from the pain in my thorax. But The Mysteries had another surprise for me.

The spirits of Altagracia and my mother sat on the loveseat in my living room. Mami was wearing a red robe, and Altagracia had a skirt that went midway down her thigh, like she used to wear when she lived in El Salao according to some seers to whom I described the vision.

"Hey, my educated little witch, how's it going?"

"Mami!" I said as I sat at her feet like a child.

"You're messing with The Mysteries again, you and your shit. Your grandma says to stop it, that you have to leave that disbelieving shit alone."

"Who's with you, Mami? She smells like flowers."

"Altagracia's with me. Listen, my educated little witch, when The Mysteries decide they want to, they'll tell you everything you need to know. We'll send you a message with someone."

"Mami, stay. I'll get you some ginger tea."

"Goodbye, my educated little witch."

"No, no, I'm not educated, I believe in The Mysteries more than the university. I believe, I really believe."

It took me hours to understand, as much as The Mysteries can be understood.

I know from my research that the day after Altagracia died in December 1999, the Spanish newspapers said that a Dominican prostitute had died of a heart attack in the park in Aravaca. But that version was called into question by some of her compatriots.

Her body was sent to El Salao. Two sisters, whom she'd helped to emigrate, didn't want to leave her in Madrid. They accompanied the coffin and gave her an old-style funeral.

Her relatives—even those who'd never met her—cried until they went hoarse, mourning in the main room of a half-constructed house, property of the deceased. Their minds were dulled by the monotonous chants of a group of professional mourners in the living room who prayed for the "soooooul of the deeeeeceased." Everyone said Altagracia's body smelled like flowers.

The men played cards in the yard, but they were dressed up and respectful, and they drank Brugal rum.

Months later, the families in the village began to give form to the legend of Altagracia the whore, the most muscular cunt in all of Madrid, Saint Martha's horse, the patron saint of women who want to go to Europe.

Her tomb in El Salao's cemetery is always covered with flowers and copies of visas authorized because of her intercession.

But this is not something I'm going to talk about now. Girl, you're nineteen years old and already wise. You don't know it, but your aunt Juanita, who is also clairvoyant, sent you to live here not just because the university is nearby and I can drop you off in my car every day.

She asked me to let you live in my house because, while I was having visions, she could see everything on her altar. And The Mysteries told her you had to complete the mission that I couldn't finish because of my history of doubting, or for whatever reason; you can tell me later so I'll understand. By the time you get here, you'll probably already know everything I'm telling you.

In any case, I'm doing my duty. Auntie said I had to talk to you about the visions. It's incredible that, though you didn't even live your first six months in El Salao because you had to go be with your evangelical parents in San Francisco, you've taken to the old wisdom with such shameless passion, as you have to the science which intrigues us both.

It's my duty to teach you, and when you learn, dear girl, Altagracia will communicate with many more women through you.

Like her, like me, you are also a favorite daughter of Saint Martha's. I will introduce you to the 21 Divisions.

I'm so moved by this mission, Lisania, that I'm writing this all down for you, because if I tried to tell you, I'd be crying too much to make any sense. I'm waiting anxiously for you to come through my door. I know that you can heal women of their most serious ills with a mere touch, that you're very powerful, and it frightens me to try to teach a younger visionary.

That's why I pray to Altagracia before a photograph of her I got in El Salao, and to Saint Martha, our mother, that they show us the way so you, Lisania, can complete the mission that the holy woman will reveal to you when you're ready.

I don't know how, but I know it's up to you to light the way for the daughters of Saint Martha who take to the road in our sister Altagracia's footsteps.

THE ROUTE

FICTION BY LUDIN SANTANA

Translated by Achy Obejas

I arrived at the Route 37 bus stop overheated from having come so many blocks. I was sweaty, but I still smelled a bit like almonds, which I like so much and use every day in all my soaps and creams. I quickly got a seat in the front of the bus so I could be comfortable and saw my haggard face in the rearview mirror. My green eyes, which usually shone, were opaque and had bags under them. My hair was uncombed, and my roots were starting to show. I felt ugly, my body uncared for and tired. I figured dancing until all hours the night before with my sister was the reason for my sorry state. I'd escaped from my husband for the first time, supposedly to try to get rid of all the stress built up over the last few days—I had a bunch of crazy ideas going around in my head that I couldn't quite pin down and carry out—but I think I'd gone dancing more to assure myself that I was still alive, youthful, and energetic.

I felt strange. I didn't recognize myself, and all the movements, the smiles, and the comments around those six hundred square meters with a dirt floor and huge trees didn't seem important to me. The sun's rays cut through the branches of a mango tree, warming my face, but I wanted them to warm my soul.

In the distance, drivers sat under a thatched canopy on empty beer crates around a billiards table, enjoying the morning's warm little breeze. I thought that, rather than friends, they were like a family that had built a lucrative and fun paradise in that corner of the capital. I knew them all very well. They weren't restless union guys who joined protests or political parties. They were, instead, living a kind of very open brotherhood, sharing their dreams of progress and prosperity.

When I looked at my watch, I realized it was getting late and the bus wasn't starting. There was no schedule to determine when each bus would leave. It could be every three or every thirty minutes. The signal that we were about to take off had always been when the driver said, "Squeeze tight like you did last night," as we filled up with five passengers on the backseat, four in the middle row, three up front, and a few others on the improvised wooden bench behind the driver. On the verge of desperation, a woman leaned her face out the window of that crazy minibus, a tinplate souvenir held together with colorful nylon strings, with open-air windows and an advertisement on the back window for a store that sold Japanese spare parts. "Man, we're full. Let's go!" she yelled.

Tabo immediately climbed aboard and started up the motor that gave meaning to his life and took others to where they needed to go to keep their own lives going.

I greeted him with restraint so he'd understand I wasn't interested in talking. He turned to me with an effusive smile. I'd never noticed how his dark and worn face showcased his perfect white teeth. It'd been days since I'd last seen him, and I noticed he'd lost weight. I learned later that he was playing a lot of softball. You could see the muscles on his arms.

I remained silent, wondering where my life was going now that the word "change" had knocked on my door. I wanted to welcome it in. I loathed my husband more than ever, or as much as ever, but I also pitied him in a stupid way that made it impossible to leave him. I was sure no one would take on an old drunk who ate on the bed and left his plate right there full of chewed-up chicken bones. I was the willing prisoner of a hairy-bellied man who didn't make me happy and hadn't been able to give me the child I wanted, an abuser who'd clipped my wings when I was fourteen years old and to whom, according to everyone, I owed "everything" and to whom, I was sure, I owed "nothing."

I glanced in the rearview mirror, careful not to draw attention, and dried a tear that had gotten away from me and would give away my anguish. In that small piece of glass I saw the reflection of the sad and luckless woman I'd become, alone in spite of the fact that I shared a home. I asked myself what had brought me to this point. Was it just the failed relationship with Joaquín? Or that I had no children? Or my frustrated desire to leave the country? I searched my surroundings for blame, but I was the only one responsible for my plight.

Just then I remembered an afternoon when I'd asked Joaquín to go for a stroll with me on the Malecón and then take me to a motel. He told me we were too old for that, to not be ridiculous. He also told me I'd gotten fat and that he wasn't attracted to me like before, and that that was why he hadn't gotten me pregnant. That evening, he left me dressed up and upset. He went off with his friends into the night and came back a mess, drunk as a skunk, throwing up all over the house.

Between the unfortunate memories that assaulted my mind and the landscape I saw repeated every day, the trip home went as usual. The radio loudly played merengues from the eighties while a few passengers closed their eyes as if they were being transported back in time. A woman with a loud and shrill voice preached the Word of God. Two big shots, one in the front and the other in the back, talked about last night's ball game. In all that din, only two people seemed incapable of distraction—a woman wearing a hairnet and reading a romance novel, and me, immersed in my inner turmoil.

I was so caught up that I almost missed my stop. On Gustavo and Churchill, I tapped Tabo and whispered, "On the corner." I got off with a great desire to just not go to the beauty shop where I worked. I didn't know where I wanted to go, but it wasn't to my job or my home.

Maybe it would have been better to keep going on the bus, to use it as therapy. When I lived with my parents and Papaíto had problems at work, he'd buy a big batch of pigeon peas and sit in the back of the yard, shelling them. According to him, that was therapy. Maybe mine was to take a ride in a miserable little bus, rounding streets and skirting corners in a congested and dusty city that still managed beautiful sunrises. I would have preferred to have stayed on at least until we got to José Contreras and Churchill, my favorite stop on the route because from up there you can see the Malecón with its radiant Caribbean waters and the obelisk that completes the picture.

I spent the whole day in a bad mood. Even the most minor thing that my colleagues or my boss said bothered me. I grumbled at everyone. Thank God they were all older than me and probably understood me better than I could imagine.

I didn't talk to any of them about my doubts, nor did I share them with my clients, whose fingers I accidentally snipped while doing their nails.

For the first time in a long time, I didn't stop myself from dreaming. That day, I fantasized about a life in New York, in that big city full of colored lights from which my friends came back wearing necklaces, with Jeeps, deported or dead in a coffin. Something told me, "Cindy, you could be one of the winners." I had a profession that paid well in wealthy countries, and I could also count on a sister-in-law and my friends to help me.

I got so sick and tired of thinking so much about what to do that when I left work I decided to stop by the house and discreetly pick up my things and go back to the childhood home that, according to my mother, I'd left prematurely and where I would be welcomed back with open arms.

I thought about calling a taxi, but they take too long, and I needed to act quickly so I wouldn't chicken out. I hired three motoconchos instead—also taxis, but two-wheelers with limited space. I loaded my bags on the front, on top of the fuel tank, and then a few boxes and other things in the back, on the rack. We worked quickly. As we left, I felt the wind in my face, and it forced me to close my eyes and at the same time renewed my spirit.

From the moment I arrived, I felt protected and loved like I hadn't in a long time. The house was the same as I'd left it more than ten years earlier. It smelled of newly cooked cornmeal, just like before. I was enveloped by the scent of vanilla and cinnamon in every corner. The walls were the same pastel colors, painted over so many times that you could peel the layers. The bed-sheets were the same too, with little multicolored flowers now faded from so many washes.

I immediately became a part of the family dynamic, helping out here and there, and I felt happy. I'd never imagined I could make that transition, which I was sure others saw as a step back. My mom was happiest, because she'd never wanted me to carry the same burden on my shoulders that she'd had to in order to keep her thirty-year marriage going. And my sister was happy because now she had a confidante to talk to until dawn and to go dancing with her on the weekends. Papaíto didn't state his opinion, but that's how he was, a man of few words. That didn't mean he disagreed.

I tried to be discreet in my escape—no one ever sees a thing if a crime or a burglary is being committed, but if a man's cheating on his wife or a woman flees her husband, then everybody's a witness and knows what she took and what she left behind. One of the motoconchistas, a friend of mine, called me from my old place to let me know that the whole neighborhood was anxiously waiting for the man I'd abandoned. They wanted to tell him their own versions of the story. Some were hanging out near the door of the bar embellishing the story, and a few others were over by the lottery vendor betting on someone else's bad luck.

He told me they didn't even let Joaquín get to the house. As he drove up with the car windows open, they started yelling stuff at him. "Your wife left you," "Looks like she took everything," "Be cool, cuz she'll be back," "That woman's a thief, like we always told you," "It's okay if you kill her, just see if she left you anything first." Everyone talked at the same time, and I could make out a few voices on the cell phone—young and old, men and women, with good and bad intentions, those who'd been real witnesses and those who hadn't seen anything. It seemed no one wanted to be without an opinion, even if they drove the poor man crazy. Whatever his faults, he wasn't a violent person, and maybe because he was twice my age in the back of his mind he had almost expected this to happen.

They told me that, devastated, he closed himself up in what had until recently been our four walls. Knowing him, I understood that he was trying to find a way to get me back in that old four-poster bed, damp and camphorous, where I'd given him what so many believed was so valuable and what to me was so meaningless—what, after all, can skin represent without emotion?

I suppose Joaquín knew that economics influence emotions in young people like me. I knew that in that hard head of his, he would try to come up with a fantastic idea, something that had never crossed his mind before. But great ideas would never come to him, such an average, common guy, so conventional and mediocre. He was so predictable that I was sure I could see him drinking many cups of coffee, wide awake, pacing around the house, waiting for dawn, which always seems an eternity when you're awake because love has gone bad.

Joaquín arrived early where he knew he'd find me. I'd just woken up from a recuperative sleep. I left the room I shared with my sister, took a shower, and got dressed. As soon as I heard his familiar voice, I started muttering between my teeth. Once we were face to face, he tried to touch my hair.

"Don't touch me. Don't you understand I don't want you near me?"

"Don't be that way. Don't get surly with your husband. Let's talk."

"Yes, daughter of mine, listen to him," Papaíto said from the kitchen.

"Woman, listen to me. I'm willing to take you back home. Everything I've given you, I'll continue to give. Let's go," said Joaquín, as if Papaíto's comment had given him strength.

Hearing such stupidity, I flung the just-brewed cup of coffee in my hand to the floor. Then I expressed myself in a way I'd hoped to never have to do.

"Everything you gave me, I left behind, even your air conditioner. I don't love you, and that's why I can't stay with you. What I want is a child and to go to New York, and you can't give me that, so go, find your own way, because I'm going to find mine."

Everyone looked at me as if I was a spoiled child, and deep down I was sad. Then I hurried away, leaving them with their mouths hanging open, because the stop for Route 37 was even further away from me there.

That morning was like every other, with the same heat and the bustle at the stop, and the same chatty morning murmurings on the bus. In the back, the radio played the same merengues I've been hearing since I was born. By chance I got to ride with Tabo, right next to him in the driver's cabin, and I felt for the first time how he stared right at me, trying to figure out what I was thinking. I caught him looking at my thighs, which were snugly sheathed in a pair of jeans a former neighbor had sent me from New York. Later I saw him glance at my bosom, but I didn't blame him. I was wearing the kind of low-cut neckline that could stop traffic. That day, the rearview mirror didn't reflect back my troubles but rather my curly hair and my sly smile.

I felt like quite the babe. I don't know if it was because of the change in my life or because I'd bathed from head to toe with three bucketfuls of water and put on my favorite clothes. Maybe both.

In spite of the obvious attraction, Tabo didn't say anything. How could he? He'd been a friend of Joaquín's since before he started driving on Route 37, when they were motoconchistas together on February 27th Avenue, without tunnels or overpasses, when dawn would get lost in the car smoke.

Twenty-four hours earlier I'd felt like an old shoe the whole way, and today we hadn't even gotten to the rotunda at Los Próceres and I felt like the sexiest and most beautiful woman in all of Peratúen and the surrounding neighborhoods. I'd taken the first step to an uncertain but different future.

I got off at the same place as always. I didn't even need to ask him to stop. I felt how Tabo was looking at me. Those daring scenes repeated themselves every day. Provocative looks and gestures were standard from Tabo, who drove the Peratúen-Fería route an infinite number of times crazed by my almond perfume.

One morning like any other—except not as hot—I got to the bus stop a little earlier than usual. It wasn't Tabo's shift. He was hanging out under the canopy, and I, feeling fresh and clean, sat by his side. I could have left on another bus, but I wanted to talk to him. It was the perfect moment to bring him up to date with what was going on in my life, which he'd probably been imagining for a few weeks anyway, but which he needed to hear from my own lips.

When we got on the bus, we started on the route right away, and for the first time Tabo felt free to put a hand on my thigh while he changed gears. From that day on, he never charged me a fare again, and he dedicated himself to flirting with me, while I flirted back with my eyes and my killer smile.

Poor Joaquín got nowhere bringing me food at work, coming to get me in the afternoons, and sending me flowers. I'd discovered the pleasure found by those women who leave what little they have and realize everything they need is in themselves.

I felt more beautiful than when I'd turned fifteen. I went dancing almost every night at the Car Wash and nearby discotheques. My sister and I had become partying comrades in arms. We lent each other clothes and always tried to wear something new.

I was no longer that scruffy girl who worked in the beauty shop and then went home to be the servant of a drunkard.

On Sunday afternoons I didn't hang out with my sister, so I could go out with Tabo. We went all over the city in his little jalopy, going slowly down Churchill to José Contreras to enjoy my favorite view. When it started to get dark, we'd take refuge in the cabins at Manoguayabo, where we'd exchange caresses even though we didn't have a steady relationship. My sister and the clients who were close to me urged me to see that he was worthwhile and to take him seriously, but I was afraid to, and I'd hedge, saying I'd decided to change my life and for that reason I wanted to avoid commitments. The neighbors talked about the supposed relationship, but I tried to hide it—until one day Joaquín came to call for me at the door of my job and I let fly.

"It's none of your business what I do with my life. What part of 'leave me alone' do you not understand? I can go off with whomever I want. Let's see if I can get the baby that you couldn't give me in ten years together. Stop these spectacles and threats. You know very well that you couldn't kill a fly and that I'm quite capable of destroying you."

I thought he'd die of shame. He didn't know what to do with himself. All that silence and everyone looking at him left him disconcerted. Since I knew him well, I was sure my words had hurt him deeply. In spite of his vices and infertility—the second perhaps a result of the first—he didn't deserve such cruelty on my part.

Talking on the phone one day with Joaquín's sister who lived in New York, I confirmed how very much I'd hurt my ex-husband, that he considered me an ingrate and a real bitch for getting involved with someone from his circle of friends, someone that he'd even helped when he was starting out.

Just before Christmas, my ex-sister-in-law came back home. Many people considered her a go-between or matchmaker for pay. She'd organized a number of marriages, all for business purposes, and she offered to introduce me to an Asian widower who worked with her at a Chinese restaurant in New York. According to her, he was looking for a good woman to marry, and he liked Dominican women because we're fiery and hardworking. I couldn't believe I could be so lucky and decided not to let that opportunity pass me by. I accepted and agreed to get in touch with the man. I didn't care if he was twice my age and had five kids. If I'd made sacrifices for so many years for a relationship that brought me nothing, what could it possibly cost me to sacrifice for one that would fly me to the city of my dreams? I jumped for joy, and we toasted with beer. I told everyone I came across I was going to New York. It would now be me who'd be sending huge packages of gifts back home.

Bit by bit, I got involved in the phone chats with the Chinese man who'd be the key to my leaving. The conversations sounded ridiculous because of my broken English, but in less than three months what had seemed a joke turned serious. The man wanted to meet me and planned to come for a visit to the island, which, from what he said, he imagined having beautiful beaches and spectacular mountains like he'd seen in the tourist documentaries. I couldn't help but think, "Poor guy, he has no idea what kind of place awaits him."

From the beginning, Tabo knew about the mess I'd gotten myself involved in from ulterior motives. He took it in stride because he was a smart man who understood my real feelings, which were quite intense, though I tried to hide them. One rainy weekend afternoon, while he played pool with other drivers at the Route 37 bus stop, I came up behind him, smiled, and embraced him from the back.

"What are you going to do when I get married?" I said in his ear.

He burst out laughing.

"I've never said we're going to get married," he said.

"I never said we're going to get married either," I said back, but in a stronger and more sardonic tone than his, and in front of his friends.

Suddenly there was the kind of silence that descends on cemeteries after six o'clock. The players finished the game and fled, leaving us alone, speechless and dying of shame. I could see in Tabo's eyes how bad he felt about the stupid way I'd chosen to give him the news. In the world we lived, a decision like mine was understandable and logical. Who would have turned down such an opportunity? The papers I was about to get were considered as valuable as a university degree in our neighborhood.

In a short time there was a wedding with toasts and cake, and even a honeymoon in a hotel in the Colonial Zone where I'd never before even imagined setting foot. There were also tears, not so much from emotion but from fear. We women dream of marrying the man we love, and when we can't accomplish it, we become even more attached to that love.

Not even a week after my new husband, the Chinese man, had gone back to New York, I went with Tabo to the cabins in "Alasca." That was a funny name we gave to our love nest. That afternoon it rained very hard, just like I like, and we made love several times. I never had to say how disgusted I was by my legal husband because it was obvious from my eyes. I took the opportunity to apologize to Tabo and confess my real feelings as he very slowly caressed my breasts and listened to me in absolute silence.

"I want to tell you how sorry I am about the stupid way I handled the marriage thing. You know it's strictly for business purposes and that I'm not the first in the neighborhood to do something like this. I've never told you before, but I love you. I love how you love me, and I don't want to lose you. You know what? As soon as I get to New York, I'm going to dump that shitty Chinaman, and I'm going to have you come up and see the snow and the Statue of Liberty and those really tall buildings with giant electronic screens that you see in the movies."

With his eyes filled with tears, Tabo hugged me and kissed my forehead. I felt that he'd forgiven me, especially since what I was doing was normal in our world. I thought that, more than once, he wanted to tell me he loved me, but the same forces from our world kept him from doing so.

After that afternoon, we made our relationship official. Everyone knew about it and respected it. We didn't need to hide in dreary little motels anymore, and now Tabo came to see me in an apartment the Chinese man had rented for me. That poor Asian man, trying to be a responsible husband, was making efforts to control me long distance, but nothing could stop me. I was a willful and indomitable woman.

There, in that new little home, is where the nausea, dizziness, and vomiting that made me so happy began. The worse I felt physically, the better I felt inside, because those symptoms meant the realization of one of my greatest dreams, motherhood. From the minute I heard the news, I couldn't stop smiling. I ate sweets like mad and touched my belly day and night. From the beginning, I felt like the luckiest woman on earth, because my mother always said, "You're never a complete woman until you give birth."

But the joy wasn't exclusively mine. Tabo, my parents, my sister, my colleagues and clients at work were also happy. And that emotion even reached New York, where the Chinese man, in spite of having adult children, was enthused about the idea of having a child with a bit of Caribbean spice. Every two weeks he'd send me a blue 55-gallon drum filled with toys, disposable diapers, furniture that had to be assembled, food, and maternity clothes. The entire neighborhood lived for the arrival of the truck that brought the drum.

No one ever questioned or doubted that the Asian man was the child's father. Not even Tabo said anything about it. Who better than me, master of my own body, to determine who was responsible for my pregnancy? The months went by quickly, just as I wanted the years to pass before I could get my United States residency. I had a room in the house decorated in blue, with the little bears that were fashionable at the time glued to the wall. Everything was ready—a cradle, crib, playpen, and stroller, all directly from Niu Yor Ciri.

One afternoon we were at the stop for Route 37. The thatched canopy above us and the surrounding ground were covered by innumerable orangish-red flowers from the poinciana. The mango tree was bearing, filled from top to bottom with succulent fruit. I was sitting on a plastic chair, bathed in sweat and with my swollen feet on top of a pair of empty boxes, trying to keep cool and talking to Tabo. Suddenly I felt some strange contractions. I couldn't finish my beer. A shiver ran down my entire body. I got goose bumps, and an indescribable fear made me unable to think straight.

"Oh, Tabo, I think I'm giving birth," I told him.

He laid me down in the back of the bus and started immediately for the clinic. The traffic was heavy because of repairs they were making on the public roads, and I couldn't stop screaming.

"Oh, Tabo, I'm going to die! I can't take any more. I'm going to give birth!" I screamed repeatedly, each time louder. "I don't want to lose this child. Faster!"

When we arrived at the clinic, I was attended by the resident gynecologist. He had on a white coat that seemed more appropriate to a butcher or watchmaker than a medical doctor. He had such a stupid face, I could barely look at him. I was told to wait for my doctor, who was at the corner, but inside I thought, "What corner?" That's when I put my fate in the hands of the guy with the stupid face and whoever chose to help with my presumable pre-eclampsia. I was dying to see my child, and I wasn't willing to wait an extra minute.

I won't deny that fear was eating at me. For a moment, I forgot all about my obsession to be a free and independent woman, and I felt totally tied to the treasure in my belly. More than anything, I wanted to live to offer the fruit of my loins a more dignified future. I wanted to go to New York to earn my own greenbacks to share.

The boy was born healthy, weighing eight and a quarter pounds. From the moment I saw him, I knew he had cheeks exactly like his grandfather and green eyes like his mother. I didn't look for any other parental traits. He was a beautiful and strong boy.

I let them take him to clean him up while I slept for a bit. I'd experienced total satisfaction even in the midst of difficulties. I had a man to love and a child who gave me a new reason to live and who'd motivate me to put up with the occasional visits from my husband, who smelled of soy and boiled cabbage but who guaranteed a better tomorrow for all of us.

I didn't care about the past. The journey had barely begun for me. I had plans, even if failure was a possibility. I had courage enough to fight for the papers that would get me abroad or to take a boat in a worst-case scenario, the guts to put bread in my baby's mouth and to wait for someone else to pay for the DNA test, and the nerve to leave a man when I no longer needed him. I'd experienced a rebirth of my dreams, had taken control of my life, and was on the road I wanted to be on, without regard to whether I would arrive or get lost on the way.

FOR A MANGO

FICTION BY MIRIAM MEJÍA

Translated by Achy Obejas

As I do every afternoon, I left work and walked the length of Saint Nicholas Avenue (now called Juan Pablo Duarte) located in a crowded Dominican neighborhood in upper Manhattan. It was the end of spring, and the sidewalks were filled with vendors offering fresh vegetables and a wide variety of fruits. Vegetables from California and Mexico, oregano from the Dominican Republic, pretty bananas from Costa Rica, mangos from the Far East and the nearby Caribbean, avocados from Colombia, plantains. A special on bunches of plantains.

I stopped in front of a supermarket just as a stock boy emptied a box of plantains onto an already big pile. A group of men and women waited for the new ones. Before the stock boy could finish, they began to pick out what they each wanted. I joined them. We leaned into the pile, reaching for those farther away that seemed to have the characteristics we were looking for. Big, green, fresh. Now and again, more than one hand would reach for the same plantain. It was a ten-for-a-dollar special, so everyone wanted to take advantage of the deal.

I put fifteen in a clear plastic bag and continued my stroll past vegetables and aromatic plants. I was waiting to go pick up my kids from their after-school program. I neared the tropical fruits, and there they were. There, tucked into boxes aligned side by side, were my favorite mangos. I approached them skeptically. I'd looked for them in vain for years. I took one in my hands. It was the same shape; it had the same color. And, above all, it had the same

183

smell. Now I had no doubt whatsoever—it was a Columbus mango, the kind that used to grow in Doña Eufemia's yard. That familiar tang almost made me drool.

As I picked out the ones I wanted, I remembered Old Femia. Alone. Enigmatic. Mistrustful, but with a huge heart. I can still remember the day that tall, skinny, ungainly woman showed up in my tiny childhood village. It was an ashy and dusty place where nothing out of the ordinary ever happened, before or after her. I remember how the elderly woman's appearance was a huge thing to most of the residents of Aguas Frescas, that dry arid region so full of cactus and guasabara. If her arrival was enough reason for adults to get out of their daily routines, it was like a magic spell for those of us still caught in the enchantment of childhood. Maybe these memories come to me framed by that marvelous fantasy we're all prisoners of when we're children.

Doña Eufemia arrived in the clear light of a radiant morning, following the path of a spring Sunday. Her very tall figure was followed by her long, lazy shadow, which looked as if it were playing hide-and-seek with the sun. Her luggage was a faded red tinplate suitcase. As she walked, all her attention was fixed on her left hand, which was wrapped around the most beautiful mango we could ever have imagined. The inviting smell soon penetrated the dry air and became part of our very breathing. From that moment, a line of children followed the strange woman's path, the procession becoming our amusing game.

Almost without thinking about it, we decided to compete for that delicious fruit. The winner would be whoever stepped on the head of her long shadow's silhouette that dragged lazily on the ground without leaving a trace. But the shadow zigzagged and evaded us. It folded into other shadows or leapt unexpectedly over our small herd. Sadly, no one seemed capable of winning the contest. It was at the precise moment when our competitive spirit had reached desperation that we noticed the shadow wasn't moving. As if hurled by a spring, we all fell on top of where the shadow stopped, not realizing it rested precisely on a puddle of water where we piled up. By the time the last of us got up, drenched in mud, the woman had already gone inside the empty yard of that abandoned house, the only place we actually respected because, according to what we'd heard, it was haunted by ghosts.

Disappointed, my playmates took off one by one. I was left alone. It was as if I were riveted to the front of that huge house. Then I saw the old woman in the backyard. She signaled for me to come in. I obeyed like an automaton, entering that feared and ghostly place. The mango was still in her hand. She asked me something, but I didn't understand. She came toward me and put the mango in my hand. "Let's plant it," she said. I swallowed the flood of saliva that the smell of the mango provoked. I watched as she dug out the dry earth. When the hole was finished, she filled it with water. Then she went on to tell me the best way to plant it. "Now you can eat it." I looked at her, stunned. I leaned over to deposit the mango in the dirt. Her hand stopped me. "You have to eat it. The seed must be sowed without the pulp." I sat down and forgot about everything, savoring the most delicious mango I'd ever had. I left the seed smooth and white. The fruit's sweet stickiness covered my hands and arms to my elbows. Mango strings adorned my dress. Then, allowing the old woman's wisdom to guide me, I planted the seed.

That day, I received a well-deserved reprimand from my parents for having come home so dirty and, on top of that, late. The next day, with my parents' permission, I went back to the house that no longer frightened me. I watered the hole.

One day, I gleefully discovered that the plant had germinated. Over time, it grew tall and bore fruit. Later I went from yard to yard repeating the ritual that Old Femia had taught me. Eventually, all the houses in the neighborhood had mango trees in their yards, and that arid zone became famous for its sweet, delicious mangos.

Lost in satisfying memories, I walked quickly toward my children's school. It had gotten late, and my children would be getting desperate. I was panting when I arrived. It was already closed. I knocked. It was a while before the security guard half-opened the door. I asked for my two children. With a sour look, he said that all the children had already gone home. I asked for the school principal. "There's no one here," he responded.

Like a madwoman, I walked for blocks around the school. I searched for my children's faces among those that passed by. Along the way, I got rid of the bags of plantains and mangos that had been weighing me down. I ran home. I didn't wait for the elevator and ran up the stairs two by two. I was panting when I got to the fourth floor. Shaking, I could barely get the key in the lock. I went in. Everything was dark. I looked for them, but they weren't in their rooms.

Crying, I grabbed the phone. I needed my sisters to come over. I was dying of shame. Where were my children? God, please don't let anything happen to them. I realized there was a message on the answering machine. The red light was flashing. I called my family. They told me to try to stay calm, but I didn't know how. I cried in desperation.

I heard steps in the hallway. It was the neighbor from across the hall just getting home from work. The phone rang, and I ran to get it. My brother, who'd just found out, wanted more information. A knot in my throat kept me from speaking. "I'm coming over," he said and hung up.

I pressed the message button, and with my heart beating out of my chest I heard my beloved son's voice. "Mami, sorry that we didn't wait for you at school. We're watching a movie at our friend Charo's apartment, on the first floor. Come get us."

I sat down and took a deep breath, but an inner anger overwhelmed me. I slammed the door on the way out. I descended the stairs slowly. I normally never spank my children, but I couldn't forgive them the scare they'd given me today. There was no escaping their first spanking. I stopped in front of the door where my kids were and raised my hand to ring the bell, but I left it dangling in the air.

I turned around and went back out to the street. I needed to calm down. I went back toward where I'd left the grocery bags. Maybe I'd be lucky enough to find them. Eating a mango would do me good.

TÍA MILENA/
MILENA TÍA

NONFICTION BY CAROLINA GONZÁLEZ

"A quien Dios no le da hijos, el diablo le da sobrinos." To whom God does not give children, the devil gives nieces and nephews. I never understood that old Spanish saying. Does it mean that kids of your own are a blessing but a sibling's offspring are a curse? Does it mean that nurturing children who will never be your own is a torture for those permanently childless? Or is it that children get under your skin, that there's no escaping the bittersweet pangs of filial love?

These questions have been very much in my mind since my sister Doris asked me to accompany her to China to pick up her daughter, her first child and the first baby we've welcomed into the immediate family in quite some time. Sitting in 16A before takeoff, I watched the video on my phone over and over. It runs two and a half minutes and shows my niece playing in her pink-and-yellow bedroom. When I shot it, she'd been in the United States just two weeks, and already she radiated comfort and joy, recognizing she had arrived in a safe and loving home. Offscreen, I pulled out all the tricks my sister and I had developed to get her to laugh on camera. I sang a silly hip-pop ditty where Will.I.Am asks a curvy girl, "Baby, where'd you get your body from?" and she responds in a breathy voice, "I got it from my Mama." In the video, Milena squeals when she hears the song, her four front teeth visible within a face-splitting grin, and she collapses in mirth on the plush rug.

We found out she loved that song in the "baby hotel" in Guangzhou where Doris and I waited out the last of the adoption rituals that took Fu Xin Ning from her China origins to a New York life as Milena Xin González. Music videos kept her amused while we took care of things. We discovered she loved beats heavy on the bass—hiphop, reggaetón, and dancehall. "She's ready for the Bronx," we joked.

Every time I sang the Will.I.Am tune, I thought of how apropos it was. Her big head, her moon-shaped eyes, her bony butt were all indeed things she'd gotten from her birth mother, not from us.

I felt self-conscious watching the video again—remembering all the times distant family, friends, and acquaintances had subjected me to cute baby videos—and thought, why in the world am I obligated to react as if this is some miracle, as if no other baby in creation has ever done these things? In my defense, I wouldn't share this video with anyone. It's my own private delight. In it, Milena picks up a small book, turns the pages intently, points to pictures of baby bunnies, and squeals again. She drops that book and two others into a red plastic bucket, walks down the hall and back, bucket in tow. By takeoff, I'd played the video a dozen times over, indulging myself in the near-empty plane, marveling at this little girl who's made my sister so happy, who I already loved so deeply. The picture wiggles sometimes, teetering on pixilated breakdown. I hit "play" one more time.

In mainstream U.S. culture, aunts and uncles have no special status. The focus is on the sanctity of the nuclear family, with some indulgence granted to grandparents and their doting. I'm always shocked when Anglo friends tell me they speak to their siblings only occasionally and know little about the details of their lives. Dominican families, even ones as assimilated as ours, are tight, sometimes asphyxiatingly so. Every member of our extended families—from second cousins to comadres to "tíos" whose blood connections we need diagrams to trace—has a place in our lives. Our aunts and uncles have a prestige rating just below grandparents. They are more than surrogate parents. They are courts of appeal, guides to mysteries too embarrassing or trivial for parents to endure, refuge from parental martial law.

For me, being an aunt means I get kids without having them. It also means I get to pass on a piece of my world, the way my aunts and uncles gave me a piece of theirs.

The plane banked south, and the early morning light made reflective surfaces below light up like Christmas—yellow, red, green, sparkling blue. I could see the shadows of Manhattan skyscrapers extending over the shimmering water. If I followed the big mouth of Rockaway up toward Prospect Park, I could almost see home.

I was headed down for a few weeks to Santo Domingo, the first home I remember. I've been going to Santo Domingo more often in the past few years. Sometimes I weasel my way onto a conference program or invent an errand that cannot be taken care of by email or surrogates. That time, there was no special reason for my trip down; it was just part of a promise to myself to make the island a regular stop in my yearly travel schedule. I had bought the plane ticket before Doris and I knew when we were going to China. And as much as it hurt to separate from this new relationship, to fly away from that sweet, round face, I went.

I'm not sure how many times I've flown that same route. I'd have to count the stamps in eight passports to get the exact number. The first one, in a long-lost passport, was dated November 1966, when my tía and madrina Milena took me from the New York winter to the Dominican tropics, from my parents and siblings to my tía Hilda and tío Monché, with whom I'd live until I was eleven. My trip and my niece's almost mirror neatly. Nine-month-old Baby Caro flew with Tía Milena from New York to a new home; fourteen-month-old Baby Milena flew with Tía Caro to New York to a new home.

Of course, our circumstances were completely different. My parents both needed to work to support themselves and four kids and to buoy families back on the island. They preferred to entrust my care to siblings fifteen hundred miles away rather than to strangers next door. Fu Xin was given up by her young mother a day after she was born and had been cared for by a foster family while she awaited adoption.

Accompanying my sister to China brought up some deep emotions for me, some I expected and others I hadn't considered. In my mind, my job on the China trip was to be calm, to offer my clear-eyed focus, to monitor what I imagined would be an intense emotional roller coaster for my sister. I think I managed that, though I'll admit the process—minus one crucial missed flight the day before we met Fu Xin—was, in my eyes, smooth. And Doris, who in our family has a reputation as a llorona, too driven by excess emotion, was lucid, self-aware, digging out practical child-care nuggets from the bottomless mommy purse she'd already been carrying for years. Most surprising to me, she adapted well to whatever was happening in what was, to us, a whole other world—China, the transnational adoption protocol and industry, the idiosyncrasies of this little person. In other words, she was fully transformed into a mom.

In the day and a half between landing in Hong Kong and meeting the baby, jet lag, logistics, and our wonder at seeing a new continent kept us focused and calm. But on the first night with her, reality settled in. When Fu Xin screamed inconsolably for hours, pointing out the window and crying over and over the only word she knew, "Mama, mama, mama," I wondered, did I cry like that, too? Did Tía Milena and Tía Hilda's hearts break as mine was breaking? Did they, too, swallow their desperation at being unable to instantly make it all better?

Like all families, mine has a well-honed repertoire of routines about each member, fables that are supposed to reveal the essence of each of us. Like some milder, browner version of the Borg, we've uploaded the stories into the collective memory, so that any of us can retell any of them with the agreed-upon details and inflections, even if the teller was not present when the incident took place.

The stories about me as a baby fall into two general categories. There are the ones that portray me as a Caribbean Athena, sprung from Zeus as a fully formed egghead, a trait that earned me my family's Homeric epithet "la niña superdotada." Then there are the ones that show me as a quirky, stubborn spirit, which started out as "voluntariosa" (strong-willed) and crystallized into "space cadet" as a teen.

In the voluntariosa category, there is my insistence on having my food compartmentalized, or as my brother Luis describes it, "in a bento box arrangement." And there is also my toddler resistance to bedtime, when I, according to my father and siblings, impersonated the Fantastic Four's Mr. Incredible, stretching out my arms and legs from under my father's grasp to latch onto the doorframe.

I was luckier than most kids sent away to be raised in more cost-efficient and culturally congruent environments. I got to visit my parents and siblings yearly, unlike so many others I've known who had only letters and the occasional phone call to sustain their filial bonds. But every trip to New York eventually came to an end, and there are also stories, less often told, about my departures. "You cried a lot when it was time to go back," says my sister Esther. "We all cried. You were so cute. We'd get used to you, and then you'd have to go."

I have no memory of this.

I have clear memories of the rituals to prepare for trips to New York. The packing days before, Tío Papocho carefully wrapping contraband fruit, bottles of rum, slabs of jalao sweet and sticky enough to yank out your very jawbone. I remember the Santo Domingo airport, the smell of disinfectant and expectation evaporating off granite floors, and the ozone-charged air at JFK in winter, the awaiting wool coats and suffocating scarves. But I have no memory whatsoever of the repeated cruelty of separation. And now that I am thinking about my niece's new life with us, I try to imagine what it must have been like for Tía Hilda and Tío Monché to see me cry so desperately for people I barely knew, for a love more abstract than the one they showed me every day. Sometimes I imagine they were secretly relieved on the plane back, thinking we could all go back to pretending I was their own daughter, the only one they'd ever have.

Tío Monché had children from a previous marriage, but their names were never spoken at home. Tía Hilda had gotten married at the scandalously late age of thirty-one, and the two never had kids of their own. So I was it—as long as my "real" parents weren't around. In Santo Domingo, they were my parents. In New York, they were demoted to foster parents, and they had to turn off their intense bond with me, act as if the relationship was secondary.

Spanish is often more precise, and kinder, in how it names relationships. "Mamá de crianza," the mother who raises you, sounds truer to the reality it describes than foster mother, which has an institutional scent. It's easy for me to think of the various aunts and uncles who raised me as madres and padres de crianza. "Foster" just doesn't enter into it.

But that idyllic situation, multiple surrogate parents full of affection and infinite patience, had some dark foundations. The contentment of my childhood depended heavily on depressed fertility among several of my mother's siblings, the side of the family most present in my childhood. Shortly after getting married, Tía Hilda had a hysterectomy. Tía Milena died from uterine cancer in her fifties. Tío Alcides was divorced before I could remember and never remarried. He saw his one daughter on Saturdays, which she'd spend at my house. Tío Papocho and Tía Lépida never married, for reasons equal parts tragic and mysterious. So their focus remained undiluted by the everyday care of kids of their own. And without my parents around, they all had near equal claim on my discipline, my instruction, my affections.

When I was young and pictured my adult life, I always imagined myself a writer. There was always a husband in that vision of the future, but the picture grew fuzzy when it came time to imagine kids. Although I knew plenty of artists with kids, I felt that women always put their art second to their children. In some ways that is as it should be; parenting is an intensive endeavor. But I was unwilling to let go of my writerly ambitions. I kept those maybe-selfish thoughts to myself.

As my thirties neared an end, I had to think good and hard about my fertility, how it, too, was winding down. I resented being unable to reason with my body. Not yet, not yet, I whispered. But my ovaries played deaf, stubbornly popping out eggs, depleting the store. I didn't want to measure every man I was attracted to by his father potential. Shortly before my fortieth birthday, no daddy on the horizon, I made peace with the idea that I would not give birth. I would not push my luck in a lab, either. I'd seen too many friends in too much pain over repeated fertility treatments and failures to complete a pregnancy. No miracle science babies for me, thanks.

I bought a one-way ticket to Tía-ville and never looked back.

A few months after Doris and Milena were settling into their new life together, I'd returned from Santo Domingo to my teaching and writing routine, visiting them as often as I could, but not often enough. One day the call came from her work number. "I am headed to the hospital, and I need you to meet me there. Olga is picking up Milena from day care, and you may have to stay with her while I'm there." The pains that had forced her to double over under her desk required surgery to take her gall bladder out and a weeklong hospital stay. I stayed in her apartment while she was gone, the longest continuous time I had spent taking care of Milena without her mother around.

Gall bladder surgery is not usually life-threatening. But a couple of times, basking in the TV white noise after Milena had fallen asleep for the night, a small corner of my mommy-mushed brain piped up, "This is a test run. This is what it would be like if I got her." Superstitious, I swatted the thought down. But it's something my sister and I have discussed. Should anything happen to Doris, I get custody. We know people sometimes die before we think it's their time. Ian, one of my sister Esther's sons, died at nineteen. A year later, my brother's partner, Brent, also died, at forty-one. It's made us more willing to prepare for the worst, because the worst sometimes happens.

When she told me she'd designated me as the custodial parent, I was un-surprised. I knew it was my duty, as the sister who lives closest. When we went to China, I already saw myself as my niece's backup parent. I thought of Tía Hilda and calculated how old she was when she got me to raise. I mis-calculated that she was forty-two, the age I was when getting Milena. She was in fact fifty-two, closer to Doris's age. I think the slip was subconscious. I am the available childless aunt, the closest among my siblings to a Tía Hilda. But repeating the contours of that relationship is difficult at best, given my career-driven, worldly life. I go out too often and spend too much of the rest of my time hunched over a computer keyboard. The same things I chose over having kids make it hard to give Milena all the time and attention she needs, the kind I got from my aunts and uncles.

I am close with all three of my siblings, but for many years and for many reasons I felt closest to Doris. She is closest to me in age, and even when I was a teenager the eight-year gap in our ages was easily hurdled. When I moved back to my parents' house for good, she and I shared a sofa bed and then a room until she married. She is the one who was assigned by my mother to talk to me about menstruation, the one I swapped clothes with and stole Elvis Costello LPs from, the one I talked to about things I was too scared or embarrassed to share with anyone else in the family.

When the adoption idea moved closer to reality, I began to think about my responsibilities to my sister and my coming niece. I promised myself to be my sister's most reliable support, the person she could count on above all. On our way back from China, drunk with baby love, I imagined visiting weekly, being a constant in Milena's life. But things have worked out otherwise. It takes me almost two hours to get to Doris's house by subway. A cab there from Brook-lyn costs more than fifty dollars. So crises aside, my visits are more like once or twice monthly. The situation is making me rethink key aspects of my life.

Moving closer to them is out of the question, too much of the sort of con-cession to family obligation expected of unmarried women. The spinster sis-ters of my mother's generation thought nothing of moving for months at a time to take care of new babies and ill family members. When I moved back to New York, Tía Hilda and Tío Monché moved in with us, and until he died and she decided to move back to the Dominican Republic to become the female caretaker for her two brothers, she was the live-in babysitter for my sister Esther's kids. In our more autonomous generation, a move driven by my sister's needs is not something I easily consider or that she feels she can easily ask. Sometimes we joke about splitting a townhouse, but in the end, she stays in the comfortable Riverdale apartment she loves, and I stay in my Brooklyn pad, near shops, parks, a farmer's market, concert halls, and museums. But without telling anyone, I've gotten a learner's permit for the first time in twenty years and vow to have my first license and car within the year.

After only a few days of close contact with Milena while my sister was in the hospital, I found my ears suddenly tuned to the voices of children her age. On the subway headed home, I heard a toddler laughing, a sound that at other times had blended into the background buzz. By the tone of the giggles, I could tell the child—I couldn't see if it was a boy or girl—was happy but tired, soon to collapse into fits of crying frustration. It's as if the prolonged exposure in such close quarters had recalibrated my sensibilities, at least for the moment. Each time I spend an extended time with Milena, I miss her with physical pangs. Me hace falta. Is this how filial love works? Like a viral infection?

In circles of single or childless friends, we often talk about catching baby fever. We notice clusters of pregnancies and joke that spending too much time around swelling bellies can result in contagion, even if there's no likely father figure around. But I seem immune. Never have I felt the primal uterine pull I see in so many women I know. In the past few years, I've even lost the regret over not having one of my own.

It's not that I dislike children. I wonder at their sprouting, at the synapses connecting, at the exponential quickness with which they figure out the world. And it's not that I want to avoid the physical drain of child-rearing. In a few days my arms and shoulders throbbed with the repeated efforts of picking up twenty-four-and-a-half-pound Milena, and the intense attention she requires made me feel like her caretaking appendage. I would not have been unhappy to have a child. But I did not want motherhood badly enough to do it by any means necessary, to do it on my own if I had to. The two relationships in which I considered having kids, well, the timing never seemed right.

I do envy one aspect of Doris's bond with Milena, one that does not transfer to me. For some years at least, Doris will never be alone. Every morning, there is "Good morning, mama," and the singing and talking on the drive to work and day care, and in the evening, projects and baths and books. Mommy and me, daughter and Doris, all the time. When I return home after spending days with Milena, my solitude suddenly feels as uncomfortable as an itchy sweater. I long to shake it off, to head back to her singing, her ear-shattering squeals at the sight of raspberries.

My love affair with Milena is not that of a first-timer. My sister Esther had three boys; the youngest is now eighteen. But I think none of us ever took our aunt- and uncle-dom seriously with them. I was eleven when my first nephew was born. Doris was nineteen and Luis twenty-one. Maybe we felt too young for the titles "tío" and "tía." None of us felt like the clearly mature people our own aunts and uncles had been. So we were laissez-faire about what the nephews should call us, and they learned to call us by our first names. That was possibly a mistake, made the relationship too casual. But now that we are at various stages of middle age, "tía" and "tío" seem like appropriate forms of address.

I work hard to help twenty-one-month-old Milena learn to pronounce the word "tía." She sometimes says "titi," a baby term for auntie common in Puerto Rico. But she has pronounced "tía" only once or twice, and I long for the title. She knows who I am and points to me when her mother asks where Tía Caro is. She even confuses me with her mother in one black-and-white photo booth strip she often stares at. For now, when she wants me to pick her up or get her something or play with her, she doesn't call me anything at all, just looks up at me and makes her wishes clear.

I compare my toddler pictures to Milena's. In both sets there are lots of high-chair shots, photos of cute outfits and combed baby hair, of playtime at home in diapers and little else. And I recognize the look on my aunts' and uncles' faces, the desire to do whatever it takes to hear that laugh again. When Milena sits in the chair made by my crossed legs and makes me read her a Dr. Seuss book for the five-hundredth time, I think of Tía Hilda, reporting proudly to my parents how at age three I'd memorized the stories in my favorite books. When Milena offers me a tidbit of chicken from her plate, I think of how much I loved Tía Hilda's thick bean purées. How all these little details add up to the bountiful love that never gets the recognition of a parent's.

If that's my curse, I'm happy to bear it. Maybe the devil knows what he's doing.

THE DAY'S LIST

FICTION BY YALITZA FERRERAS

Carlos was still alive when his parents called me to bring his toys to the hospital. Isabela explained that he had fallen and hit his head while at a birthday party but was expected to be fine. "He will want some of his things when he wakes up," she said on the phone.

I arrived at the emergency room with two trucks, a teddy bear, a pad of construction paper, and crayons. His parents, doctors, and nurses were scattered around him like they had all just been in an explosion, dazed and trembling. He was dead.

The Carlos who lay in the hospital bed still had his long, beautiful eyelashes that reminded me of dark wings flapping when he fluttered his eyes closed before he went to sleep. I watched Isabela pat those lashes down on his cheeks. She ran her hands from his forehead, down to each eyelid, the tip of his nose, then his lips, over and over. "But he's still warm," she said.

Her husband, José, who had been holding Carlos's hand, was silent. He let go of his son's hand, patting each finger down individually, then took a step back from the bed, put both hands on his head, and grabbed two fistfuls of hair.

I dropped the bag of toys and heard the trucks and box of crayons thump together when they hit the floor. It wasn't a loud sound. I was probably the only one who heard it.

One of the nurses put her hand up in front of me as I moved toward the bed, unsure whether I should be allowed closer. In the midst of everyone's grief, the nurses scanned my body for markers of wealth, looked at my worn clothes and brown skin, and determined I was probably the family's worker in some way.

"I have his toys," I said, as if he would ever need them, but I couldn't think of anything else to say.

When I picked up the bag again, my consciousness moved from the crayons shifting against each other within their own box, up from the bag, its handle, my arm, through my bones, and up and out through the room and over the ocean and over to my island, and through the dream I had before I left for Spain, the one that held promise and told me that everything was going to be all right.

I felt like a brown stain that had seeped through layers of pale sheets. With every step tentative like a guilty toddler's, I went up to the foot of the bed, moved the bag of toys from my right hand to my left, and did the sign of the cross. I was going to say a prayer for him but then decided to do it later—I shouldn't have been standing there with the family for so long. I thought it improper to touch him, but when I put my hands down I brushed the top of his toes, which felt like little corn kernels under the blanket.

I had to help José walk Isabela through the hallway to the private room where they were moving Carlos. I had never touched her in the entire year I had been working for them. There in the hospital, I almost called her Isabela when her legs gave out from under her. As I held her, I could feel the sweat coming through the armpits of her silky blouse. A few weeks before, Carlos had asked me, "My mamá's name is Isabela, and I call her Mamá, but why do you call her Señora?"

"Because she is the lady of the house. She is special."

"Are you special?"

I laughed, shook my head, and said, "I am not special, Carlitos." I pinched his cheek and added, "You are."

I helped Isabela inside the room, and then I knew to step outside of it. As more parents who had been at the birthday party arrived without their children and their nannies, I retreated farther away from the room. Eventually I ended up down the hall, crying, resting against a soda machine. I didn't know what to do with myself while I waited, but I understood I had to just stand nearby until I was needed. I pulled out that day's list from my pocket to see if I had done everything. The last item said: *Carlos will have had birthday cake at the party. Make sure he doesn't eat more sweets before he goes to bed.*

I wanted to call my family and make sure everybody was still alive, but my day off wouldn't be for another week. I was number ten of fourteen siblings, and nine of us were left. Even though I knew my mother hadn't planned on so many, I wanted to tell her that it was good she had all of us—Isabela was left with nothing. I even wanted to talk to Pedro, my husband, whom I didn't love.

One of Isabela's friends walked over to me looking stricken and said, "Make yourself useful."

She told me to get coffees. I was usually very quick, but this time I didn't move or say anything right away. For only a second, I looked her in the eyes, as if we were equal, as if the tears in our eyes united us in some way. This woman had servants too, so my hesitation prompted her to ask, "Do you need money?"

"Yes, Señora," I answered.

A year earlier, when I had first arrived in Madrid to work for the Alarcóns, they were in between nannies, waiting for a new one to arrive from England. They needed someone more cultured, a white woman, to be around Carlos. They had not been waiting for me, a nun-trained Dominican domestic who was hired to cook and clean.

I had been next on the church's list of the women who wanted to go abroad. We supported the whole town with our Spanish pesetas. Besides being able to make as much money in one week—even after the usual paycheck deductions of rent, food, and airfare—as most people made in Vicente Noble in a month or more, everyone knew that those who returned from Madrid looked and smelled better, newer.

The nuns taught me about kitchen appliances I had never touched before, like blenders and toasters. They showed me how to act correctly and taught me the social rules, the most important one being "Don't sleep with the husband!" which made me very uncomfortable coming from a nun. I knew that wouldn't be a problem for me. Pedro was all I could get because I wasn't very good-looking. I wanted someone to come back home to besides my family, someone to build something with, so I tried not to think about Pedro marrying me for sponsorship. My mother had told me, "Keep him, because who knows when or what else will come along. You just need a man to give you children."

As I was making chicken with rice for dinner on one of my first days, trying not to ruin it by making it too Dominican (too much parsley) and not Spanish enough (more garlic), I overheard Isabela yell at José, "Are you going to fuck the next one? Tell me. I need to know before I call the agency."

"Calm down, woman," José answered.

He then shushed her, which just made her angrier.

I guessed that José's response wasn't convincing enough, because Isabela decided that they would not hire a new nanny and that she would play a more active role in her son's life, since her work as an interior decorator was sporadic. The next day she told me, "You'll help out, at no extra salary of course, because it won't take up too much of your time. It will just be silly little things, like helping him get dressed and taking him to the park and things like that."

That was also the first day she gave me a note—handwritten instructions on her monogrammed paper. She left these for me every day, even if some of the day's instructions were identical to ones from the day before. She wrote out the lists at the dining table while I made breakfast. The lists told me to *sweep the sitting room, but carefully, don't hit the furniture legs with the broom or you will scratch them*; or *don't sweep too fast, you will release too much dust into the air*—as if she had ever done any of these things herself. As soon as I read the first one, I knew what the lists were really saying: I am reminding you of your place in life, so don't even attempt to entice my husband into sleeping with you, and do not love my son more than is required for you to take adequate care of him, but be emotionally involved enough to risk your life for him if necessary.

It had been my idea to take Carlos to the Museo del Prado just a few blocks away from the family's apartment. At first he just ran around, and then he escalated. Part of the bargain Carlos and I had negotiated was that I would hold his hands up the steps to the Entrada de Goya doorway of the museum, and then I would let him go, following closely behind. He ran in between all the people, grabbing asses, skirts, and coats. He had to touch every security guard chair whether a guard was sitting in it or not. If the chair was empty, he climbed up on top, then performed a little convulsion that launched him off the seat. He draped himself on each of the ropes that hung in front of the paintings, while I held him to prevent the rope posts from buckling. My biggest fear was that he would somehow launch himself onto a painting and damage it. Occasionally someone would move toward him when I approached, not understanding why I would be running after this white child.

He pointed to paintings with battle scenes and pretended to shoot people, his hand forming a small gun as he spat out blasting noises. One day he stopped in front of Velázquez's *Las Meninas* and said, "She looks little and big," then started laughing.

I never knew why he thought that was so funny, but he seemed to enjoy looking at the infanta Margarita, the five-year-old princess in the painting. Like him, I admired her childlike face and what appeared to be adult formal royal dress. She reminded me of Carlos and many other wealthy Spanish little boys in Madrid, dressed in vests and ties as if they were miniature gentlemen.

I pointed out the young boy on the lower right of the painting, his foot casually placed on top of a dog.

"Why is his foot on the dog?" Carlos asked.

I had to think about it. Why would Velázquez paint this? "Because his foot hurt," I answered.

"Why does his foot hurt?"

"Because he runs too much. If you run too much, you have to rest your foot, too."

"I want a dog."

"Okay, let's go." I pulled him away from the painting. I didn't want the dog idea to linger in his head. Dog walking would've been added to my list of chores.

When we went to the museum again, we sought out paintings that portrayed children, dogs, and other animals. On each visit after the first, I brought crayons and construction paper so that we could sit on the floor to sketch along with other people who did the same. Carlos looked up often, pretending to draw the paintings, to imitate me, drawing basic shapes and squiggles meant to be animals. Carlos commanded me to recreate the paintings, but it was a hard thing to do with crayons, which he insisted I use.

He had been impressed by my ability to draw the animals and sometimes came up with challenges that commanded me to "draw that zebra head on this cow and put it in a car" or any other combination he dreamed up, laughing hysterically at the results. I taught him how to draw by holding his small fist around a crayon.

Whenever I drew a dog, he liked to put the construction paper on the floor and step onto it. "Look, Gracia, my foot is on it," he said giggling.

"Is your foot hurt?"

"No!" he screamed and slid around the room on the drawing.

He used to leave crayons outside my bedroom door.

In the days after Carlos's death there were times when I wanted to leave the house but felt that I shouldn't. For the first time since I had started working for the family, I was finishing work early at around eight or nine p.m. Isabela stayed in her room. She wasn't eating very much, but I made soups, which José or her mother brought in to her. I mostly cooked for José, who was around more than he used to be. He seemed sad but stoic, and I wondered if he was different when he wasn't at home, what he did to relieve his grief. I moved around the house quietly. In my room at night, I watched the small black-and-white television. It seemed like every channel featured talk shows hosts who ranted about how to keep people like me out or what to do with the ones who were already here.

"How do we keep these people from ruining our country?" they asked, and, "How do we control this problem?"

To me it sounded like, "How do we stuff them in a drawer or a closet and only take them out when we need to use them?"

Many of the talk shows discussed the murder of Lucrecia, a Dominican domestic from Vicente Noble. I watched a segment where the host went out and asked "typical Spaniards on the street" their opinion on current events. When asked what he thought about the murder, a man dressed in a business suit answered, "The problem isn't the neo-Nazis who killed her, it's that the Dominicans and the Filipinos and the Africans gather in the city squares, and

Madrileños don't want to see that." I guessed we were becoming too visible, multiplying in numbers too quickly, like vermin.

On my first day off two weeks after Carlos died, I snuck out the side entrance of the house (the entrance I had always been required to use when I wasn't in the company of Carlos) as if it wasn't my day off. I went to Plaza Corona Boreal to conduct my usual Sunday business: making phone calls at the locutorio; going to Restaurante La Cueva to listen to merengue, drink café con leche, and talk about Dominican news (mostly about Lucrecia in the last few months); and then passing by the apartment of Lina, a woman from Vicente Noble whom I had met in Madrid. I didn't want to stay out too late, so I decided to skip La Cueva in case there was something Isabela wanted me to do that I hadn't known I was supposed to do.

I walked into the locutorio and looked at the two clocks on the white-tiled wall labeled Dominican Republic (7:38 a.m.) and Spain (12:38 p.m.).

I could feel the tears welling up in my chest when I heard the first ring. When Mamá answered the phone on the second, I was already crying and struggling to tell her what had happened to Carlos.

"He was so little."

Why was I crying like this? I had seen little ones die from malaria or dengue fever back home. My own mother had lost babies.

"I will go to church and light a candle for him."

"Thank you, Mamá."

I thanked her for having compassion and for not asking me why I cared so much. I continued, "Did you receive the clock yet?"

I had been asking her for weeks. I didn't spend too much money on it because I didn't know if it would arrive. Dealing with the postal system in the Dominican Republic was like playing the lottery—you felt like you won something if you received a package.

"It needs batteries," she said. "Why didn't you send it with batteries?"

"I don't know. I forgot."

"But, you should have just sent them. You should have sent the clock ready for us to use. It probably costs you nothing over there to buy batteries."

She was right, but I thought about how I never had any money left over for me. The clock wasn't important—it was just something I thought my mother would like. I had forgotten the batteries, but I had put a note in the box that told her to leave the clock on Madrid time. That detail had seemed the most important to me.

"I'm sorry. I'll send it right next time."

"There's one more thing."

I took a deep breath and leaned my mouth into the receiver. I was usually very aware of germs, especially since I had moved to Spain. I cleaned everything until it gleamed so that the Alarcóns had nothing to complain about.

"What's the matter? Are you still crying? Calm down."

"No, no. I'm fine." I didn't want to be scolded again.

"Don't tell Pedro I told you, but he's been going to the cockfights. I can't control him. Can you send more money next time?"

"Put Pedro on the phone."

"No, Altagracia. Listen to me. Do not say anything to that man if you want to find him here when you get back. You have to let them do these things."

"Then why are you telling me?"

I wasn't sure if I wanted to find him there when I got back. When I was told I was leaving for Madrid, Pedro went to get a loan to pay the bribe for a speedy marriage license. He figured I'd be able to pay it off when I started sending money back, and he was right. We were driven to the courthouse in the back of a platano truck and officially got married by signing our names on the certificate with a Bic pen on a gray metal desk. I was on a plane a month later. The nuns asked me if I wanted a small church service, just me, Pedro, and the priest, but I said no. I didn't want to lie to God in the face.

The way it usually worked was that one day you start calling the man your husband, and then everybody would nod their heads and say, "Oh, I see," and that's it, you're married. The church didn't like this, but all they could do was deny you communion. All it really meant is that you were having sex with him, and you get pregnant, and you move in with his family, or he lives with yours. If he ends up in your house, then it's not just you cooking for him—it's your mother and your sisters, too. Another man in the house, another man to help with money, except that like all the other men, Pedro could barely help himself with the money he sometimes made loading avocado trucks. My mother didn't have a real marriage. She had never had a marriage license and neither did the woman my father left her for. Marriage certificates were for rich people or for people in the capital.

When Pedro got on the phone, he asked, "What happened to the boy?"

"He fell at a party and hit his head. He was only four."

"What's going to happen? Are you working?"

"Yes. I'm working." I thought about the meals I cooked that Isabela didn't eat and the toys I no longer needed to pick up around the house. "Of course I'm working. How are you?"

"Are they going to pay you less money now?"

"Did you hear me? I asked you how you were. What are you doing? How is the house? Is the foundation down yet?"

I fed Pedro, my mother, my brothers, and my sisters. I was building all of them a cement house right next to the wooden shack. Pedro was overseeing the construction. He'd decided that was his only job.

"The house is fine. Have you talked to them about a job for me?"

I paused and looked around me before I answered. There were women on phones crying, telling their sons, daughters, mothers, and husbands that they missed them. I didn't miss what my family had turned into.

"Their son just died! And you want a job? You're not even helping the men that are building our house. What do you know about construction?"

"Just send more money. I know you have it."

"Maybe if I don't send the money this time, then you can find some other way to pay for your fights."

I hung up without saying goodbye. I would let my mother deal with him. I was glad I didn't have any children to lose with Pedro.

When I walked into Lina's apartment, I was greeted by the smell of the chicken in the sancocho, hair relaxer, and nail polish. She earned money in various ways by arranging work for the women and by hosting a salon in her apartment doing hair and nails for Dominican women on Sundays. Whenever she went back home, she left with a suitcase full of Spanish shampoo and face creams, and on her return she brought back Dominican Mirta de Perales beauty products, making money coming and going. A woman known to be a prostitute was picking up her shipment of beauty products.

Someone said, "You bought a lot."

"Well, you know. I have to keep things up. The products here don't work for my hair, but the men sure like to grab it. So, you know, you have to keep it a little bit soft."

Lina answered, "You know how to work it, woman," and laughed with her while the rest of us nodded politely. The woman never lingered much. There was a hierarchy even among us workers.

Pedro was still on my mind. I had used Mirta de Perales products to wash my hair on my wedding day, but the conditioner I used seemed to make my hair bigger and fluffier in a way that magnified the fact that I was no beauty, that I didn't have a particular feature, say, like my hair, that one could point to that would be at all attractive to anyone. But here in Madrid, with no one to look at me, why try?

The women were lively, happy to be around each other. They cooked, talked about available cleaning jobs, and arranged for the transport of goods back to Vicente Noble. Letters were carried for free, but not gifts. For that you had to pay and reserve the space in the suitcase very far in advance. Some women were saving up to open small grocery stores or beauty salons back home. I wanted to open an art school. With all that money going back, there were still not enough schools, especially to teach something so frivolous.

There was a small altar in the corner with a picture of Lucrecia surrounded by candles with saints on them, a small Dominican flag, and a dried-up white carnation. As usual, the women were dressed more colorfully than most Spanish women, some wearing yellow or red pants. It was a scene that I wanted to paint one day. Dressed in black pants and a black sweater, I sat down like a crow that had descended into a shower of confetti.

They debated whether to bring up excessive working hours to employers, but they already knew the answer to that question.

"The new law says that we are supposed to work no more than nine hours a day," one woman said. "And a total of forty hours a week."

Another one asked, "Which one of you live-ins works under sixty hours a week?"

"Ay, shut up," someone said. "We're going to call you Che Guevara from now on." A few made a sound somewhere between a sigh and a tired, half-hearted laugh.

I thought about what it would be like to work forty hours a week. I thought about how Carlos had sought me out. How even when I was exhausted I had let him take me by the hand and lead me to his room, where his books and crayons were out on the floor waiting for us to draw animals.

All those museum visits had come at a price. Isabela paid for the museum, but it was time spent away from performing my duties around the apartment. It meant that Isabela added more on my list of things to do for that day.

"Did my Carlitos have fun at the museum?" she asked him and then turned to me, "You must've had fun too?" Whenever we returned, Carlos ran into the house, gave her a hug, then proudly handed one of his scribbled construction sheets to her, while I quickly went into my room to put on my work uniform.

Sometimes she seemed annoyed that I wasn't around to answer the phone or sew a torn seam, yet she seemed happy that I was doing something cultured with her son. I was at fault for not being able to do both at the same time. Going to the museum meant that I sometimes went to sleep well past midnight, even though I had to get up at six the next morning.

"She used to clean me," Carlos had said of the maid before me. "But she didn't color with me." How do I explain that to these women?

"Hey, Altagracia, you haven't been here in a while. We were starting to worry."

"The boy I work for died."

All the women started talking at once.

"Oh my God."

"Poor little thing."

"God rest his soul."

"How did it happen?"

And finally, "What are they going to do with you now that the boy died?" one of the women asked. "You know they are going to try to pay you less money, right?"

I didn't tell them that my salary was never increased when I started taking care of him.

"Thank God you weren't the one that was with him when he died. Can you imagine that?"

I had imagined that. I knew that Isabela probably wished it had been that way, that I had been the one with him. I was still not completely sure what happened at the birthday party, but from the snippets of conversation I heard at the house, it sounded like any fall, among the many times children fall. I knew Isabela was blaming herself for it, and maybe even José was blaming himself, too, or they were blaming each other. I didn't want to think about it, but I would've watched him so closely, like I always did, that it's possible that he would still be alive. Maybe Isabela thought so, too.

When I got home, I went straight to my room. As I took off my shoes, I heard the buzzer that Isabela uses to summon me. I hesitated before putting on the smock over my clothes that signaled I was on duty, but I put it on anyway. I went into the kitchen, and Isabela was standing there in a robe, but she wore lipstick, and her long brown hair was pulled up with a glittery comb.

"Are you going out, Señora?" She hadn't left the house in the two weeks since the funeral.

"Come with me."

She turned around. I followed behind her, wondering what I had done wrong. The house was so clean it looked like no one lived in it.

She walked me toward Carlos's room. When she entered, I stopped before the door. The last time I had been in the room was when Isabela's mother asked me to help her find the right shirt to go with his burial suit. His grandmother grabbed toys to put in the casket with him—some of them weren't his favorites, but she didn't ask me. I think he would've liked to be an artist, and I would've selected his crayons. I couldn't go to Carlos's funeral. I stayed home and made appetizers for those who came to the apartment afterwards.

When I stepped into the room, I saw what looked like a flat Carlos on the bed. Isabela had laid out his clothes—a jacket and a shirt nestled within, pants with a belt inserted through the loops, and the white band of underwear peeking out from inside.

"Where are the sneakers I bought him? I can't find where you put them."

I saw a sock coming out of each pant hole.

Isabela had bought him new sneakers the day before he died. They were still in the box, so I hadn't put them out with the rest of his shoes. I walked to his closet, reached up to the top shelf, and took the box down. I removed the tissue paper from inside each one and handed them to her, first the left, then the right. She tied the shoelaces into a bow, placed them on top of each sock, hesitated for a second, then tucked each sock inside each sneaker.

I stood there silently. I didn't know what to say to her. I wanted to ask if she needed anything else.

"Close the door behind you," she said without looking up at me.

"Yes, Señora," I answered without looking at her.

I didn't know if Isabela would need me for anything else, but it didn't matter. Carlos would've been starting preschool tomorrow. I guess that's what the outfit was for. I left the house and went toward the museum. It was only going to be open for another hour. I went straight to *Las Meninas*. Art students sketching on large pads looked at me when I sat down on the floor among them. I felt self-conscious there without him. I looked in my bag for a piece of paper and a crayon. I pulled out one of Isabela's lists. I normally didn't have them on me during my day off because I hated any reminder of work when I wasn't at the house. This was a really old list. One of the items on it said: *go through Carlos's shoes and take out the ones he has outgrown (but make sure he's wearing socks when you try the shoes on him, and don't forget to take out both shoes, I don't want any mismatched pairs in the closet).*

I turned the paper around and started sketching the infanta Margarita. I spent extra time on her face and especially her eyes, trying to capture what I thought her spirit had been like in real life. I drew Carlos next to her holding her hand—a tiny prince next to the tiny princess. My drawing of him didn't really look like him. It hurt to spend too much time rounding out his cheeks, or even drawing his skinny sticklike legs, but that was okay for now. I tried to draw them little and big at the same time.

CONTRIBUTORS

MARIVELL CONTRERAS is a past president of the Asociación de Cronistas de Arte de la República Dominicana. With a degree in social communication, she has published and edited content for various newspapers and magazines. She is chief editor of Enterato.com and works at TV Dominicana. Her stories have been anthologized in *Narrativa contemporánea de Monte Plata, Cuentos del beisbol,* and *Meter un ¡goool!* She has also published three poetry collections: *Mujer ante el espejo, Hija de la tormenta,* and *El silencio de abril.* Other publications include *Feria de palabras, La chica de la Sarasota: Cuentos de la calle, La flotadora,* and *El sabor de las letras.*

KERSY CORPORAN has been writing poetry and short stories since she was a teenager. Her love of literature and writing led her to attend Columbia University's Teachers College, where she earned her MA in English education. She has led workshops in teaching writing, culturally responsive teaching, and issues of social justice. Kersy especially enjoys helping teens tell their stories and currently teaches high school in northern New Jersey, where she resides with her husband and daughter.

ANGIE CRUZ is the author of two novels, *Soledad* and *Let It Rain Coffee.* She has published short fiction and essays in magazines and journals including *Callaloo,* the *New York Times,* and *Kweli.* She has received numerous grants and residencies, including the New York Foundation of the Arts Fellowship, the Camargo Fellowship, Yaddo, and the Macdowell Colony. She is one of the founding members of the National Book Foundation's BookUp program and editor of *www.asterixjournal.com*. She was recently awarded the Elizabeth K. Doenges Visiting Artist/Scholar Fellowship from Mary Baldwin College. She teaches creative writing at the University of Pittsburgh and is at work on her third novel.

RHINA P. ESPAILLAT has published ten full-length books and three chapbooks, comprising poetry, essays, and short stories, in both English and her native Spanish, as well as translations from and into Spanish. She has earned numerous awards, national and international. Her most recent publications are a poetry collection in English titled *Her Place in These Designs*, and two books of Spanish translations, *Oscura fruta/Dark Berries: Forty-Two Poems by Richard Wilbur* and *Algo hay que no es amigo de los muros/Something There Is That Doesn't Love a Wall: Forty Poems by Robert Frost*.

DELTA EUSEBIO was born under the sign of Aquarius. She likes children, animals, and home-cooked meals. She also likes storytelling, reading, and dreaming. She studied education and got a master's in social education and sociocultural presentation because she didn't like her own elementary and middle school. She teaches and tries to make sure the students don't get bored. She studied personal development in Chile and creative writing in Argentina and received a masters in art therapy from the Instituto de Arte Terapia Analítica Integrativa de Madrid. She says that when she writes and does art therapy, she's soul making.

NORIS EUSEBIO-POL studied sociology at the Universidad Nacional Pedro Henríquez Ureña, where she also taught. She did postgraduate studies in rural sociology at the Latin American Commission for Social Sciences and in massage therapy and stress management in Baltimore, Maryland. Her teaching experience also includes the Instituto Tecnológico de Santo Domingo. She has done considerable research on rural organizing and struggles. Her articles appear in the book *Movimientos sociales del Caribe*, the journals *Ciencia y Sociedad* and *Estudios Sociales*, and national newspapers, and at www.cavernacristalina. blogspot.com. For many years she was part of the team for the radio program *Matutino Alternativo*. She's currently the director of Editorial Funglode.

YALITZA FERRERAS was a 2014–15 Steinbeck Fellow at San Jose State University. She received an MFA in creative writing from the University of Michigan, Ann Arbor, where she won the Delbanco Thesis Prize. Her writing appears in the *Colorado Review* and *Wise Latinas: Writers on Higher Education*. She is currently working on a novel and a collection of short stories.

CAROLINA GONZÁLEZ is a writer and teacher who has worked in academia, media, and the arts for the past two decades. As a journalist, she has covered education, immigration, politics, music, and Latino culture in various alternative and mainstream media outlets. The guidebook she coauthored with Seth Kugel, *Nueva York: The Complete Guide to Latino Life in the Five Boroughs,* was published in 2006. Currently she works in communications for the union 32BJ SEIU, continues to work independently on radio projects, and teaches at the Milano School for International Affairs at The New School. Her essay was written in 2007; Milena is now nine years old.

FARAH HALLAL was born in Salcedo, Dominican Republic. She is a poet, prose writer, cultural activist, publicist, and promoter of reading and writing. She has published three books of poetry: *Sol infinito* (1994), which won first prize at the VI Feria Científico-Cultural at the Universidad Nacional Pedro Henríquez Ureña; *Una mujer en caracol* (2009); and *Borrándome* (2013). Under the Alfaguara Infantil imprint she published *Sábado de ranas,* which won the Premio Nacional de Literatura Infanto-Juvenil Aurora Tavárez Belliard. Her children's novel *Un adiós para mamá* was awarded the Premio El Barco de Vapor 2013. In 2015 she published the children's story *Las gallinas son eléctricas.*

ÁNGELA HERNÁNDEZ is a writer and poet whose work has been translated into English, French, Italian, Icelandic, Bengali, and Norwegian and included in anthologies in the United States and Europe. She won the Cole Prize for the Novel in 2002 for *Mudanza de los sentidos;* the National Story Prize, given by the Secretary of State and Education in the Dominican Republic, in 1997 for "Piedra de sacrificio"; the National Poetry Prize, given by the Secretary of Culture, in 2005 for *Alicornio;* and the National Story Prize, given by the Ministry of Culture, in 2012 for "La secta del crisantemo." She is a corresponding member of the Academia Dominicana de Lengua.

JULEYKA LANTIGUA-WILLIAMS, managing editor of *Next America* (Atlantic Media), is a journalist, writer, editor, and former college professor whose writing and editorial work has appeared widely in newspapers, magazines, and books in the United States and abroad. She earned an MFA in creative writing from Goddard College and an MS in journalism from Boston University. A Fulbright Scholar, she has served as the communications director for TEDx-Fulbright, and for over a decade was a nationally syndicated columnist with *The Progressive* magazine's Media Project.

ANA-MAURINE LARA is a national award-winning novelist and poet. She is the author of *Erzulie's Skirt* (2006), *When the Sun Once Again Sang to the People* (2011), translated by Emilia María Durán Almarza, and *Watermarks and Tree Rings* (2011). Her poetry and short fiction have appeared in numerous literary journals and anthologies. In 2013 she guest-edited a special edition of *Aster(ix) Journal,* "Ra(i)ces: Black Feminist Encounters." She received her BA from Harvard and her PhD from Yale. Currently Ana-Maurine is an assistant professor of anthropology at the University of Oregon.

ERIKA M. MARTÍNEZ, recipient of a Fulbright Fellowship and a Hedgebrook Writing Residency, holds an MFA in English and creative writing from Mills College. Her writing has been adapted for the stage and has been featured in the anthologies *Wise Latinas: Writers on Higher Education, Homelands: Women's Journeys across Race, Place, and Time*, and *Second Sense of Place: The Washington State Geospatial Poetry Anthology*. Her work has also appeared in *Muthamagazine.com*, *Consequence* magazine, and the *Afro-Hispanic Review*. She has taught creative writing in the Dominican Republic and is the editor of the annual *Middle & High School Voices* for the National Writing Project in New Hampshire.

MIRIAM MEJÍA, a Dominican writer living in New York, studied statistics and sociology at the Universidad Autónoma de Santo Domingo. She has published *Crisálida* (1997), *De fantasmas interiores y otras complejidades* (2004), *Garabatos en púrpura* (2007), *Piel de agua* (2008), *Aristas ancestrales* (2010), *Mujeres en claves* (2010), and *. . . y la imagen se hizo verso* (2012). She also coedited *La palabra rebelada/revelada: El poder de contarnos* (2011). Her work appears in the anthologies *Di aroma di café* (2006), *Antología de cuentistas dominicanas* (2007), *Voces de la inmigración: Historias y testimonios de mujeres inmigrantes dominicanas* (2007), and *Para no cansarles con el cuento* (2015).

RIAMNY MÉNDEZ is a storyteller, in journalism and literature. She was a 2012–13 Fulbright Humphrey Fellow in Journalism and Gender Studies at the University of Maryland. In 2008 she won the Rafael Herrera Cabral Prize given by the Fundación Global Democracia y Desarrollo (FUNGLODE) for her work as coauthor of the series "Desarrollo Humano." In 2009 she took second prize in the Fifth Annual Journalism Contest for Stories about Childhood and Adolescence, sponsored by UNICEF in the Dominican Republic. She coordinated the Dominican part of a research project titled "Responsibility and Transparency in Ibero-American Civil Society," sponsored by a nonprofit alliance. She has a degree specializing in international relations from the Latin American Faculty in Social Sciences (FLACSO), a regional educational organization established through UNESCO.

JEANNETTE MILLER is a poet, prose writer, essayist, and art historian born in Santo Domingo. She has published four books of poetry, *El viaje* (1967), *Fórmulas para combatir el miedo* (1972), *Fichas de identidad/Estadías* (1985), and *Polvo eres* (2013); four story collections, *Cuentos de mujeres* (2004), *A mí no me gustan los boleros* (2009), *El corazón de Juan* (2012), and *La verdadera historia de María Cristo* (2015); and a novel, *La vida es otra cosa* (2006). Her work has been translated into English, French, Italian, and Portuguese. She has written for the newspapers *El Caribe* and *Hoy*. With a degree in letters from the Universidad Autónoma de Santo Domingo, she was the third woman to receive the National Literature Prize in 2011.

SHEILLY NÚÑEZ was born in Santo Domingo and received her law degree from the Pontificia Universidad Católica Madre y Maestra in Santiago de los Caballeros, where she also participated in the literary group Ateneo Insular. She received various national literary prizes for prose between the ages of seventeen and twenty. In 2004 her book of stories, *Los Elementos*, was the winner of the Young People's Story Contest at the Santo Domingo International Book Fair. She currently practices law but continues to write and wait for her writings to be published.

JINA ORTIZ received her graduate degree in creative writing at the Solstice MFA Program at Pine Manor College. She is the coeditor of *All About Skin: An Anthology of Short Fiction by Women of Color* (2014). Her poetry has appeared in publications including the *Afro-Hispanic Review*, *Calabash*, *Green Mountains Review*, *Worcester Review*, the *Caribbean Writer*, and *Solstice Literary Magazine*. She has received residency fellowships from organizations such as the Art Omi/Ledig House International Writers' Residency, Virginia Center for the Creative Arts, Vermont Studio Center, and the Can Serrat Residency in Barcelona, Spain, as well as grants from the Worcester Cultural Commission and the Highlights Foundation.

SOFIA QUINTERO, a self-proclaimed Ivy League homegirl, is a writer, activist, speaker, and producer. Her first three novels, written under the pen name Black Artemis, are included in the *Encyclopedia of Hip-Hop Literature*. Quintero also writes "chick lit," erotica, and young adult fiction under her real name. She has been featured in the *New York Post*, *El Diario/La Prensa*, the *New York Daily News*, the *New York Times*, *Latina*, and *Upscale*. Kirkus called her latest novel, *Show and Prove*, "powerful and thought-provoking, an homage to a climactic hip-hop era." To learn more about her and her various creative and political projects, visit www.sofiaquintero.com.

DULCE MARÍA REYES BONILLA was born in Santo Domingo and migrated to Brooklyn in 1989, then to Miami in 2011. She is a black global citizen and intersectional activist, nonfiction writer, translator, copyeditor, MA-level sociologist, and educator. Her English stems from "pollito:chicken," *In Tune*, NYC worlds, and CUNY faculty. She has studied with the Center for Writing and Literature, VONA, ALP's Tongues Afire, the New School, and IWWG. She has been published in *Colorlines*, *50 Ways to Support Lesbian and Gay Equality*, *Revista ABPN*, the *Gotham Gazette*, *Divagaciones bajo la luna*, and *Desde la Orilla*. In 2001 she was named to *El Diario*'s "50 Mujeres Destacadas."

LISSETTE ROJAS, a journalist with a literary vocation, loves to bring stories to life with her number 2 pencil. She uses her prose to draw out life around her, searching for meaning in the details. In 2009 she won first place in the Radio Santa María Story Contest with "La niñera y el grito." In 2008 she received an honorable mention in the International Story Contest at Casa de Teatro for "En territorio de niños herejes" and in the Alianza Cibaeña Story Contest for "La mosca que haría temblar a Suiza y otros cuentos."

NELLY ROSARIO was born in Santo Domingo, Dominican Republic, and raised in Brooklyn, New York. She holds a BS in engineering from MIT and an MFA from Columbia University. She has received numerous awards, including the Sherwood Anderson Award in Fiction and the Hurston/Wright Award in Fiction. Rosario tells the story of generations of Dominican women in her debut novel *Song of the Water Saints*, which won a PEN Open Book Award in 2002. Rosario has served on the MFA Program faculty at Texas State University and is currently assistant director of writing for the Blacks at MIT History Project.

LUDIN SANTANA was born with a missionary soul in San Pedro de Macorís. She's considered herself a poet ever since she can remember but has had the opportunity to venture into stories, eventually being named a finalist in various national contests, including an honorable mention in the Feria Científico-Cultural at the Universidad Nacional Pedro Henríquez Ureña in 1997 for "Rosalia." She has a degree in marketing and a master's in management from the Instituto Tecnológico de Santo Domingo, which has allowed her to work in the pension and insurance sectors, a social ministry that complements her writerly vocation.

LEONOR SUAREZ was born in the Dominican Republic and moved to Washington Heights in New York City at the age of eleven. She received her BA in Latin American literature from Wesleyan University in Middletown, Connecticut. She completed her MFA at Columbia University, where she wrote her first novel, *Lent Sacrifice*. She is currently working on her second novel.

SHEREZADA (CHIQUI) VICIOSO was born in Santo Domingo. She has a degree in sociology and Latin American history from the City University of New York (Brooklyn College). She earned a master's in educational programming design at Columbia University and studied cultural project management at the Getúlio Vargas Foundation in Rio de Janeiro, Brazil. She has written and edited content for various newspapers. She received the Caonabo de Oro prize in 1988, the Gold Medal for the Most Distinguished Woman of the Year in 1992, and the National Theater Award in 1997 for her play, *Wish-ky Sour*. She is the author of five poetry collections, eight plays, and a collection of essays. Currently she is working on a screenplay.

PERMISSIONS

The editor thanks and acknowledges the following authors and the publications in which their work first appeared:

Marivell Contreras: "The Queen of Chá" was adapted and expanded from the original, which first appeared in Spanish as "Repeto a la Reina del Chá" on *Mapa Literario de Santo Domingo*. Copyright 2009. Reprinted by permission of the author.

Delta Eusebio: "The Big News" was adapted and expanded from the original, which first appeared in Spanish as "El notición" on *Mapa Literario de Santo Domingo*. Copyright 2009. Reprinted by permission of the author.

Noris Eusebio-Pol: "In Chinatown" was adapted and expanded from the original, which first appeared in Spanish as "My vida y el Barrio Chino" on *Mapa Literario de Santo Domingo*. Copyright 2009. Reprinted by permission of the author.

Farah Hallal: "The Immaculate Finger" was adapted and expanded from the original, which first appeared in Spanish as "Un dedo inmaculado" on *Mapa Literario de Santo Domingo*. Copyright 2009. Reprinted by permission of the author.

Ángela Hernández: "The Yielding Paths" was presented in Spanish as "Los senderos elásticos" during Dominican Story Week in Madrid and appears in her collection *La escritura como opción ética* and in the anthology *Pensantes*. Copyright 2002. Reprinted by permission of the author.

ACKNOWLEDGMENTS

First and foremost I thank the Dominicanas who believed in the importance of this project and submitted their stories. From its inception many not only contributed their writing but dedicated their time and effort to helping me with the search for a publisher. The women in this book shared their connections and conducted outreach to spread the word about the compilation. I even received in-kind design services to launch a website. Bringing this book into the world was a collaboration and fulfilled my dream of creating a community of Dominican women writers. I am grateful for their patience as the timeline for the work kept getting extended. But most of all I thank them because in their work I found reflections of myself; I found home on the page. Even though my work as anthologizer is complete, I will return to these narratives again and again.

A tremendous thank-you to Julia Alvarez for supporting this project since our first meeting, then reading the final manuscript and sharing her words; to Edwidge Danticat and Junot Díaz for their advice and affirmations; and to Achy Obejas for translating the stories from Santo Domingo and helping us move toward publication.

I would like to recognize the support of the Fulbright program, which made it possible to spend an academic year in the Dominican Republic to conduct research and an open call for submissions. I owe special thanks to Elmaz Abinader who proposed the idea for this collection and guided me through the entire Fulbright application process. Carlotta Caulfield, Eric B. Martin, and Christian Marouby also provided crucial assistance as I prepared my proposal materials. In addition, I am grateful to Daisy Cocco de Filippis, Nelson Santana, and the friendly staff at the Dominican Studies Institute Library who generously dedicated time to answering my questions and offering suggestions as the project took shape.

In the Dominican Republic, I was warmly received by Frank Báez, Giselle Rodríguez Cid, and Fatima Portorreal. Without their generosity my transition to life in the capital would have been much more difficult. At the Universidad Autónoma de Santo Domingo I thank Basilio Belliard, Rocío Billini, Paulino Chevalier, Rafael Guillermo Díaz, Eulogio Javier, Ramón Morel Félix, and Jenny Montero for opening their doors to me, introducing me to Dominican literature, and connecting me to the literary circles within and beyond the academic community.

Thanks to Domingo Abreu, Nelsy Aldebot, Soledad Álvarez, Valentín Amaro, Aurora Arias, Dinorah Coronado, Nexcy de León, Ibeth Guzmán, Mary Ely Peña-Gratereaux, Ylonka Nacidit Perdomo, and Sylvio Torres-Saillant for forwarding the call for submissions to their networks and offering outreach suggestions. I also thank the many people who had lengthy conversations with me, either in person, on the phone, or over e-mail, about editing, translation, and publication: Marinieves Alba, Neelanjana Banerjee, Jennifer De Leon, Jinky de Rivera, Carolina De Robertis, Carlos Decena, Lisa Factora-Borchers, Cristina García, Julio González-Ruíz, Minal Hajratwala, Nathalie Handal, Summi Kaipa, Marcela Landres, Mahmud Rahman, Pireeni Sundaralingam, Antonio Tillis, and Patricia Tumang.

I am indebted to Meg Petersen for championing this endeavor as well, and motivating me through every difficult moment since we met in Santo Domingo. She encouraged my development as a teacher of writing, which strengthened my editing skills and instilled in me a dedication to the National Writing Project. I am also grateful to Cruz Bueno, María Hortensia De la Cruz, Patricia Liranzo, Elisania Núñez, and Dora Tezanos. Their enthusiastic feedback and encouragement helped me overcome the daunting task of organizing and compiling the submissions.

Many thanks to M. J. Bogatin and Geoff Piper for empowering me through contract negotiations; to Lemny Perez and Michael Santiago, who were generous with their artistic vision; and to Ann Marlowe and Susan Starr for their invaluable feedback.

I have been blessed with wonderful friendships that have sustained me throughout this entire process. Thank you to Aimee Bruederlee, Sharline Chiang, Yalitza Ferreras, Linda González, Daisy Hernández, Leslieann Hobayan, Meeta Kaur, Rachel Afi Quinn, Joy Taylor, and Nina Zolotow, who have all assisted in multiple ways. They not only wrote recommendations, read content and proposals, provided feedback, reviewed applications, and contributed financially, but have been there to share the joys of this process, nourish my creative well, lift my spirits through the disappointments, and keep me sane.

Generous donations from the following friends and family members helped finance the translation of stories into English: Selma Abinader, Jennifer Leeney Adrian, Rebecca Alcalá, Ynez Arce, Miguelina Beras de Weber, Sonia Bolanos, Stephanie Brown, Sara Campos, Carmen Cenko, Ching-In Chen, Caiti Crum, José Frank Cuello, Edgar David, Laura Joyce Davis, Jasmine Dawson, Tanya Dommel Kaanta, Elaine Eng, Eugenio Fañas Pantaleon, Rob Fleischer, Kim Foote, Angela Gilliam, Kathie Giuffrida, Jessica Greenman Muenter, Kristi Guevara-Flanagan, Laura Hane, Melanie Hilario, Carol Hill, Patty Hirota-Cohen, Ofelia Huergo, Ron Iozio, Diana Ip, Susan Ito, Pearl Kan, Jane Kaplan, Alexandra Kostoulas, Jaclyn Kuwada, Maximus Lewin, Michelle López, Monica López, Jacqueline Luckett, Martha Manno, Alejandra Martínez, Nelly Maseda, Donna Miscolta, Carinne and Mark Niemann, Virginia Niemann, Ora Nwabueze, Evie and Izzy Peterson, Danielle Pugh-Markie, Ajay Rao, Sujani Reddy, Kerry Reichs, Nilsa Reyna, Ivelisse Rodríguez, Editha Rosario, Elena Sánchez, Yvette Santana-Taveras, Tanya Saracho, Joy-Marie Scott, Derek Sevier, Danielle Smith, Sreedevi Sripathy, Yvelette Stines, Kathryn Stutzman, Erica and Michael Thornton, Giovanni Vásquez, Elodia Villaseñor, Paola Vita, Meghan Ward.

When the Fulbright funds ran out, my family offered food to eat, beds to sleep on, and corners to write in. Thanks to the Cuello-Tavarez family, the Beras-Cuello family, and to Blanquita Cuello; they all took such good care of me in Santo Domingo. I am grateful for the never-ending love and prayers of my mother, Mercedes Cuello, my sister, Melissa Iglio, and my brother, Francisco Martinezcuello. Even though scattered across the United States, their caring words were always only a phone call away. Thank you to my father, Agapito Martinez, who cooked and cleaned for me during the final stages of this project, which coincided with the last month of my pregnancy. I deeply thank my husband, Paul Niemann, whose love and kindness make it all the more possible for me to pursue ambitious projects such as this one.

My sincere gratitude goes to Lisa Bayer, Elizabeth Crowley, and the entire staff at the University of Georgia Press for their enthusiastic support. Thank you for taking us through this final phase and making sure the voices of Dominican women reach a wider audience.